The World of the
Contemporary Counselor

The World of the Contemporary Counselor

C. GILBERT WRENN
Arizona State University

LYNN LEONARD
Research Assistant

Houghton Mifflin Company · Boston

Atlanta · Dallas · Geneva, Ill. · Hopewell, N.J. · Palo Alto

Photo Credits

p. x	Christopher S. Johnson
p. 14	Nancy Cheser
p. 40	Ellen Siddons/Stock, Boston
p. 64	Christopher S. Johnson
p. 92	Christopher S. Johnson
p. 124	Christopher S. Johnson
p. 142	Mike Mazzaschi/Stock, Boston
p. 160	Christopher S. Johnson
p. 180	Christopher S. Johnson
p. 210	Donald Wright Patterson, Jr./Stock, Boston
p. 246	Christopher S. Johnson
p. 268	Stephen J. Potter/Stock, Boston

Selections from "The War Between Young and Old" by Arthur Miller
are reprinted by permission of International Famous Agency. Copy-
right © 1970 by McCall Publishing Company.

Printed in the U.S.A.

Library of Congress Catalog Card Number: 72-4800
ISBN: 0-395-13901-5

Contents

Preface

A preface is often designed to help the reader to understand the writer. This book as a whole attempts to contribute to this understanding — the first few pages of Chapter I describe what I think is important about counselors, and this is certainly "me" speaking, not the profession; I often state a personal opinion or belief so that the reader reacts to me, not merely to an idea.

The main theme of the book is that the counselor should know the world of the student, or whoever the client may be, and in particular the world of reality outside of the school walls. Often the reality-world of the student is not the same as that of the counselor. The book is a modest attempt to bridge such a gap. This gap is widened by differences in age, by differences in the subcultures in which client and counselor were reared, by differences in day-by-day habits of feeling, thinking, and living.

Many books have been written about the human being and his behavior, few about the shifting world of values and the increasing pressures of one's environment. The term "a rapidly changing world" may be seen as a cliché, but it is one which arouses many defensive reactions: "We have always had change, what is so remarkable about that?" "You won't find *me* accepting every new development; most of them will go out the window, anyway"; "Well, I *know* what will work, I haven't had all these years of experience for nothing." These are easy escapes, reassuring retreats, comforting cocoons.

The rate of change in values, beliefs, and patterns of social living is an accelerating one; the slope of the curve is logarithmic, not arithmetic. I think that students, or the young, or members of the counterculture, appreciate the rapidity of change more clearly than do many counselors. This book is designed to jar the reader a bit, perhaps to make him less complacent. The "real" of the world must be *his* real. I tend to echo G. K. Chesterton, who wrote: "I believe in being in hot water. I think it helps to keep you clean."

Another theme of the book is to make clear that my world is not necessarily the world of the reader or the world of anyone else. A great many facts are presented and some trends are suggested, but consistently I have tried to propose that "I say this," not "it *is* this way." Carl Rogers taught me this years ago. When I say "I think" — not "it is" — the reader is free to accept or to reject any statements. I am not propounding ultimate Truth, but truth with a small "t," and the reader may accept or reject in terms of his truth. I am, of course, clearly hoping that my truth will make sense to the reader and be useful to him, but I use no sledge-hammer blows to force my views upon him.

One further point might be made. What I write may seem elementary indeed to some well-read students, but to such readers there may be satisfaction in finding that someone else supports their thinking. To others, some of the proposals and conclusions will seem "far out" — the reader couldn't disagree more. This will not disturb me. If I have agitated a neuron or two that has been quietly slumbering I will smile gleefully! James Russell Lowell wrote with great insight: "New occasions teach new duties; Time makes ancient good uncouth. They must upward still and onward, who would keep abreast of truth." This is again truth with a small "t." Truth is forever emerging, never fully found.

Acknowledgments

I have learned during eleven years of editing a psychological journal and another eleven years of editing some 40 textbooks that a book is the product of many people besides the original writer. "Acknowledgments" are more than an expected formality; they are the recognition of a basic reality.

Because this is a personal kind of book, one in which, beyond any others in my experience, I have tried to share myself with the reader, my first acknowledgments are personal rather than professional. They are acknowledgments to people who have quite literally made me what I am, during the period of this writing and sometimes over a much longer period. These are people who have influenced not only my thinking and my writing but what I have become as a person.

First is Kathleen, my companion and my wife for 46 years, my loving critic and my constant support; one who has vastly increased over the years my sensitivity to people and to beauty.

Next is Robert, our counselor-psychologist son, patient, insightful, compassionate; not only a son, but a satisfying companion and colleague.

My pastor, Edwin Grant, is a man from whom I have learned much during the past six years — much about the depths of life's meaning, much about putting new wine in new skins rather than into the old ones.

Lynn Leonard has been my assistant in the research and the writing of this book, creative and loyal, a discriminating yet considerate critic; one who has influenced me as well as the book. My debt to her is great.

I am indebted to many graduate student advisees over the past 36 years, particularly some 80 Ph.D. candidates, and more particularly my former teaching assistants: Willis Dugan, John Butler, Walter Johnson, Lyle Estensen, Clarence Mahler, Jorgen Thompson, Clyde Parker, Elvet Jones, Beulah Hedahl, Joseph Bentley, and Jack Rossman. Sue Lund and William Farquhar were also assistants for somewhat shorter periods of time. From them I have learned more of the meaning of perseverance, awareness, and original thinking.

I would be remiss not to acknowledge the contribution made since 1964 by many staff members and graduate students at Arizona State University in increasing my openness to others. They have given me both unselfish love and critical appraisal; they have taught me that I dare risk myself with others.

On a more professional basis, I am indebted to the several readers and critics of the manuscript of this book as it progressed from stage to stage during the past three or four years. Dugald Arbuckle (Boston University), Robert Gibson (Indiana University), Helen Shiels (University of Natal, South Africa) and Arthur Resnikoff (Washington University) read the complete manuscript in its next-to-last draft. They gave many suggestions that reduced the inconsistencies and increased the clarity of the writing. Joseph Bentley (University of Utah) read the first eight chapters. His comments resulted in a complete rewrite of Chapter I as well as a combing of the manuscript to reduce the instances in which there was an unwitting "laboring of the obvious."

Particular chapters of the manuscript were read by Sanford Davis, Robert Heimann, Wayne Maes, and Jeffries McWhirter, all of Arizona State University. I am grateful for their support and their helpful comments. Two graduate students, Mary Lou Kincaid and Douglas Gaston, of the same university, made a careful reading of the full manuscript from the point of view of graduate student readers. Their endorsement of what was new and helpful to them gave me encouragement, their identification of what was unclear resulted in numerous changes. Edwin Grant, earlier mentioned, and Nancy Derrickson, librarian and Ph.D. candidate, made many suggestions from their wide reading on youth and society, for chapter references that I would not otherwise have considered.

From June 1968 to June 1971 I had an appointment as Distinguished Professor and Educational Consultant at Macalester College under a term endowment subsidized by Dewitt Wallace. I am appreciative of the freedom given me in that assignment to work on this book.

Doreen Fitzgibbon was the careful typist of the several drafts of this manuscript. She not only caught errors and inconsistencies but contributed to clarity of thought. I am indebted to the publisher's editorial assistant responsible for this manuscript. I would like to acknowledge her by name, for she called to my attention many places in which wording and phrasing could be improved and new ideas sharpened, but I understand that it is not the policy to do so. In any event, great thanks both to her and to the three Houghton Mifflin editors with whom I have worked over the years.

May I give to all of these the old Gaelic blessing: "May the road rise to meet you, may the sun shine warm upon your face; and until we meet again, may the Lord hold you in the hollow of his hand."

C. Gilbert Wrenn

CHAPTER I

What This Book
Is All About

INTRODUCTION

Perhaps a writer's most difficult task is to provide a "set" for the reader. What is the book about, what can one expect and not expect? This is not a book about counseling, except for the "Implications" sections and the last two chapters. It is for counselors as people. I have a conviction that it is as persons that counselors are significant. What they know about their world and the worlds of their clients, who they are as living, loving, angry people are what is important.

Some years ago I wrote about "the encapsulated counselor." This is a counselor who unwittingly spins around himself a cocoon of a very small professional world, an unsatisfying, limiting world or a pretended world, one that isn't really there. This book is an attempt to provide an antidote for cocoon-spinning. The world is magnificent, complex, and wonderful but it is also a shrinking, polluting, brutal world. Both the positive and negative aspects of the world are real, and I've been trying to keep my eyes open to them. This book is a personalized sharing with the reader—of values, beliefs, facts, and loves.

My sharing is with the reader as a person. Most of the first ten chapters could also be a sharing with salesmen, social workers, teachers, citizens—as much as with counselors. Each of the earlier chapters has a section on the implications of this sharing for counselors as such. But the body of the chapter is written for people, Americans perhaps, whether counselors or not. (Throughout, the generic term "man" is used for the counselor as a matter of simplicity and convenience.)

Basic to my being-in-the-world is a wide range of reading. Some of it is skip-and-jump reading, to be sure, but I catch glimpses of the wide, wide world—and I want the reader to be there with me. I am fascinated by the future. I have an insatiable curiosity about what might happen, not only in our world but in our universe! So I dream and lean out into the future and into space. Some people are fascinated by the unpredictable slot machines at Las Vegas, but my excitement comes from gambling with dreams and projections about what might happen in the world. I'll "hedge my bets" by relying on facts and figures. So the reader will get them too. What is their meaning for now, for trends, for the future? These questions hold mystery for me that I "play" at solving.

This book is a "teaser," to use the label given by an anonymous critic of the manuscript. I hope it will make you want to explore more deeply than I have done in this spot or in that. Hence the suggestions at the end of each chapter. I make no claim to in-depth investigations—I hope you will go deeper where you will.

I have another problem. In writing a book intended for reading by counselors (and perhaps others) I face at once the question of just who is my audience. The 60,000 or so professionals who carry that title (50,000 of them in schools and colleges) range widely in age and setting. The difference in setting, of course, be it school, college, hospital, prison, social agency, government, or business, is peripheral. All counselors, by definition, have a central responsibility for dealing with people who have decisions to make, confused feelings to release, understandings of self and others to clarify, behavior to modify. People are at the core of all that counselors do, but the kinds of people involved vary with the setting. So I do have to be concerned about the variety of settings in which prospective readers may work.

The variation in age and experience of my reading audience is more difficult to handle. The older counselors on the job, or those who have returned for graduate work after some years of experience, are likely to differ markedly in attitudes and values from counselors-in-preparation, some of whom may be in their early twenties. To the older ones I will be saying, "Try to understand the contemporary world of youth, as I am trying to understand it." The younger ones are *in* that world or so close to it that some of what I will be saying may belabor the obvious. Occasionally, I am sure, I will be reflecting on an issue which is immediate and troublesome to the younger counselor but strange and remote to the older counselor. It may help me at times to address a point specifically to "the younger" or "the older." Bear with me then as I attempt to visualize such a varied reading audience as counselors on the job in various settings and counselors-in-preparation. Nor can I assume homogeneity of outlook in either group. Some experienced counselors are very much with the world of youth, while some younger ones, preoccupied with their own hangups, may have difficulty in understanding anyone slightly younger than they are.

As I have said, this book is not about the counseling process or the professional knowledge and skills required of the counselor. It is directed at the need of the counselor *to attempt to understand contemporary youth and the world in which they live.* This is one of the two major responsibilities of the counselor. Of course if the client is an adult then the need is to try to understand *his* particular world, conditioned as it is by both the number of years he has lived and his unique pattern of experience. Sometimes the need is to understand an older counselor's conflict between the world in which he was young and his contemporary world.

A corollary of knowing about the world is the need to know *how to deal with this new knowledge,* to understand what new counseling emphases and processes grow out of this new world. In a word, how does the counselor's role assume new proportions?

The second major responsibility of the counselor is *to attempt to understand himself and his relation to the world around him.* It must be anticipated that the world of the counselor and the world of the client coincide only in part. The professional task of the counselor is to reduce the gaps between them so that communication can be meaningful. "To attempt to understand" (not "to understand") the other's world and "to reduce the gap" (not "to close" it) are deliberately chosen words in the preceding sentences. One can live in the other's world only in part— ever. The same reservation is applied to the counselor's understanding of himself. This is never fully accomplished; it is a lifelong task. I am certainly not the person that I was ten years ago, nor are you. Do I understand the present "me" well enough to relate to my environment effectively, and in particular to seem real to others? This must be my continuing attempt as a person and as a counselor.

If the counselor has a task of *knowing,* he has also the need to *care.* In the first ten chapters of this book the importance of knowing is empha- sized. But knowing and caring are not independent. Does the reader care enough to *want* to know, to try to understand the values and the social world of his youthful client or the particular world of his older client? The reader has a second concern: where does he as a person stand in this contemporary world, how close to or how far from the world of his client? Although the chapter titles do not always convey so complex a message, knowing is a form of caring. Knowing and caring about himself is as important as knowing about the world of his clients. The last two chapters carry the title "Caring," but caring is assumed throughout. Rollo May's powerful book *Love and Will* has a chapter on "The Meaning of Care" (pp. 287–306), and I want to introduce both the book and the concept to you at the very beginning. (See References at the end of the chapter.) The counselor must not only know about but care about relat- ing to the world of youth. More of that will be discussed in the last two chapters.

It is indeed difficult in the early seventies to write meaningfully about counseling without becoming involved in the labor pains of our era and of our society. Change of an often stressful and painful nature is more and more becoming a reality. The comfort of former gestation periods has disappeared almost entirely, and society wrenches hourly in labor pains. The dizzying speed of technological development is accompanied by threat to our most comfortable values. True, today we worry less about "sinfully" violating an immutable value. But in place of the guilt of "sin" there is the void of having nothing meaningful enough to worry about, or the question "what is significant?" Experiencing such uncertainty can be more distressing than experiencing guilt.

Older counselors may also experience more than a little pain as they watch the established educational structure collapsing around them. The traditional structure includes the required courses that are "good for everyone," prerequisites which theoretically reduce the incidence of academic failure (which is viewed as a disgrace rather than as an experience with valuable learning outcomes), extensive examinations which call for a reflexive regurgitation of what has been learned, letter grades which are reported to parents as symbols of success. These and many other widely used practices are coming under fire. So too is the wise and definitive counselor who has the answers for his clients. What we have fondly adhered to in much of our school tradition is clearly seen to be increasingly irrelevant to today's school and college youth, and to the world in which they live.

It is easy to delude ourselves into thinking "Things will *certainly* quiet down soon." But that is the most dangerous of illusions. I find it hard to believe that our present agitations of the spirit—the flurry of new technologies, new concepts, new beliefs that are thrust at us daily— are temporary at all. Life is not characterized by certainties. Uncertainty will be the warp and woof of our daily life for at least a decade or two, and probably henceforth. Some people reason that the seventies, following in the wake of the turbulent sixties, will be a more stable period. It is not starting out that way. We are only in the introductory phases of a period which will continue to be changeful, stressful, and painful— perhaps at an accelerating rate. Alvin Toffler's *Future Shock* makes that very clear. (See References.)

Life consists of learning to live with ever-increasing uncertainty. This prospect does not trouble me. I have lived through a sweeping depression and three and one-half wars. True, the war years were more strenuous for me than the depression, but the earlier struggles prepared me for the later ones. What I have done before, I can do again—perhaps better. And so can anyone who belongs to the family of man.

At this point the reader is asked to turn back and review the Table of Contents in the front of the book. As I have said, the contemporary counselor can be truly contemporary only if he both knows and cares about significant areas of living. The areas of knowing to be considered in this book are not the conventional ones—the counseling process (individual and group), interpreting information about the client to him, serving as a source of educational and vocational information, dealing with educational and personal crises, etc. These areas of knowing are dealt with, often thoughtfully and skillfully, by other writers. "The world about us" is my particular concern but with no suggestion that process and skills are not also important. The more neglected areas of knowing that appear significant to me would start with "changing values," although in a more logical sequence the social conditions that lead to changes in values might well be considered first.

Recently I led a weekend retreat for some fifty adults, and the discussion of changing values in our society was painful for many of them. But for many readers younger than the people I had at the Retreat, the pain is already recognized—for some there is just a simple acceptance of change with little pain involved. Remember, though, that while you may be youthful enough in spirit to accept changing values, there are many others in your life who find such an acceptance a painful process—one to be resisted. In this book we will look first at critical changes of value in our society (Chapters I–V) and then turn to current conditions in some of the more significant societal areas.

VALUES IN FLUX

At the risk of being too elementary, we might consider that any discussion of values raises an immediate question: "What are we talking about? What do you mean by values?" For this is a comprehensive term, one which is broad enough to constitute a major dimension of philosophy, called axiology. "Value" is also a very ordinary word. The question, "What value do you place upon this, or what is it worth to you?" could mean either life value or value in terms of dollars or cents. Sometimes value means respect: "I value what you say very highly." Or it can refer to a life style, a total way of living: "His sense of values is not very high."

"Value" can mean what one desires, or it can refer to what one should desire. In the first sense, values are human preferences. They are descriptive and normative; they are the way people *are.* These values change with social conditions and are a normal dimension of social conditions. In the second sense, values are goals or standards, what people *ought* to be. These values are resistant to change because in one's thinking they are often endowed with a sense of changelessness. These values may be lofty and provide appropriate goals. On the other hand, they may be totally unrealistic and a dead weight upon change. One way out of the latter dilemma is to say that if there are immutable values, they then require expression in terms that are meaningful in a given period and to a given society. (See also page 160.)

Hierarchy of Values

Each of us has a hierarchy of values, an ordering from high to low of that which we believe to be important in life and, more specifically, in *our* life. This hierarchy orders our behavior. If "being honest" is higher in our hierarchy than "having money," then we will not act dishonestly to obtain more money. But if "money" means more to us than "leisure," then we will work overtime even to the extent that we injure our health. These are small, ordinary, workaday values. They shift in emphasis in terms of changing personal need and changing situations. They influence our behavior from hour to hour.

More comprehensive values such as "Belief in the integrity of each person," or "People are more important than things" also influence us. Sometimes these are merely stated values which do not affect our behavior even though we affirm them. Often we affirm "I believe in peace above all" and then engage ourselves in a violent argument to defend our belief! Or we state we believe in "each man's integrity" but proceed to treat children or friends differentially as they vary in intellect or power. It is so easy to believe in the "complete integrity of each child" and then treat the bright, clean child with more dignity or respect than the malnourished, untidy one. Often we are not consciously hypocritical in espousing values that are then violated by our behavior, but an observer of our behavior could point out the discrepancy. We should be grateful for this insight of the other person, but often we are not!

Change in Values

The heading "Values in Flux" suggests that values change. This is an assumption and a critical one for all that is said in this book. In this writing I assume that values change—all values, any value. The presumed worth of any concept or experience is subject to change, particularly in its position in a person's hierarchy of values. *Money* was once "more important" than *time* in my personal hierarchy, but now time is the more valued of the two. Perhaps both have been superseded by *achievement* that is personally meaningful.

This assumption of dynamic changing values is, of course, not accepted by many who assert that there are immutable, unchanging values. Often these are values that are so broadly stated and generalized that their application to behavior requires much interpretation. Still, to many, these values are changeless. For me, although it does not have to be so for you, nothing is changeless. Social conditions, growth in population, technological developments, scientific findings, and changes in philosophical concepts all affect the value or worth of any concept or experience. These factors particularly affect the relative value of one experience as against another. "Relative values," as opposed to "absolute values," is a distasteful concept to some. I opt for relative values as well as changing values, but the reader is free to judge whether my later arguments justify such assumptions. A lucid and careful analysis of values as such and of values in relation to counseling is given by Peterson. (See References.) One should note, also, that there is a serious and continuing search for universal values. The position of the relativist is challenged by many, particularly some of the humanists with whom I feel a degree of affinity (see Laurence N. Solomon, "A Note on the Ethical Implications of Values Research," *Journal of Humanistic Psychology,* Spring 1970).

What I propose to do is to examine values in terms of the areas of greatest conflict. There are conflicts in value between cultures and between subcultures in a given society (white versus nonwhite, poor versus affluent, those with much time in school versus those with little time in school, etc.). Perhaps of even greater significance to a counselor are the assumptions of worth that divide the younger and the older generation, youth and the Establishment. The counselor is very likely to be of a different generation from that of his client, and this may seriously retard the development of a counseling relationship. A generation is technically a matter of some 20–25 years, the time interval between the birth of parents and the birth of their children. From the point of view of today's children and youth, however, half of this time or even less constitutes a psychological gap of much significance. With the accelerating rate of change of all sorts, a 25-year-old counselor and a 15-year-old youth are living in different worlds. Stated differently, the world the counselor lived in when he was 15 years old is vastly different from the world of his 15-year-old client. These worlds differ not only in technology and social conditions, but in many value assumptions.

The Counterculture

Every generation has seen some of its basic tenets challenged by those of the up-coming generation. Much has been said pro and con about the current "generation gap." The arguments against the assumption of a gap appear to me to be rather defensive, although perhaps it is the term that is a misnomer. There is for me, however, in a somewhat distinctive fashion, a "prevailing culture" and a "counterculture" of considerable significance in today's world.

The counterculture consists of a comparatively small percentage of any population group. It is certain to be larger among: (1) the younger members of the population, (2) those who are dissatisfied with life and hostile to it, and (3) those who are intellectually, and perhaps experimentally, inclined. Recently I spoke on traditional value assumptions, and the fact that they are being challenged, to a mixed age group in an experimental church situation. I had used the terms "youth" and "adult" several times in contrasting the prevailing culture and the challenges to it, each time feeling a little uncomfortable in having to explain that the concepts of youth and adult were not based entirely on chronological age. One member of the group resolved the situation by commenting that this group in this particular church was much more attuned than the average to the counterculture. That was why they were in this particular church rather than in one of the more conventional churches. Members of the group ranged from 25 to 65 years in age, and for them it was entirely true that age had little to do with the extent to which they, as individuals, were questioning many of the prevailing value assumptions.

To be remembered, however, is that when we speak of the prevailing culture and the counterculture, we are thinking of a population ratio of perhaps 60–75 percent in the prevailing group and 25–40 percent in the "counter" group. That the counterculture embraces fewer people may be misleading. The smaller group is a powerful force and is not to be discounted on the basis of its minority status. Its influence is felt widely among youth and, because of its active expression, its thrust goes deep into society. The new culture is physically distinctive because many of its advocates differ in dress and life style, but beyond this they differ in basic values related to the nature of humanness, the meaning of life, and the importance of feelings. The youthful culture sometimes embraces a mysticism which is often experienced with the fervor of religion. It attacks the prevailing culture; it contends that industrial societies are weak in human purpose; and it believes that the gap between ideals and performance has never been greater.

The prevailing culture, on the other hand, just as vigorously attacks the new. It openly scorns the new life styles (while simultaneously adopting some of them such as sideburns, beards, and bright clothing!). This culture points out to youth that without the economic achievement of the older culture there would not exist the financial security and the freedoms that support the new, that allow time and energy to focus on the "new."

These two cultures and the division that is involved are often marked by intolerance, anger, and fear. Members of the prevailing culture attempt to ignore the existence of the counterculture, pretending "business as usual." The counterculture, on the other hand, often acts upon the delusion that it can "start from scratch," make all things new. Rationalizations on both sides are often conceived in terms of the "ought" and the "should." One never materially changes what *is* by wishing that it were not. Many arguments are based upon a turning away from the realities to a consideration of what should or should not be. The latter is a much more comfortable stance. One can argue to heart's content and with great ease for *what ought to be,* whereas dealing with *what is* may be most uncomfortable and demanding.

Value Areas

For the purposes of this book, we will examine the challenge made by the counterculture to the prevailing value assumptions in eight areas. This is an opportune time for such an examination. The counterculture contains many national leaders, and the vigor of the protest is at its peak. On the other hand, because the prevailing culture is less sure of its fixed values than has been true for many past generations, adults and conventional youth seem to be more open to the influence of the counterculture. I confess that I cannot prove this, but there are many straw-in-the-wind indicators, not the least of which is the violent antipathy of some to the counterculture, suggesting their realization that they are vulnerable to its influence.

Admittedly, my selection of the value areas that we will examine is quite subjective. It reflects only my estimate of what are the most crucial elements in our changing culture to be considered by the counselor. These areas represent the trends within our society within which, I believe, the counselor must attempt to understand both himself and his clients.

In this selection of crucial value areas I could have examined the tried-and-true values of our American heritage: (1) self-determination, (2) consent of the governed, (3) equality of opportunity, and (4) dignity of the individual. There might be a complete agreement on these by young and old as some of the desirable goals of our nation. There would probably *not* be agreement between the two cultures on the extent to which these goals are being reached or the extent to which implied values are being violated.

Or I might have gone the moral route. A 1969 editorial in *Life* magazine provides an interesting contrast of "old" and "new" moral values expressed in terms of sins:

THE SEVEN DEADLY SINS

OLD LIST	NEW LIST
Pride	Selfishness
Covetousness	Intolerance
Lust	Indifference
Anger	Cruelty
Gluttony	Destructiveness
Envy	Irrelevance
Sloth	Hypocrisy

Closer to my frame of thinking is the list of "emerging values" given by Paul Nash in an issue of the *Boston University Journal* Fall/Winter 1970. He sees them as changing from the values of (1) puritanism to enjoyment, (2) self-righteousness to openness, (3) violence to creativity, (4) politeness to honesty, (5) bureaucratic efficiency to human relationships, (6) "objective truth" to personal knowledge, (7) ideology to existential decision-making and action, (8) authority to participation, (9) tradition to change.

Choosing present behaviors rather than national ideals, and attempting a social-psychological orientation rather than a moral one, the eight areas finally selected represent those that are to me areas of basic conflict. Some of these areas will be "resolved" (diminished in degree of conflict) sooner than others—some in five years, some in ten, some never.

Value Assumptions Being Challenged

The value placed by adults on past experience

The assumption that there must be implicit respect for authority

Assumptions regarding the war and patriotism

Assumptions regarding the place of women in our society

The assumption that work is a virtue and that leisure must be justified

Adult assumptions regarding the major function of sex in our lives

Adult assumptions regarding drugs—legal and illegal

Changing assumptions about the meaning of life

References for Exploration*

Fabun, Don. *The Dynamics of Change.* Prentice-Hall, 1967.

Gardner, John W. *Self-Renewal.* Harper and Row, 1964.

Green, H. *I Never Promised You a Rose Garden.* Signet paperback, 1964.

Heinlein, Robert A. *Stranger in a Strange Land.* Berkley Medallion Book, 1961. (Much more than science fiction—the book is also adventure, politics, philosophy, and an amazing psychology.)

Hoffman, Hans. *Discovering Freedom.* Beacon Press, 1969.

Keniston, Kenneth. *Young Radicals: Notes on Committed Youth.* Harcourt, Brace and World, 1968.

Maslow, Abraham. *Toward a Psychology of Being.* Van Nostrand, 2nd ed., 1968.

May, Rollo. *Love and Will.* W. W. Norton, 1969. (This is already a classic.)

Morris, Desmond. *The Human Zoo.* Dell Publishing Co., 1969. (A profound yet an invitingly written description of man in the intense urban environment, where he behaves similarly to animals restrained within the confines of a zoo. The author of *The Naked Ape* describes us in terms of having moved from tribe to super-tribe, status to super-status, sex to super-sex; he analyzes minority groups, learning, creativity and the lack of it. It is difficult to cite this book as a reference for one chapter, it is appropriate for several.)

"New Life Styles for Americans." *Society,* Special Issue, Feb. 1970. (This journal was formerly called *transaction.*)

Peterson, James A. *Counseling and Values.* International Textbook Co., 1970.

Roszak, Theodore. *The Making of a Counter Culture.* Doubleday, 1969.

Toffler, Alvin. *Future Shock.* Random House, 1970.

*The only footnote you will find is this one. It seemed essential to tell you that the seemingly casual nature of these lists of chapter references is deliberate and not accidental. In these lists I want to share with you books, journals, and films that I thought might become resources for you. Most of them have meaning for me. I have not read all of the books nor seen all of the films, for in some cases I trusted the judgment of friends and have put *their* favorites in the list. For a few other items, the quality of the author insured the quality of the book. All of the journals I do know, and they are included in the hope that I might introduce you to a new one that would open up another dimension of thinking for you.

The references roughly follow the topic of the chapter. Some I could have placed in any one of several chapters. In this first chapter I have introduced you to some of my best "friends" regardless of whether or not they fit the chapter! The number of references in each is held to a minimum. A voluminous bibliography always frightens me away.

Some of the books and films are on the solid conservative side, while others represent "future shock." Including both is deliberate. Some are classics or are currently popular and you will have read them, of course. Fine! We have friends in common. A little fiction and science-fiction have crept in—each one says something that I think is significant or that stirs up the imagination.

I hope that some of the references suggested will add to your enjoyment as well as to your understanding.

CHAPTER II

Changing Values 1:
Past Experience, Authority,
Patriotism

THE VALUE PLACED BY ADULTS ON PAST EXPERIENCE

There seems little doubt that the value of past experience is decreasing for both young and old. Although heavily relied upon in the educational systems of both primitive and advanced societies, learning from the past experiences of others is less meaningful than ever before. The reason lies in two kinds of realities: (1) The accelerating rate of technological and social change makes the world of older people and their experience in that world much less relevant than ever before; (2) decrease in the extent to which the two generations have similar value assumptions causes the younger person to question what the elder says has been "good experience for him." What the adult learned twenty years ago was learned in a world quite different from the world of today—different in technology, degree of urbanization, level of affluence, international relations, stance of minority groups, and attitudes toward work, authority, personal responsibility, etc.

Of course distrust by the young of the relevance of their elders' experience has been present in every generation. But the young generally *listened* even though they disagreed. Many youths listen less now because they sense the fast pace of change far more than do their elders. They hear older people talking with surprise or disbelief about phenomena or behavior they take for granted. In the ten-year period between their twelfth and twenty-second years (say, 1960–1970), they have seen more change in social areas and attitudes than their parents saw in three times that length of time (say, 1930–1960). This, in spite of great technological change, a depression, and a world war. In the past ten years vast and rapid changes have occurred in space exploration, attitudes toward the military-industrial complex, incidence of violence, attitude toward war, concern for the rights of minority groups, awareness of poverty that is widespread in an affluent society, drug usage, cost-of-living escalations, voting rights of youth, and the questioning of authority. These are but a few in a wide-ranging constellation of changes with which today's youth have grown up. These things, woven into the lives of youth today, are still strange and threatening to many adults. As the young hear adults rejecting the very things that are normal reality to youths, they lose confidence in what adult experience has to offer them.

"Learning from experience" is a commonly used expression which most often means learning from one's own experience. "How much has he learned from this experience?" is a legitimate question. Learning *is* experience. One learns to behave similarly again if the outcome is a

16

"pleasant" one—if there is satisfaction of some need in a manner appropriate to oneself or praise from another. One also learns not to repeat behavior if the outcome is "unpleasant"—if one is punished or ignored. Personal experience then, in action or thought, is familiar to all as a major means by which learning takes place.

Vicarious learning, learning from others, is a different story. Much of our school curriculum is based upon vicarious learning. But this is still subdivided into learning from others' present and learning from others' *past.* It is learning from the past of others that seems increasingly less reliable as a resource for the young. Much of the curriculum seems to the young to be more relevant to others' past than to their own present, to say nothing of their projected future. Anecdotal material introduced by such statements as, "Now when I was a girl . . . " or "My father always told me . . ." gets little farther than the eardrums of the young.

It is both realistic and sad that the experience of the older generation is thus discounted by the younger. It is realistic because we actually have little to say from our past that is relevant to the present; it is sad because parents and teachers, *when relying upon their experience as a source of help,* feel less and less helpful to the young owing to the fast pace of change. There are many different ways in which the young desperately need the older generation: for affection and trust, for patience with youthful fumbles, for influence and wisdom to change the present in the direction of the future, etc. But offering past experience, in and of itself, is not one of the ways.

To use an analogy, many adults are seen by youth as oarsmen in a *rowboat,* moving forward while facing the rear and moving into the future while facing the past. And so urgent is the adult's need for movement that he seldom stops rowing long enough to sight what lies ahead. The young prefer the *canoe* in which they can paddle facing forward, needing to glance only occasionally to the rear to see how far they have come and from where. To carry the analogy a bit further, the young need the old to paddle on the other side of the canoe, with both of them facing forward. The energy of both is needed. On the other hand, the presence of an oarsman and a paddler in the same vessel is seldom proposed as a desirable combination, but it is all too common a phenomenon in the world of the two generations.

There is danger in an analogy; the resemblance may appear more accurate than it actually is. The advantage to the young, be he counselor or client, in always facing forward is not clear-cut. Much can be gleaned from the past to strengthen the present and thus provide hypotheses for the future. The past has much to teach us, but it must be a distilled past, composed of selected social and personal learnings that are relevant to the present. That many youths are rejecting the past unfortunately is as true as is their complaint about their elders. Perhaps today's youth will never learn from the past as much as have previous generations. But oarsmen *are* needed—to face backward critically, to sift out and study what have been the basic conditions of society that have caused periods of war, of economic depression, of technological forward spurts. Some of these causal factors will doubtless be present in future decades. Although it cannot be proved they will be, the stakes for survival are high enough that society cannot afford to miss a bet by ignoring the past.

The Generation Revolt

Reluctance to learn from the past is not a new phenomenon. Every generation has known generation conflict. Louis Feuer reasons from the past in his *The Conflict of Generations* (see References) and concludes that the present youth protest will be no more effective in producing change than were the protests of earlier generations. I reason otherwise. This generation's protest has some very distinctive characteristics. Perhaps there is a point to be made here that will affect our understanding of all changes of value, not only the value of experience.

Today's student demonstrations, for example, occur in a world that has never existed before—a world of relative affluence, of instant and omnipresent communications, of minority groups that are bold enough to speak out, and of a host of colleges and schools that are no longer for the elite but for the multitude. If one wished to hazard a guess on the rather distinctive causes of this generation's student revolution, the following might be listed:

1. A rejection of many of their parents' goals of life as superficial, unrealistic, and materialistic.

2. The irrelevance of much *formal* education in comparison with the relevance of the *informal* education inherent in television, travel abroad, a wide range of reading choices, the mobility of families within our country, etc.

3. An awareness that youth today are much older in knowledge and experience than were their peers of a generation ago, and yet they are not given a proportionately greater chance to participate in determining the nature of their formal education.

4. The power of numbers possessed by youth, who are feeling that power. In 1970 the median age of the United States population dropped to its lowest point since 1940—27.9 years of age. This

means that there were as many people in the "young" group, under 27.9 as in all the rest of the population put together. For the year 1970 within the crucial age range of 15 to 25, there was a sizable contingent of 36 million people, 25 million of whom were eligible to vote ("Characteristics of American Youth," *Current Population Reports,* January 1972).

5. The desire of youth for quick results in social and educational change because rapid change is the order of the day in many other dimensions of our culture—science, technology, communication, transportation, family life, new occupations, etc.

6. The triggering effect of outspoken black, brown, and other minority groups, with their sense of social injustice, upon the white majority group disaffections.

7. A willingness of youth to take more risks in demonstrating their resistance to the status quo—they worry less about jobs than the youth of previous generations, and economic survival seems more assured. (This, of course, may change markedly during the 1970s.)

8. The uncertainty and disagreement among adults regarding what is "right," despite their seeming dogmatism. This confusion creates a vacuum in the world of values and certainties. Youth thrust in, seeking values that are as yet unrecognized.

One characteristic of this generation's revolt against adults is that *neither side is really hearing what the other is trying to communicate.* There is dialogue, often under crisis conditions, but listening to the other does not necessarily mean that one *hears* what he says. Sometimes the words used by the young sound strange and vulgar to the elders, and those used by the elders sound hackneyed and hypocritical to the young. All of this has happened before, of course. But social and economic conditions of today seem more appropriate for action by the young: the young are more knowledgeable; the time intervals between crucial technological and economic changes are shorter; there is a deeper sense of both acknowledged and unacknowledged guilt and frustration upon the part of parents, which makes them vulnerable. There is more of all this than in previous generations. Leonard Gross in *1985, An Argument for Man* (see References) sounds a more hopeful note. He argues for the growing integrity of his generation and says to his sons, "Don't underrate the Silent Generation." Because parents are unhappy, they are increasingly willing to communicate with unhappy youth.

A series of assumptions? Yes, but it could be that this generation's protest will last longer and cause more dramatic changes than ever seen before in a "conflict of generations." Delaying such developments, however, will doubtless be the more immediate reaction of our society to the activism of the 1960s—a reaction of severely repressive measures against further demonstrations and rebellions. The early signs are already being seen in the 1970 and 1971 actions taken by school boards, college trustees, and state legislatures. In addition, parents seem to sense the gap less clearly than do their children. In a study at the University of Southern California, for example, 80 percent of students in the sampling testified to the reality of a generation gap, but only 50 percent of their parents admitted that there was a "real" gap.

Another factor to consider is that there are more than two generations involved in this conflict or lack of agreement. As a result of the increasing longevity in America, we may now have three generations existing in the same family at the same time, even though not often in the same house. We have more elderly people in this country than we have ever had before, as well as more young people. Young people, of course, have increased in numbers more dramatically than have the elderly. For example, in 1964 there were 2.8 million who had attained the age of 18. A year later the number had jumped to 3.8 million (those born in the postwar spurt of 1947), an increase of more than a third in just one year. This was the peak increase, of course, but the 18-year-olds will increase slowly but steadily in number each year throughout the 1970s, reaching a figure of 4.2 million in 1980 ("Population Estimates and Projections," *Current Population Reports*, November 1971). There is little guesswork about such figures—these people are already here. And most of these millions of young people have "gap problems" with two other generations, not just one.

By the same token, there are more parents living well beyond the youth stages of their children. As recently as the turn of the century, the average family was likely to be broken by the death of one parent before the child left home. The generation conflict was lessened if for no other reason than the effect of this high mortality rate. Currently, however, many families have three generations alive and kicking. This means that the parents of today's youth must keep communication channels open in both directions! Certainly the present generation conflict seems considerably more complex than previous ones.

THE ASSUMPTION THAT THERE MUST BE IMPLICIT RESPECT FOR AUTHORITY

Young people have always questioned parental authority—whether openly or not. This is the only way the child can grow up and become "his own man" or a self-responsible woman. Under conditions of normal personality development, this questioning becomes increasingly explicit as the child becomes an adolescent. For the very small child, saying "no" represents the only way he can establish his own identity, can see himself as a self distinct from the personalities of his father, mother, and siblings. Often a period of negativism develops somewhere between the ages of two and four when the child is trying out a new dimension of existence. He says "No!" to everything.

Another and even more critical upsurge of negativism takes place at the beginning of adolescence. Sometimes this occurs even before puberty, around the later years of junior high school. The young person now becomes annoying to teachers as well as to parents. Up to this time teachers might have assumed that rudeness, surliness, and defiance were reflections of the home culture. In a sense the child could be excused and the parent blamed. But this adolescent rebellion is more apparently a part of a re-emerging self for which the youth is responsible—and the school partly so. Furthermore, the rebellion and negativism are directed against school as well as home, teacher as well as parent. This negativism is more than frustrating to school personnel, it is threatening. Many wonder, "What haven't I done, or what have I done, to bring *this* upon me?" The thoughtful teacher or counselor goes further to say, "How can I help this nonconforming (by adult standards) boy or girl to conform at least in part to the school requirements and expectations? How can I help him become *self-responsible* within a System without his being seriously bruised or even crushed by the System?"

It is true that the intensely individualistic youth must learn a *degree* of conformity if he is to survive in a society that will place some restrictions upon him. One hopes that institutions which exist to serve youth will become responsive to pressures for change. Schools, however, find it difficult to allow societal change to affect educational change without a crippling lag in time. They are never "caught up." The author of *Future Shock* puts it very bluntly: "Our schools face backwards toward a dying system, rather than forward to the emerging new society. Their vast energies are applied to cranking out Industrial Men—people tooled for survival in a system that will be dead before they are."

So students in high school and college resist the authority of the school even as they have resisted the authority of the home. The school thus plays its part in the widening circle of resistance to authority. During the early 1960s the resistance and the demonstrations were primarily at the college level, but the phenomenon spread downward into the high schools and probably will continue to spread into the preadolescent school situations. A 1970 study of urban high schools found that 85 percent of them have had some sort of disruption within the preceding three years. A study made of university freshmen indicated that about

30 percent of them had participated in student protests at the high school level. High school protests centered around matters relating to the immediate school situation, such as disciplinary rules, school services, dress codes, curriculum policy. Increasingly the college population's resentments are directed against some of the broad economic and social dimensions of our society. The reasoning in either case is the same, a resentment against the assumption that everyone must give implicit obedience to constituted authority. Later I will say more about the nature of resistance in both school and college, but the factor that arouses the most immediate concern is the amount of violence associated with such protests.

The Nature of Violence

Violence against people and institutions is a social phenomenon in its own right. Some people use violence because they are hostile enough to lash out against anyone, not particularly caring what the outcome might be. Some people are socially irresponsible and get satisfaction from destroying, a feeling that leads to unabashed vandalism. Some people are violent only when they are drunk and have enough relaxation from their inhibitions to try to hurt those whom they resent.

Violence is an inherent characteristic of most societies, civilized or primitive. Civilized society, which acknowledges the inevitability of violence, sternly restricts it. The right of self-defense, for example, is not absolute. Violence is condoned when it is leveled against a "breaking and entering" intruder but not when directed against one who is committing trespass. The law recognizes the validity of personal retribution, but only when it is a judicial act, not a personal one. In our modern civilization, violence is recognized as a common psychological phenomenon. For instance, there is a Violence Clinic in the Massachusetts General Hospital that treats the chronically violent or those who fear they will "break over" and become violent. Then, too, we have legalized violence called war, and we have socially approved violence in the occasional treatment of criminals or those suspected of crime. Violence at one time was the approved method of dealing with the insane.

Violence is a social phenomenon which, while extending back through the ages, is still peculiarly contemporary in some of its manifestations. There is little doubt that a model of violence is set by war, particularly a war in which "the enemy" is unknown or does not follow established rules. The war in Vietnam demonstrates that what we cannot achieve by negotiation we try to achieve by killing. We thus elevate the model of violence as the means of achieving desired ends.

Discussion of the research on violence in TV programs is like the discussion of research on smoking cigarettes—you can find what you look for. For example, one set of research studies exposed angry subjects to film violence and to the open display of guns in the room. Such exposed subjects responded by consistently giving more electrical shocks to their laboratory partners than did control subjects who were not exposed to the violent stimuli. There has been a lot of whitewash about violence on the TV screen. We have not ended that chapter of study yet.

A statement could be made that every generation has seen violence and read about it. True, but this is the first generation of "media" children—those bombarded daily with the sights and sounds of violence on the TV screen. This says nothing of their ability to handle their agressions while propelling three to four thousand pounds of steel down the highway. To the frustrated or angry person, driving an automobile almost invites violence as, indeed, does war. A disturbing trend in the American outlook is the association of violence more with property damage than with people damage. A study by the Institute for Survey Research (University of Michigan) revealed that 68 percent of a large representative sample of men associated violence with civil disorder but only 27 percent associated violence with crime; 85 percent see looting of property as violent, but only 35 percent see police shooting of looters as violent. Is this an unwillingness to accept, as fact, man's brutality to man?

The Nature of Authority

Whereas there is sadness when youths question experience, there is alarm when they question authority. It is accepted, although regretfully by many, that children will question the authority of parents or of teachers. Young people today go further and question the authority of school or college as a social institution or the authority of societal precepts that have been written into law. At this point the specter of "civil disobedience" appears, and all of society becomes frightened. What is neglected is the realization that our youths do not fight law and order as does the acknowledged criminal, who gets what he wants at whatever cost. The criminal does not question the law, he violates it for completely selfish ends. On the other hand, with many of this generation the questioning is profound: "Is this law *right*? Is it just? Do I have to violate myself in order to respect it?"

To be sure, some youth violate the law in the same manner as the criminal, engaging in senseless and destructive violence. But these, I believe, represent a minority of the youth who engage in civil disobedience. Many more question the "rightness" of a draft law in a time of "peace," for example, or the rightness of election registration procedures that discriminate against a minority, or the rightness of an ordinance that forbids demonstrations of what one believes in or objects to. Youth question the unqualified legitimacy of all constituted authority in much the same fashion as they question the value of past experience.

"The civil disobedience of youth" may have a nasty ring to it, but one could guess that to most adults it is the "disobedience" that sounds worse than the "civil." For the young are supposed to obey, these adults believe, else "what is our society coming to?" Present conditions of coercion, discrimination, complacency, neglect, elevation of the import- ance of material things—new things, big things, many things—make youth ask the same question, "What *is* our society coming to?" This is youth speaking. I don't know how "right" they are, I merely know that they are, that they are important, that they are more likely to be "with" the technological and social conditions of this era than I am. We would do well to listen to them.

Many youth question authority because justice looms larger. Much of the present authority seems unjust or dehumanizing to them. It isn't that they haven't a conscience; it is that they have an intensely personal conscience. So the question arises, "Which conscience do I listen to when the two seem to be in conflict—social conscience (the integrity of the law) or personal conscience (the integrity of me)?" One must keep in mind that civil disobedience has a long and honorable history in our country. Think of our early revolutionary forefathers who secured our independence, the suffragettes who won citizenship rights (voting) for women, the abolitionists who contributed to the freeing of slaves, Thoreau the idealist who inspired Gandhi. All of these engaged in civil disobedience, in violating the law.

Civil disobedience is a violation of the law, but it may also be an attempt to establish principles of justice, to rectify legal wrongs. It was Rhinelander, a law professor at Stanford University, not a rebelling youth, who said: "A free society commits itself to the principle that law and order by itself is not enough unless this law and order incorporates justice." Hitler had plenty of law and order; so did Stalin and Mussolini. If law and order were enough, then a totalitarian state would do a better job than a free society. George Woodcock wrote: "While there are still men who disobey in the name of justice and decency, humanity is not enslaved. When the duty to obey without question is accepted, that is the moment of freedom's death." James Russell Lowell used picturesque language to say much the same thing: "In private and personal wrongs, we do well to put on the meekness of the lamb; but when some great injury is done to virtue, all they are asses which are not lions."

Thus, there is no *legal* justification for a defiance of authority (civil disobedience), but there may be a *moral* justification. I do not want to whitewash all of youth's defiance; there are ugly aspects to the justification of disobedience and to the manner in which disobedience is expressed. But civil disobedience may be morally justifiable if it: (1) is for a principle, not a person, (2) is for something that proposes a move forward so that the disobedience is more than merely negative, (3) avoids violence to the person and to property of others, and (4) embraces the willingness to pay the penalty for law violation. These are exacting criteria, but I believe that many young people would abide by them if the generation "in authority" would accept them. Van der Haag in his thorough and thoughtful article on "Civil Disobedience" (see References) makes this same distinction between moral and legal duty and provides a careful statement of some other conditions under which civil disobedience is morally justifiable.

A lessening of respect for authority, or a defiance of it, is not limited to the youth of the United States. At least twenty-five of the countries of the world, including Japan, France, England, Russia, Sweden, India, Mexico, as well as the United States, have experienced student rebellions. Many of these have started out constructively but have developed into violent and undisciplined situations. Such violence may result as much from the methods of those who opposed the demonstrations as from bumbling or cynical leadership of youth. Perhaps the key lies in the fact that rebellions have most often been directed against some symbol of adult authority such as universities or state houses where the young feel they have been denied participation in the governance of institutions that vitally affect them. The young resent the fact that laws governing the education, the behavior, and even the lives of the 16- to 20-year-olds are made by men and women in their 60's, 70's, and 80's in our national Congress and by those only slightly younger people in our state legislatures (no age limit for politicians!). The young people who can be drafted to risk their lives in warfare or imprisoned have had until 1970–71 no voice in the laws that thus dispose of their lives. They also resent the tendency of the university or college to specify what they must take to become educated; they want a voice in determining what "being educated" means to them.

Here, again, the TV has played a vital part. From the ages of four to six and onward, the young are exposed via television to what may well be a biased picture of the evils of authority and its restrictions on personal freedom. The law may win out eventually in each film but only by a tortuous process in which the viewer is thoroughly exposed to law violation and violence. The young learn all of this long before they learn that limits are a necessary condition of freedom and that without limits there is no freedom.

As I ate lunch today in my study and was at about this point in my writing, I read a poignant editorial in my university's student newspaper *(The State Press).* "Someone out there," the writer commented, "is starting to notice the 41 million individuals who are between the ages of 15 and 26; someone is working on a national youth policy that will lower the voting age to 18, lower the age of contractual responsibility, etc. But what good will this do," asked the writer, "if the adults of our world don't trust us? We will still be living in a world of distrust and being 'put off' regardless of our improved legal position." Perhaps, the editorial went on, the civil disobedience exhibited by youth is a cry for attention. "Listen to us," they say. "We have ideas, we want to share the world with you, not be on the outside looking in." "But," said the writer, "our generation in fighting for recognition must recognize two things that are unacceptable to responsible members of a free society, whether young or old—violence, which is often a prelude to anarchy—and the desire to control rather than to share in control."

This sounds responsible to me. So does an Associated Press story which quotes a university student-body president, Pat Steiner, as saying to his elders: "You brought us up to care about our brothers, you brought us up not to run away from injustice but to recognize it and fight it. And now you castigate us. You castigate us because we think and we care. You demean our consciences, the consciences for which you are largely responsible. And you insult us by describing our protest as social fun."

Not all statements of young people are as reasoned and thoughtful as the two illustrations just given, and certainly not all their behavior is. Yet we are easily shocked by the lack of consideration and occasional violence exhibited in the rejection of authority. It is easy to fall into two traps: (1) to generalize from the obvious few to "all young people" and (2) to assume there is "no reason" for what is done. Even if we do not make this last assumption, we still may fail to inquire as to the reason or to listen to it if given. We are frightened by the common disrespect of youth for authority, frightened and threatened, and we respond emotionally, out of fear. This is not the response that will enable us to learn and therefore to contribute to control.

Nor do I think that the younger generation is against authority *per se.* Youth react differently to someone who is *an* authority *on* something and to someone who is *in* authority *over* others. The first they trust, particularly an authority on a topic that is meaningful to them. The other they may distrust, saying, "Who gave him authority over me, how did he earn the right to have such authority?" George Leonard has prophesied that "The Seventies will most likely see a plunge in the value given to power-over-others."

Leonard would, I believe, agree with sociologist Thomas Hoult who, in discussing the four major social problems of growth, technology, capitalism, and authority, said that our present crisis was compounded of (1) a breakdown in our environment and (2) our experiencing of "a widespread rejection of established authority and the manifest inability of our traditional institutions to solve pressing problems." (A 1971 Phi Kappa Phi initiation address to be published in the *Phi Delta Kappan.*) These are strong words, but they indicate that current problems of authority and social institutions are crucial enough to have become the leading concern of scholars as well as of youth.

ASSUMPTIONS REGARDING THE WAR AND PATRIOTISM

There is a reasonable hope that by the time this book appears any substantial investment of American people and American lives in the Vietnam situation will be ended. Under such an assumption the question may well arise, "Why discuss the Vietnam war which is past—why beat a dead horse?" In more personal terms, why do I raise this sensitive question?

Even though the Vietnam war may be ended in its physical sense, or substantially so, the scars of the war will remain with us throughout the lifetime of this generation. The war itself is bad enough, with its shocking loss of hundreds of thousands of the most vigorous men of many countries and the most brutal, indiscriminate killing of women and children in modern history (high-flying bombers and guerrilla mortar shells do not spare the innocent). But there is more than this. Vietnam has become a rallying point for those who object to the assumption of the prevailing culture that when war is demanded by a government, the individuals necessary to man the guns and the planes and the ships respond without question to their government's call.

There are many reasons why this war has proved so controversial, and I need not review them here. It can be concluded, however, that this is the first war since the War Between the States more than a century ago that has thoroughly divided the American people. We say this "war," but war has never been declared. The younger generation has become increasingly suspicious of the national motivations back of this particular armed conflict and our part in it, but distrust of the war is not restricted to youth. Far from it. Among adults there are "hawks" and "doves" as well as a middle-of-the-road majority (again speaking in 1971 terms). Hawks, however, have not been all of one mind. Many do not like the war but think we should get it over with at all costs and stop the bloodshed. They dislike war but think an all-out effort is the quickest way to end it. Other hawks are motivated by an intense fear and hatred of Communism and feel that no price is too great to stop the advance of this system of thought. They wish the United States to be seen as protectors of the weak and defenders of those threatened by Communism.

The doves, on the other hand, seem frequently more concerned about human beings and human lives than about the political implications of one system of government versus another. Some of the liberals of our country are strictly humanists who are more concerned with people than with governments. These same humanists declare that we have no right to sacrifice the bodies and minds of our young people for the sake of *any* political idea or threat.

The doves have said that the hawks were elevating political suspicions and fears above the lives of our people, while the hawks have replied that the doves were sentimental about matters of war and were "soft" on Communism. The hawks were sure that peace with less than total submission of the opposing Communist forces would mean a victory of Communism as such. It would also result in the world's concluding that the United States had come off second in the clash. Here enters our national pride which has, of course, disturbing political implications. Here also is youth's concern that we shall not espouse a point of view which elevates the state above the individual.

Such arguments, widely distributed through the mass media, have influenced young people of draft age even beyond their concern for their own welfare. More recently there has developed a deep distrust of what has been called the military-industrial complex. Mulford Sibley in reviewing Seymour Melman's book, *Pentagon Capitalism* (see References) wrote:

> The tentacles of Pentagon capitalism are far-reaching indeed. More than half the research money of the nation is at its disposal and some two-thirds of the scientific, engineering and planning talent. Colleges and universities are beholden to the war machine in numerous ways. Labor unions do its bidding, often gloating in new so-called defense contracts. Congress is subject to its continuous pressures, since it employs some 339 lobbyists and expends about $4 million a year just to influence the national legislature. What chance do peace organizations have against such massive power? The wonder is that they accomplish as much as they do.

The amazing fact is, of course, that all this elaborate panoply has been sup-
posedly developed to accomplish an end that cannot be attained. For there is
little doubt that national defense by military methods is impossible. Melman
recognizes and emphasizes this again and again.

"At present," he rightly says, "each of the great nuclear powers can destroy
the other, and neither can prevent the other from so doing—and this holds no
matter which one moves first." New instruments of destruction continue to
supplant the old, at astronomical costs, despite the fact that "new weapons-
systems, adding to the already enormous stockpiles of overkill, can only dimin-
ish the security of all."

The fantastic waste of the system is, of course, known to those who have read
the Proxmire committee reports. Melman estimates the waste from May 1963 to
May 1964—on the basis of General Accounting Office figures—at $10 billion
(*The Minneapolis Tribune*, August 9, 1970).

The Draft

Most of our American wars have been associated with the draft and
with draft resistance. What then is different about the resistance to the
draft law that has prevailed during the period of the Vietnam conflict?
One difference has been already defined—young men were drafted in
this situation to fight an undeclared war that did not involve the direct
defense of our own country and that ideologically was debatable in its
consequences. There are other differences: (1) the young people of this
generation have shown more distrust of prevailing political and legal
expectations; (2) those of draft age have been personally concerned
because of what they knew to be the heavy casualty rate, a casualty rate
which was identified with a country alien to their knowledge and background; (3) the draft obligated them to enter a way of life which for
many was seen as dehumanizing and the antithesis of their personal interpretation of the meaning of existence. Many young men, therefore, have
resisted both the war as such and the war in terms of how it brutalizes
the participants. To some this psychological wounding of war seems
more abhorrent than the possible physical maiming. They were asked to
sell out not only their lives, but their souls.
We have had draft resistances before, of course, but this one has been
quite widespread. It has involved many young people who were thought
of as "responsible" because they were attending colleges and universities
and came from "substantial" families and backgrounds. In 1967 there
were 29,000 investigations of the Selective Service violations, and 763
convictions (by 1969 the figures were 32,000 and 887). I have not
thought it worthwhile to compare the proportion of people engaging in
draft evasion in this war with the number who opposed, say, the Civil

War or the Revolutionary War because historical perspective does not help us particularly at this point. What we know now is what has been happening for the last ten years in this country. This is our vivid memory and this is the crux of the questioning of values. In 1972 the draft appears to be on the way out, but the memory lingers on and the scars of the 1960's will still be evident throughout the 1970's.

Responsibility to One's Society

For young people there has been an intermingling of value assumptions regarding war in general, the Vietnam war in particular, the use of the draft, and one's responsibility to society. Youth have been feeling that they are not only substantial in numbers but well informed and possessing a certain culture of their own. For this reason it seemed particularly unfair to them that they were old enough to fight, possibly to die, yet not considered mature enough and responsible enough to vote.

The U.S. Congress changed this in 1970 for the national elections. At that time only three states gave 18-year-olds a voting franchise in local elections, but the national referendum of 1971, which resulted in the Twenty-sixth Amendment, changed this too. The concept of legal age is a curious one. In the United States a young person has not been legally an adult until the age of 18 if a female, 21 if a male. This age of 21 is a throwback to the Middle Ages. In that not too dietetically robust society, a man was not considered an adult until he was physically strong enough to don armor and use a heavy sword. Hence 21, when one's body was physically strong, became the dividing line. Such a concept of adulthood is today wholly outdated. Today's young person is an adult by age 17 or 18 in every sense of the word except legally and (to a degree) educationally. He is physically taller and stronger at 18 than was the 21-year-old of the Middle Ages and of course knows a thousand times more about himself and the world around him. But he has not been "of age," although legally he could be drafted to fight the nation's wars. This paradox frustrated the youth of the 1960's as I am sure it did the youth of earlier generations.

Although 18-year-olds are substantial physically, most of them have not reached the end of their educational road. They need more time to prepare for life's full responsibilities (such as military service!). With 60 percent of our high school graduates entering college and with increasing pressures for a high school education as a minimum for all who would seek employment, the tendency toward prolonged education will increase from decade to decade. So full psychological adulthood will come late. I am suggesting in Chapter X a change in the pattern of education that might bring "adulthood" earlier. On the other hand, the tendency to marry before completing basic schooling makes this kind of maturity more attainable. Although youthful marriages are "frowned upon" and are often unstable, people who marry young achieve a kind of marital completeness that is at least temporarily more satisfying than is their educational completeness or their full legal recognition.

It is this confusing question of adulthood—physically, legally, educationally, and maritally—that relates closely to the young person's sense of social responsibility. If people of the counterculture—in this case mostly those who are younger—question the assumptions of the war as such and the use of draft as such, it is reasonable that they also question the assumed values regarding one's implicit responsibility to his society.

John Gardner is well known for his concern about the "renewal" of our societal institutions and his fear that we can well become subject to the same decay that has destroyed preceding civilizations. His concern for society goes deeper; he fears that our failure to bring social institutions into line with human life and human needs will result in a breakdown of the relationship of the individual to society. He writes that traditionally we have spent much time exhorting the individual to act responsibly, but have done too little about designing the kind of society in which he *can* act responsibly (see References for Chapter 1).

It is this lack of consistency that the young today see so clearly. They have been considered responsible enough to carry out their government's orders in times of crisis, and yet not responsible enough to participate in determining the kind of society which they are defending. In this the young see a parallel between the authority of the parents from whom they have been liberating themselves throughout their adolescent years and the authority to which they must now submit in terms of the federal government and political decisions within that government.

In questioning the war and an individual's responsibility to the call of his government, youths are accused of being irresponsible. They are said to be unpatriotic. It is true that many youths are resistant to what they consider to be a jingoistic (boastful, bellicose) patriotism. I think that they confuse patriotism with nationalism—and many adults do the same. Columnist Sydney Harris has recently distinguished between the two in such a meaningful way that I quote his statement in full. Both older and younger generations might read with profit. He wrote:

> Most people fail to understand the difference between "patriotism" and "nationalism."
>
> Patriotism is wanting what is best for your country. Nationalism is thinking your country is best, no matter what it does.

Patriotism means asking your country to conform to the highest laws of man's nature, to the eternal standards of justice and equality. Nationalism means supporting your country even when it violates these eternal standards.

Patriotism means going underground if you have to—as the anti-Nazis in Germany did—and working for the overthrow of your government when it becomes evil and inhuman and incapable of reform. Nationalism means "going along" with a Hitler or a Stalin or any other tyrant who waves the flag, mouths obscene devotion to the Fatherland, and meanwhile tramples the rights of people.

Patriotism is a form of faith. Nationalism is a form of superstition, of fanaticism, of idolatry.

Patriotism would like every country to become like ours, in its best aspects. Nationalism despises other countries as incapable of becoming like ours.

. . . .

Similarly, the word "Americanism" must not be narrowed or flattened or coarsened to apply only to one flag, one people, one government. In its highest, original sense, it asks that all men become patriots to an idea, not to a particular country or government. And this idea is self-government by all men, who are regarded as equals in the law.

This is why American patriotism—properly understood—is the best patriotism in the world, because it is for all the world, and not just for us. To confuse it with nationalism, to use it for ugly purposes, is to betray the dream of those who made it come true. (Sydney Harris, in the *Arizona Republic,* June 22, 1971.)

A similarly vigorous definition is given by William P. Rock in the following passage:

What is the new American patriot? He is surely not a flag waver. He is devoid of nationalism because he realizes that before one belongs to any nation, one belongs to humanity. . . .The new patriot is always re-creating America by challenging those institutions, whether of society or of the spirit, which are oppressive. . . .America is great because America has the structural girth to contain the shocks resulting from its search for a new identity, because Americans have, I believe, the courage and the wisdom to challenge the established and to accept the new. (William P. Rock, "Alienation: Yes; Patriotism: Yes," *The Center Magazine,* November–December 1971.)

Mr. Rock lived seven years away from the United States, justifying his alienation; he returned to rediscover America and become a patriot.

A REFLECTION

Not long ago my wife and I were watching a TV program when something sad happened. The master of ceremonies, close upon the last notes of a beautiful and moving song, came on to the screen to lead a few seconds of applause in a casual and almost bored manner, then swung at once into the announcement of the next number on the program. He had insulted his audience (or at least the audience of us!) by not appreciating what the song might have done to those listening. It had apparently done nothing to him. I wanted to savor it for a few seconds, to wonder at its beauty, but he was intent only in the announcement of the next number. Perhaps I would have been also, had the racing studio clock been staring in my face. But it made me pause. How often have I done that in writing—raced on to the next section without pause or reflection?

When I pause at this point, I see that I have been writing about three areas—experience, authority, and patriotism—in which the most vigorous assailers of these prevailing value assumptions are the young. In these areas, although not in all areas, the counterculture is primarily a youth culture, the prevailing culture being supported almost entirely by older adults and some younger ones who follow their parents without much questioning. Claims of "experience," "authority," and "patriotism" are the chief weapons of the elder in keeping the younger "where they belong"—in seeing that the young person learns from and obeys those who are older.

I differ in my personal feelings about these three topics. I am sad when others don't want to learn from my experience and only ask about what I know. My experience is more real to me than my knowledge. Perhaps I am only seeking a chance to talk about what I have learned, perhaps about who I am (how infinitely interesting one is to oneself!), but I think it is more than that. Only as I share *me* with the other person will he share himself with me, and thus we move closer to each other. Besides, I *have* learned some things and I might even put what I have learned into their language if they would hear me. So I grow pensive and feel less useful as I ponder the experience question.

There is excitement for me in my discussion of authority. Can we help make this challenge constructive? It is the way change is made. So much in the old structure needs modernizing, or is the structure (the institution) to be left intact while we make the process more related to the present? I worry about violence, but accept it as a reality to be dealt with. I would like to channel anger into being *for* something, not merely against. Anger may be necessary as a motivation to change. So I still worry about the authority question, but am hopeful. Can we help youth to be selective in resistance to implicit obedience to authority—not to treat all forms of authority as enemies to be fought? Shared power, not focused power?

My feeling about the Vietnam war and what it has lead to in the lives and attitudes of youth consists of anger and frustration. We should not have gotten our nation into a condition in which so many young people have come to doubt the national purpose and integrity. War is not the only national situation prompting distrust by youth, of course, but it is a major one. And their confusion about the draft and other obligations to their country has not been helped much by the sight of national leaders calling each other names over the war. No, I get restive when I think of youth and the war—and maybe a little fearful. We so badly need loyalty for national survival—there is much to be proud of in our nation. Can we cut out the cancers before they spread further?

There is no "typical" reader, of course. If there were one, I would guess that he might be negatively impressed by my lack of assurance in some of these areas, my inability to say that this is "right" and then to hop on the bandwagon to support it. I have also only assumed that others would see rapid change as a kind of reality, not to be necessarily embraced and enjoyed but to be lived with and understood. Perhaps some of you readers don't like current changes, deny their validity, fight them. Then my treatment of change will bother you.

For some of you I may have seemed too partial to youth, tending to see their virtues and failing to criticize their excesses and injustices. I admit this bias also. So much more is being said about what is wrong with youth that I have tended to look at the other side of the coin. For still others of you, of course, I am really a confirmed Establishment man, patriot as well as patriarch, making noises as though I thought I understood youth. Well, my noises are earnest even if not always as wise as I would like to have them.

IMPLICATIONS FOR THE COUNSELOR

Changes in value assumptions that are taking place suggest two broad areas of concern for the counselor.

The Counselor's Values

A first concern is that the couselor examine his own hierarchy of values and check it against the contemporary scene. I do not suggest that the counselor must change his values to meet changing assumptions, but rather that he attempt to increase his openness to the intrusions of change. A feeling of great certainty that what he now thinks is right and is right for all time can become a simple rigidity. It is too easy to retreat into a secure castle of one's own construction and close the gates to all that might disturb. It is healthy to be disturbed, for this means that one is required to think, to test assumptions, to question thoughtfully the bases for conduct. It is more realistic to confess confusion than to parade conviction.

On the other hand, admitting confusion could be interpreted as justifying having no convictions, no assurances of vital values. I must anticipate at this point what I want to discuss more carefully later, that one can be *committed* to values and goals even though they are tentative. In fact, one must be committed to be real, but the commitment may be to values which are seen as subject to modification, as changing with experience. "Tentativeness and commitment" paralleling each other are powerful principles, presented more fully in the third section of Chapter V, pp 103–105.

The Client's Values

The second area of concern is the acceptance of the client's right to be *different* in his values. This difference between the values of the client and those of the counselor is often a difference between generations or between cultures. Always, of course, the values of the client are the product of his life experience, unique to him and often markedly different from the experience of the counselor. The 30-year-old, middle-class, socially accepted, college-educated counselor cannot be expected to understand in all cases the values of a 16-year-old, ghetto-reared, socially-rejected boy or girl or those of an affluent, socially amoral, parentally-rejected youth. In fact, experiential understanding of another is rare. What is most important, however, is that the counselor accept the client's values as being as real and as "right" for him as the counselor's values are for the counselor. There is too frequently a tendency to protest inwardly, "He can't really *mean* that," when the value expressed by the client is in sharp contrast to a related value held by the counselor. The point is that the client does mean that; his value assumption is as justifiable to him as yours is to you.

So far I have said nothing about the counselor's responsibility for helping the client to examine a given value assumption, particularly if the value is likely to result in behavior harmful to another or to society. He has such a responsibility, I am sure, differing widely from client to client and varying often with the client's psychological readiness to examine values. Basic to the success of any such confrontation, however, is the counselor's acceptance of the "right" of the client to have different values. If a counselor enters into a discussion of another's point of view with the implicit assumption that he is "right" and the other is "wrong," failure is assured. The result is an argument. More than this, it is an argument that is morally indefensible because you deny to the other person the claim to rightness that you assume for yourself.

I experienced such a denial during a 1970 discussion of the Vietnam war with a fellow-trustee and friend. She was shocked when I suggested that the immediate withdrawal of all American troops (her assumption) was not necessarily the only way out, that there were other alternatives. I confessed to being not totally sure of any of the alternatives. She was sure, however, and was convinced that I hadn't read the most appropriate materials or been thinking enough about the subject. When I said, "But couldn't I read the same materials that you read and possibly come to different conclusions?" her answer was a surprised, "Of course not, how could you?" The conversation became strained for a time. I had "lost" her and she had lost me. Because of our affection for each other, we finally got together again, but I am sure that she now is less assured of my wisdom. I, on the other hand, was disappointed that she denied my "right" to think differently even though I have since come to accept more fully her point of view. When this situation develops between counselor and client, something happens to the counseling relationship.

Dealing with Differences

I am sure that learning from another's past experience, having respect for authority, and feeling responsibility to one's government are battleground areas for counselor and client if the counselor allows them to become so. He can be so sure that he is right that his convictions become a threat to the client. He can be so sure of his convictions that he denies the client the innate right to be different. He may believe firmly in these premises: "My past experience has taught me so much that I would like to share; respect for authority is essential to an orderly society; responsibility for others and for the government that sustains us is necessary for survival." These and related convictions have roots deep within us. Can we permit others the "right" to differ on such crucial issues? To admit that (1) we cannot be sure of the permanence of all that we now believe and (2) a different point of view on the part of another is reasonable and defensible for him, is to lay the groundwork for a meaningful dialogue with students. The counselor as a person has the right to have convictions and to express them. As a *counselor,* however, he must be professionally judicious in the interests of his client as to the circumstances under which he "sounds off." Sometimes it is not the content of what he may wish to say but the tone of voice in which he says it. Should a counselor ever attempt consciously to influence a client? Of course, but with caution. What is sauce for the goose (the counselor) may only by coincidence be sauce for the gander (the client). Without question, a counselor influences a client in all sorts of subtle ways: tone, body posture, the questions asked, etc., without realizing that he is doing so. If he is sure that he has a strong conviction that may "come through" as an "I am right" feeling, he might well warn the client of it and thus reduce the degree of imposition.

What can you as a counselor do directly to help a student on matters of history, authority, and patriotism? One thing is to show the student that you think these are vital dimensions in modern life. This means more than listening to the student's views and encouraging their expression. It means also that *you* think about these areas, come to some conclusions regarding values that should not be lost—or values that can well be played down. Perhaps thinking means social action upon your part. Have you ever *done* anything about supporting positive values in these areas or fighting the negative ones?

I have introduced a new note here. Not only might the counselor listen to a student's values, not only think about his own, but also do something about them. "Doing" may mean the counselor's sharing with a student what the counselor sees as positive. Listening with understanding is not the counselor's only function here; sharing with the student his perception of positive values in a particular area is another responsibility. Once the counselor has listened to the client and is still seen as accepting him, then he can share personal insights and convictions with little danger of the imposition of values mentioned earlier.

This is tricky ground. How can one be sure that "sharing" is not seen as an attempt to influence? One cannot be sure, but sometimes the risk must be taken. How else is the client to see that there are positive values in an area that he sees as only negative? It may be important that he (or she) hear these expressed by someone in whom he has some degree of trust—trust because that person has listened to and accepted him. And these positive values need to be weighed by the client along with his awareness of the negative ones. If there is value in short-range historical perspective, if authority can at times be a protection of liberties, if loyalty to one's country means loyalty to her virtues and not her vices, how can the client appreciate these if we fail to share our insights with him? If your statement of the positive is not accepted, do not push or feel offended. The other person's choice is *his* or *her* choice, just as I have tried to say to you: "Read and choose. My voice is only my voice. If you disagree, you haven't lost ground with me, perhaps you've gained ground because you have listened!"

References for Exploration

Becker, William H. "Autonomy vs. Authority?" *Christian Century,* Sept. 30, 1970.

Berrigan, Daniel. *No Bars to Manhood.* Bantam Books, 1970. (A great book by a man of courage and dedication.)

Blatz, W. E. *Human Security: Some Reflections.* University of Toronto Press, 1966.

Evans, Robert A. *Belief and the Counter Culture.* Westminster Press, Witherspoon Bldg., Philadelphia, 1971. (A multimedia package with poster-illustrated book and two 30-minute records of counterculture music.)

Feuer, L. S. *The Conflict of Generations.* Basic Books, 1969.

Fuller, R. Buckminster. *Operating Manual for Spaceship Earth.* Pocket Books, 1969.

Gross, Leonard. *1985, An Argument for Man.* Norton, 1971.

Kennen, George F. *Democracy and the Student Left.* Little, Brown and Co., 1968.

Mead, Margaret. *Culture and Commitment.* Doubleday, 1970.

Melman, Seymour. *Pentagon Capitalism: The Political Economy of War.* McGraw Hill, 1970.

van der Haag, Ernest. "Civil Disobedience" *National Review,* Jan. 21, 1972, pp. 29–39.

The Hat (cartoon film). 18 minutes. Mass Media Ministries, 2116 N. Charles St., Baltimore, Md., 21218. (Delightful film about the stupidity of letting others decide things for us.)

The Magician (film). 13 minutes. Mass Media Ministries, 2116 N. Charles St., Baltimore, Md., 21218. (A fantasy involving a circus magician and children taught to use guns and to kill.)

The Merry Go Round (film). 20 minutes. Contemporary Films, Inc., 267 W. 25th St., New York, N. Y., 10001. (A biting commentary on the difference between the sexual attraction and experiences of a particular boy and girl and the logical comments on the subject made by Ann Landers [columnist], Dr. Albert Ellis [psychotherapist], and Mary Winspear [sex educator].)

Epple, Ron. "A Great New List of Short Films." *Media and Methods: Exploration in Education,* March 1971, 7:23–38. (An excellent reference on short films for study or for use with students. The article annotates each of 249 films, gives source, length, and price. In the selection of these films attention was given by Epple to the artistry of the presentation as well as the significance of content. Some are "far out" but they are intended to jog the imagination into action. I have selected only a few. Another source has been *Short Films in Religious Education*—the great majority of which are on social and psychological issues— by William Kuhns. George A. Pflaum, Publishers, 38 West Fifth St., Dayton, Ohio, 45402. Last supplement, 1969.)

CHAPTER III

Changing Values 2:
Women, Work

ASSUMPTIONS REGARDING THE PLACE OF WOMAN IN AMERICAN SOCIETY

One of the striking social phenomena of the past few years has been the change in the status of women in our society—in the family, in the occupational world, in political life—a change of status that has been unaccompanied by any marked change in the woman's perception of herself. Yet this is where it must start. Women must see themselves as persons, equal in personhood to men. This must precede, it seems to me, any expectation of change in men's perception of women. Men find it difficult to see that equalitarianism, so important in our assumptions about what it means to be an American, must apply to the two sexes specifically as it is assumed to apply to people generally.

How Women See Themselves

With all the brave talk about women's new freedom, the reality is that only a minority of women seem to want it. Only a distinct minority of women are vocal and active about changing the woman's perception of herself. President Nixon's "silent majority" of citizens—those who have the power to influence but who are too apathetic to use it—can be matched by the silent majority of women. They comprise 53 percent of the population of the United States (5.4 million more women than men in the United States in 1970, up from only one million more in 1950), yet the majority of *this* majority are hesitant to speak up for themselves. They seem to want no change in role despite a marked change in status. Women have more formal education than ever before (later noted is the increasing proportion of women in college); more have careers out of the home as well as in the home (a later section gives more attention to the place of women in the labor force); they "stand taller" in the world both socially and literally (today's average woman is almost one inch taller than her mother and—surprise!—an inch slimmer in the waist.)

Although still discriminated against in terms of salary and appointment or promotion to top ranks, women in increasing numbers have proved themselves as jurists, professors, physicians, architects, and as having capability in all fields. No major occupational area is now closed to women. This was not true a relatively few years ago. It was only in 1964 that civil rights legislation made it illegal for employers to discriminate against employees because of sex. But much has happened since then.

42

The widespread use of the Pill has given women sexual independence: they can now choose to have children or not, how many, and when. Women are increasingly active in the political scene—witness the number of women in the national Congress.

This changed status is recognized by many women who still see their main role as being loved and looked after by men. The Women's Lib movement appears to be focusing upon encouraging women to change their self-perception as a necessary prelude to bringing about changes in men's perception of women. As I mentioned at the outset, this seems both wise and necessary. The Business and Professional Women's Club has long fought for equality with men in jobs, salary, promotions. But Women's Lib, the National Organization of Women, and the Women's Political Caucus of the 1970's have a dynamic quality about them that surpasses both in numbers and activity anything seen for some decades.

Perhaps this very vigor frightens some women. When the subject is raised, Women's Lib often is rejected by women themselves. Below are some comments made by women about themselves (cited by Miriam Allen deFord, "Women Against Themselves," *The Humanist,* January 1971):

> "Women were better off when the only taste they got of the competitive world was in cutting each other's throats over a cup of tea."

> "Everything about us man has made—not woman. Women have got to be kidding when they say they want to help run this world. They are fighting a losing battle if they hope to equal men."

> "I would rather that my husband have more prestige at his career and I be only the lady of the house."

> "I don't care for women's liberation. I prefer the strong arms of my husband about me."

One wonders why, but perhaps the answer is simple. They have been conditioned for generations to see themselves in restricted roles, conditioned to "lean upon" men, often even to belittle themselves. From the cradle women are taught that it is *feminine* to be passive and submissive. A young woman friend of mine recalls the bewilderment she experienced when she defeated the boy genius in her fifth grade by "spelling him down" in a spelling match. She was bewildered, but he was not. He had the answer. "You're not very feminine. Girls shouldn't beat boys."

In our culture mental health is defined in terms of assertiveness for males and dependence for females. It is somewhat frightening to realize that 53 percent of the voting populace has been thoroughly trained in dependency. Erich Fromm has analyzed the potential harm that can come to a nation in which the majority have been taught to escape from the responsibilities of freedom by fleeing to or welcoming a state of dependency.

Of the differences between men and women known to be innate within the structure of the body, few, if any, appear to bear upon the personality dimensions of independence, self-respect, or autonomy. When one gets beyond physical differences between the sexes, the evidence points clearly to *social conditioning* as the cause of the distinctions between men's and women's attitudes toward themselves. An exception appears to be the large increase in boys at puberty of testosterone, which is associated with aggressive behavior.

This conditioning process has been evident for centuries, both in America and elsewhere. In 1792, English feminist Mary Wollstonecraft observed that "women are told from their infancy and taught by the example of their mothers, that a little knowledge of human weakness, justly termed cunning, softness of temper, outward obedience, and a scrupulous attention to a puerile kind of propriety will obtain for them the protection of men." Anyone who has viewed the television series "The Wives of Henry the Eighth" will recognize the probable accuracy of her statement. Later in the United States (1838) Sarah Grimke tersely wrote, "I ask no favors for my sex—all I ask of our brethren is that they take their feet from off our necks." Still later, in 1856, Elizabeth Cady Stanton stated, "We shall never get what we ask for until the majority of women are openly with us; and they will never claim their civil rights until they know their social wrongs. . . ." As the president of the National American Women Suffrage Association, Elizabeth Cady no doubt knew firsthand how difficult it was to get women to unite and claim their birthright.

The quotes above were used as illustrations in an interview with a prominent Women's Lib spokesman of today, Gloria Steinem (in *Redbook,* February 1972). She is encountering the same resistance voiced by Elizabeth Cady. Steinem attributes the cause of the resistance to the fact that many women believe they *are* inferior to men. "The worst punishment society inflicts on all second-class groups is to make a group believe it is second class." Philip Slater (in *Redbook,* February 1971) found this astonishing attitude of inferiority when he taught a course on the generation gap to middle-class women who had college-age children. Slater reported the women's response to his desire for a discussion approach to be "Who wants to talk to a bunch of women?" with obvious self-contempt.

Many women see themselves as appendages only, not as persons. Some even attribute their status to a "divine plan." An Indiana housewife who was interviewed by Vivian Cadden (*Redbook,* February 1972) proclaimed, "God made women for a reason and I think we should fulfill that reason. He made us to be a helpmate to men. I think we should be as God created us. Keep a clean house and take care of a man's meals and his clothes. After all, he's earning our bread." This statement illustrates what happens when an individual is convinced she is an appendage, existing only to play a role.

The July 1971 issue of *Mademoiselle* carried an article entitled "Female Sexuality: What It Is and Isn't." The article was in essence a round-table discussion between celebrities as diverse as James Dickey, Germaine Greer, Erich Segal, and the entertainer Viva. I was particularly struck by Viva's comments. She said, "If I knew what the male point of view is on sex, then I might know what the female point should be." She went on to deplore the fact that there are so many male points of view. "I wish they'd get together on it. . . . Then we could have a female point of view. . . ."

Here in a nutshell is the point that many feminists deplore. Women have learned to define themselves only in terms of men and most often by assuming the characteristics and opinions that are seen as being opposite to the male's. In other words, self-identity for many women is a matter of reaction rather than of "proaction." As a counselor I am always uneasy when I find a person who is totally dependent upon another's response to him or her, and who is willing *to alter himself* in reaction to it.

Part of the evidence for women's being man-defined rather than self-defined can be seen in the marriage vows. "I now pronounce you man and wife." These are not parallel terms. In essence it says, "I now pronounce you *person* and *role*." To say, "I now pronounce you husband and wife" would be to wed one role with another. Only the statement "I now pronounce you man and woman" would unite two fully functioning persons rather than person and appendage or role and role.

Esther Woo, in "Theology Confronts Women's Liberation" (*America,* March 13, 1971), points out that in a "male culture, females are necessarily looked at from a relational point of view." She goes on to say, "Men who discriminate against women most cleverly deny any 'human nature' to women by effectively limiting them to a relational role." Woo asserts that "there is but one human nature taken in itself. Male and female are modes of relation." To see nature as pertaining only to males eliminates half of human nature. In a philosophical sense, the feminist

movement can be seen as in the mainstream of the Humanist tradition.
It seeks a wholeness, an integration, a move away from fragmentation
into male and female parts.

Sexuality

In the recent reading I have been doing about women, I have been
struck by the lack of attention paid to women's sexual needs. For
instance, a lengthy article by Elizabeth Braly Sanders ("What Do Young
Women Want?" *Youth and Society,* September 1971) made no mention
of female sexual desire and need. Perhaps this omission occurs because
large numbers of women receive little sexual satisfaction (*Psychology
Today,* July 1971 and February 1972). Perhaps part of the responsibility for this lack of sexual satisfaction lies with men who take it upon
themselves to define what a woman's sexual response is or should
be.

A powerful article on "Sex and Equality" by the well-known team
of William H. Masters and Virginia E. Johnson is found in *Redbook* for
March 1972. The article is rich in content and covers a wide range of
topics. In their description of male-female relationships Masters and
Johnson detect a shift in the power structure of the sexual act. "Traditionally sex is something a man does to a woman. More recently it
has become something he does *for* her. Either way, he alone is responsible for making the experience good, bad or indifferent." The authors
go on to describe the ideal sexual situation in which partnership, not
power, is the dominant concept. "What men and women achieve
together benefits both—the very quality of life, *as it is individually experienced,* can be immeasurably augmented by a fully shared partnership."

In a chapter entitled "Understanding Orgasm" appearing in *Family in
Transition,* Susan Lydon says, "Women's sexuality, defined by men to
benefit men, has been downgraded and perverted, repressed and chan-
neled, denied and abused until women themselves, thoroughly convinced
of their sexual inferiority to men," would probably be dumbfounded to
learn that there is scientific evidence that women *can* get more pleasure
than men from making love.

Lydon's chapter outlines the Freudian psychoanalytic concept of the
female sexual response, which became a codified myth in our culture.
This theory holds that the clitoris is the leading erogenous zone for
females, but that in order for the transition to womanhood to be complete, the clitoris must abondon its sexual primacy to the vagina. The
clitorally-oriented female was termed by Freud to be "psychosexually
immature." Not until the 1966 study by Masters and Johnson was

evidence marshaled to refute this view. Unfortunately it will take a long time to undo the damage which this myth caused. When women truly enter into sexual intimacy in order to please themselves rather than because "he wants it," "it makes him happy," or "I hate to deny my husband" (*Psychology Today,* February 1972), a truly gratifying sexual relationship will be possible for both men and women.

Both Sides of the Coin

In the preceding pages I have taken some pains to summarize some of the views held by the protesters among modern women. Many of the statements cited are "Women's Lib" statements. I intended them to be. It seems important that the protesters among women be heard as well as the protesters among the "youth" of our counterculture. Most of the persons cited are certainly of this same counterculture, with the focus centered upon sex roles rather than youth roles. Discriminations, based on age (of both the young and the old), race, and sex are of one kind. Each questions the equality of dignity and worth among people for the irrelevant reasons of age, color, and sex. (In the next chapter I give attention to another kind of sex discrimination—that directed against men and women who find sexual satisfaction in ways that others label unnatural.) It has been easy for me to express points of view that represent "Her Majesty's Loyal Opposition." In this I have been greatly helped by Lynn Leonard, my research assistant, who, although not a Women's Lib member—are you, Lynn?—knows the literature on women better than I do. She provided me with excellent paragraph summaries, some of which I have used verbatim.

The other side of the coin must also be examined. Some women, certainly some married women, are happy the way they are. They are quoted disdainfully in some of the preceding paragraphs because they are happy and do not want to be disturbed—quoted by women (most often) who are not happy with the status quo and who *are* disturbed by it. What troubles me most in the area of sexual equality are the injustices against women in the occupational and economic dimensions of life. These are perpetrated by men and should be rectified. If, on the other hand, a woman likes her married life, her marriage role, and discrimination doesn't bother her, then give her freedom to be content! If she doesn't want to fight other women's battles, then I think I must respect her right to be herself as much as I respect others who are fighting sex discrimination. There is danger that the aggressive women's movements may become agents of polarization among women, while men sit back and enjoy the spectacle.

No, the major battle, to me, is for men and women to work together to right the serious economic inequalities between men and women.

Employment and Promotion Practices

It is true that women have made some gains. During the 1960's we witnessed the acceptance of the first female jockey and many female cab drivers. There are also a few professional fields in which women have made inroads: the social sciences, psychology, health technology, physical and occupational therapy, recreation work, personnel work, accounting, mathematics, and statistics. On the other hand, women still account for only 7 percent of the physicians and only 3 percent of the lawyers in the United States.

The May 17, 1971 issue of *Newsweek* told the story of Joe Porter and Mary Gardner, magna cum laude graduates of Harvard and Radcliffe, respectively. Both received their Ph.D. in Shakespearean studies. *Newsweek* reported that the only difference in their academic records was that "Mary's was slightly better." They sent out 100 job applications to colleges. The result was that Joe received 8 firm job offers and Mary received none. Though the colleges offered no explanation, Joe Porter stated that "Mary is a woman and I am a man and there's no other way to explain it."

The same article gave the statistics on promotion practices in academia. Women comprise one-fifth of the faculties of the nation's 2,600 colleges, but they are bunched at the bottom of the professional ladder. They tend to be frozen at the rank of instructor or assistant professor. In 1969–1970 at Stanford University, 30 percent of the instructors were women, but only 1.6 percent of the full professors were women; at the University of Michigan the corresponding figures were 40 percent and 4.3 percent. Harvard's faculty includes 582 male tenured full professors and 3 women tenured full professors. Berkeley has not appointed a woman to its music faculty since 1943, to its sociology faculty since 1925, or to its psychology faculty since 1924. Only 2.6 percent of the department chairmen in the colleges and universities are women.

Sex *per se* is denied as the basis for such discrimination on academic faculties. Most often a desire to avoid nepotism is the reason given, and this is an effective deterrent to the promotion and tenure of women Ph.D.'s, a large percentage of whom are married to Ph.D.'s. Yet this discrimination does not seem to work to the man's disadvantage; where husband and wife are on the same faculty, the general practice is that the husband gets the promotion and tenure.

Economic Disadvantage

Working women numbered 31 million in March 1970, yet today women workers are seemingly more disadvantaged than they were 30 years ago. In 1940 they held 45 percent of the professional and technical positions in the country. In 1969 they held only 37 percent of these positions. This is true despite a large increase in the proportion of women in the total work force (half of all women between 18 and 64 years of age are in the labor force).

Most women are working because of pressing economic need. In 1970 about half of all working women (48 percent) were either single, divorced, or widowed, or had husbands whose incomes were less than $3,000 a year. An additional 22 percent were married and had husbands with incomes between $3,000 and $7,000. (In 1970, in order to maintain a low standard of living for an urban family of four, an income of $6,567 was needed.) Thus, 70 percent of the 31 million women were working from economic necessity. (*Underutilization of Women Workers,* U. S. Department of Labor, 1971.)

In the face of this, it is disturbing to find that the woman who works full time is three times as likely to earn less than $3,000 a year than is her male counterpart. In 1955 the median earnings of a woman working full time year round was 64 percent of that of a male in the same category. By 1970 this had dropped to 59 percent. (*Fact Sheet on the Earnings Gap,* U. S. Department of Labor, 1972.) Many people are not disturbed by these statistics because they assume that women are not the sole breadwinners for the families. Yet 37 percent of all families at the poverty level are headed by women. Women head 1,934,000 impoverished families. ("Characteristics of the Low-Income Population in 1970," *Current Population Reports,* U. S. Department of Commerce, November 1971.)

The January 1972 issue of *McCall's* carried an article by Ralph Nader entitled "How You Lose Money By Being a Woman." Nader's article pointed to one clear fact: Whether a woman spends her life as a homemaker or chooses to work, the net result is less money for her in her old age. The average annual private pension for an unmarried woman is $200–$665 less than the average benefit for single men. Social security benefits for older unmarried women average $115 monthly as compared with $145 monthly for older unmarried men.

The older married women is no better off. A widow is generally excluded from receiving her husband's pension benefits after his death and is entitled to only 82.5 percent of her husband's social security benefits. However, husbands receive 100 percent of their benefits if they outlive their wives. Nader asks, "Are a woman's needs really 17.5 percent less than a man's?"

The net result is that the 7.5 million widows and single women over 65 constitute the poorest segment of our society. In 1970 half of these women had yearly incomes of $1,888 or less.

Conclusion.   There is much yet to be done to reduce discrimination against women in both jobs and income. (A step in this direction was taken with the passage in the U. S. Congress of the equal rights bill, which will become the Twenty-seventh Amendment if ratified by 38 states. All modifications were defeated, despite Senator Sam Ervin's [D., N.C.] assertion that passage of the bill would "repeal the handiwork of God.") Nevertheless, it is still "a man's world" and it is here, the world of work, that men can employ, pay, and promote in terms of performance, regardless of sex. On the other hand, women must move toward an assumption of equality with men in personhood. To continue the assumptions of subordinate status and dependency does an injustice to the dignity of the person. Perhaps women have a responsibility to "speak up for themselves" and to reduce, ever so slowly perhaps, the sharp differences between the man's culture and the woman's culture in our society.

A 109-item questionnaire on the roles of men and women, attitude toward Women's Liberation, and sexual relationships, completed by 20,000 readers of *Psychology Today* cannot be easily summarized. There are 15 tables of data, 12 pages of discussion, and 20 or so vividly personal statements. The report deserves careful and thoughtful reading; the reader will see his own feelings reflected more than once. Perhaps the last paragraph should be quoted:

> Ambivalence, conflict and resistance always travel with transition. Respondents show that women's liberation has a long way to go, at least by the movement's standards. At the same time, they are moving toward a reintegration of values that may, in the long run, be the most revolutionary change of all. Many young men are breaking out of the male mystique: they get primary satisfaction from their family and love relationships, and they are beginning to consider their wives' happiness in making career decisions. The women, in turn, get great satisfaction from work, yet do not want to sacrifice the warm gratification they find in love and family. In short, both sexes are moving toward a happy integration of what Freud said all healthy human beings should do well: love and work. (Carol Tavris, "Woman and Man," *Psychology Today*, March 1972, p. 85.)

As part of its continuing series on the liberation of women, *Redbook* featured in its April 1972 issue the questionnaire, "How Do You Feel about Being a Woman?" This questionnaire was designed for *Redbook* by Dr. Tavris, senior editor of *Psychology Today*. A preliminary report on the results of this questionnaire is planned for the August 1972 issue of *Redbook.*

THE ASSUMPTION THAT WORK IS A VIRTUE AND THAT LEISURE MUST BE JUSTIFIED

Youth (and some adults) are questioning the work ethic. In present-day America, however, only foolhardy youth and very courageous adults would be presumptuous enough to throw down this particular gauntlet. Work is born and bred into our very bones; "a hard worker" is written more often into current job recommendations than any other phrase. Such a phrase is more significant than any other today *because* some people are questioning the superior value accorded it. To attack this value is to threaten the very foundations of our existence—particularly in North America and those areas of the world that lie within the North Temperate Zone. Perhaps the value is especially prominent here because of the variable climate where at one time one could work only "while the sun is shining" and before "winter's blasts" hit the workers.

To some people any questioning of the work ethic seems both heretical and unpatriotic. Such questioning is labeled "heretical" by some because they feel it is "God's will" that we develop the world he has given us. Work is seen as an important part of our character since no goal of life is more important than achievement, etc. Questioning the work ethic is further labeled "unpatriotic" by some who feel that we must keep faith with our hard-working forefathers, that we must retain leadership in technology and industry in order to protect ourselves against "aggressors" and other external threats. People may hate their work but do not admit it. Work is "manly" or "womanly"; you are *supposed* to work. I, on the other hand, *like* to work! I get my greatest delight from achieving, whether it be getting the stubborn top off a jar of pickles or finishing the first draft of an article. I sigh with satisfaction, smile pleasantly to myself, feel slightly more worthwhile. It is possible that the dissenters respond in a similarly human way upon completing a task. Those who are disturbed at youth's questioning of work *per se* seldom stop to examine the reasons for such dissent and the nature of it.

Is it work that is being questioned or the kind of work? Is it work or our deification of it? If we listened, we might hear echoes within ourselves of some faint mutterings about "Work, work, all of the time, that's all I ever do. Where is it getting me? I am older every day and life is passing me by." These are likely to be whispered complaints, suppressed by conscience. Or, such complaints are forgotten if we are sedated by imbibing alcohol, swallowing a tranquilizer, losing ourselves in front of the "boob tube," or accepting praise for our industry from some faithful soul upon whom we can always count. But however we meet our doubts, if we have them, we are critical of those who raise the issue. Young people do not "know the value of a dollar." They have too much—they are lazy. We reason that since they have never witnessed mass unemployment with its soup lines of the hopeless and jobless, they cannot imagine the financial and psychological importance of having a job, of having work to do.

But the hunger and despair of joblessness are not all that youth have failed to encounter. Youth often encounter men who derive nothing more than a paycheck from their jobs. What is more, the young notice that many men seem to *expect* nothing more. Thus it is entirely possible that it is not work *per se* to which the young have an aversion. Perhaps it is the meaninglessness of most work that disturbs them. Or perhaps it is the seeming indifference to this lack of meaning which arouses their feeling that the "reasons for living" of many adults are superficial.

Like all youth before them, today's young people are concerned with the heart-searching questions of "Who am I?" and "Why am I here?" Yet seldom before have so many had so much time free from labor in which to ponder such problems. In Athens during the Golden Age of Greece only a quarter of the population was "free," but Greek culture and vocabulary reflected a society that was oriented to leisure. Today the usual concept of leisure is "free time"—time off the job. In Greece, *work* meant un-leisure. More than this, work was negative— the Greek word "work" had the same root as the word for "sorrow." It was a curse, nothing less. The gods were contemptuous of mankind and condemned them to toil.

Today we appear to be well on our way to achieving a degree of leisure which will far exceed that known by the Greeks. In 1967 the Southern California Research Council predicted that by 1985 the per-capita income (including children and nonearners) in noninflated dollars will be almost double what it was in 1965. From this prediction it is possible to infer that we will work half as much for the same income. This will be achieved either by taking a six-month vacation, or working a two- to three-day work week. The trend toward a shorter work week is well under way, with the four-day week now being tested as one alternative. Early in 1972 it was estimated that some 700 firms employing 150,000 people were "trying out" the four-day work week (see Riva Poor, *4 Days, 40 Hours*). But unlike the Greeks, we do not define work as "un-leisure." In Hebrew the word for *work* and *worship* is the same, and traditionally we have tended to deify work.

In America today we have not relinquished our deification of work—but we are questioning it. Note the analysis of why people become work addicts in the 1971 book by Wayne Oates, *Confessions of a Workaholic* (see References). Not all of the motivations toward overwork are commendable. Work is not a curse, but neither is leisure. We are currently ambivalent about leisure, although there are many for whom employed work and leisure are antithetical. We have not been a nation that has accepted leisure easily. Leisure must be fought for, won. Even then, it is not as worthy as work. The moral value given to work has not been matched by any moral value attributed to leisure. For leisure means pleasure, and pleasure is likely to be "sinful," wasteful, or at least not useful. This is the heritage that my generation has given to the younger generation. It has been said many times that North America has no tradition for leisure—it has only a tradition for work. "I've *earned* my vacation," "I haven't done enough," "He works so *hard*" (praise) are commonly used phrases that represent this attitude.

The History of Work Concepts in America

We can understand how our generation has inherited this reverence for work. Our early forefathers brought over from Europe a strong *religious imperative* for work. They built a *pioneer* society from which an *industrial* society developed.

The religious motivation toward work as a virtue received a mild impetus when St. Thomas Aquinas developed a system of guilds and corporations based upon the value to society of the work done. Until the days of Luther, however, work was still second in importance to prayer and contemplation. The present life was less important than the life to come.

Luther set a new tone. Work was not only essential, but it was carrying out God's purpose in one's life. Calvin went further and saw work as required by God. It was the major reason for living—man's work was to bring about the Kingdom of God. Idleness was a sin, and toil of all kinds was a virtue. An outcome of this emphasis upon the sacredness of work made possible the success of modern industrialism and modern capitalism as substitutes for the Kingdom of God.

This view of work as both essential and required of man meshed beautifully with the pioneer conditions to which our ancestors fell heir. Here "work as a virtue" became translated to "work as survival." The nonworker in our strenuous pioneer society was a liability, whereas he or she who worked contributed not only to self-survival but to the survival of others. Work was necessary in the most compelling sense although not necessarily virtuous in and of itself. Always there was much to do, and he who did not carry his share of the load was criticized.

This feeling about work as necessary was a useful carry-over from geographical pioneer days to industrial pioneering and to the development of an industrial society. Machines needed tenders and repairmen, and they required factories to make them. Labor was imported in large supply for the factories and mines, just as slaves were brought in from Africa to work the plantations. Work of all kinds was now honored in a sense which went beyond the stamp of religious approval. A man was thought capable of rising to any height if he worked intelligently enough and hard enough, no matter what the job.

The industrialization of our society, however, brought about a further and somewhat unexpected development. The determination of worth and status now became not only a question of work but of the *kind* of work. This distinction came soon after the mechanically generated energy of steam engines displaced the biologically generated energy of human muscle. Muscle became less important, the brain more so. Status then was derived from the particular occupation in which one was engaged because this determined the kind and the presumed "quality" of work done. There is little doubt that the hierarchy of occupational status present in our country early in this century would be a radically different one had we not developed into the mature stages of industrialism.

Thus it came about that status was achieved largely by means of the money possessed (the fruits of one's work) or the prestige of one's occupation. *Work* was now replaced by *occupation* as a means of determining one's significance. Generally one worked to succeed in an occupation, but it was the kind of work that counted, not merely work itself. In fact, when one used his brain to reduce or avoid physical work, it was counted in his favor.

Questions Are Raised

All of these earlier reinforcements to the justification of work as such are now being questioned. Religious motivations have become focused more upon social justice and individual integrity in which work (toil) plays less part than *intent* of work and the quality of human relationship involved.

The pioneer days of necessity are gone—there is no longer either "work for physical survival" or "more work than anyone can do." The film *America: The Edge of Abundance* proposed that we are now in a transition period between the pioneer days of necessity when there was so much to do and a future period in which the central significance of life will no longer be paid employment. Such a shift portends concern for rapid occupational changes requiring retraining and/or relocation. Rather than thinking of work as the major consideration, men will have an increased concern for insurance against unemployment and old age. In the future a "parceling out" of the "necessary" work will be imperative. There is a great distance between these concerns and the work concepts of pioneer days.

The basic justice involved in modern industrialism (dependent most often but not always upon capitalism) is being seriously questioned by more members of our society than just the young. Sometimes the questioning is indirect in the form of complaints against the insulting depersonalization of urban industrial life, the increasing air and water pollution resulting from the "advances" of technology, and the increasing tension in crowded inner-city living. Often there is a direct questioning of the social ethics of modern business and industry with their focus on power over many in the hands of a few. What is resented is the dictation by these few of how, when, and where a man shall work. Often there is little regard for what such dictation does to the individual's sense of significance or sense of self-determination.

Man needs to work; a life of complete leisure would be unsatisfying. (The statement will arouse skepticism on the part of some readers! "Just give me a chance at complete leisure, I'll take the risk," would be their reply.) My proposal is based on specified definitions of both work and leisure that are given in the latter pages of this chapter. Anthropology enables us to follow man as he evolved from a vegetarian gatherer of roots and berries, to an omnivorous hunter with specialized tools for obtaining meat, to a cooperative member of an agrarian or pastoral society. Throughout this long history we see clearly that the ability to secure food for survival was an ability which man enjoyed demonstrating to others. Modern fishing and hunting stories are but pathetic imitations of the boasting done by primitive man when he engaged in what was truly a survival effort! George Pettitt writes of the primitive Arunta of Australia: "When the band came together for its evening meal all shared in what was available, but the successful hunters of the day bustled around the fire with beaming faces; the unsuccessful ones sat quietly at the outer edge of the group." (George Pettitt, *Prisoners of Culture,* 1970.)

There is little in our society today to provide these personal satisfactions from "survival work." Few produce food directly, and few of those get any satisfaction from seeing the products of their work satisfy the hunger of those who eat it. The *evidences* of work done are impersonal and symbolic. Few see the finished product of their labor, few get satisfactions other than money as a symbol of their work product, and often here the reward is a symbolism twice removed—a check which represents money which represents work! Job satisfaction studies place economic security high on the list, but it may not be at the top. Dimensions of psychological security such as personal control over conditions of work, kind of supervision, companionship with others on the job, significance of his own or his group's contributions to society may be rated above money as job satisfiers.

As man loses control of both the product and the process in work, he feels estranged from the outcome. In this state of alienation he no longer feels in control of the external world, his home, or his family. Highways, once proudly viewed as evidence of man's ability to subdue the earth, now encompass and constrict him with chains of asphalt and concrete. Once man's voice was the sole authority in his own home. This enabled him to feel like king in his own castle. Today other authorities invade the home, and no psychological moat is able to stem the armies of authorities who invade his privacy via the mass media. Children are no longer the product of the father's sole guidance. Hence they are less predictable and controllable. When these children accuse their father of being a mere "cog in the machine, the system," he feels he has received the final blow. Even as he points to the house, the car, and other tangible proofs of the value of work done, he senses with his children that this proof is too many steps removed from the work itself.

It may be that the satisfactions of work must be enjoyed before the satisfactions of leisure can be realized. Leisure is no more of a panacea for a decreasing number of work opportunities or lack of satisfaction on the job than are improvements in work environment or unemployment insurance. Youth worry about meaningless work or work toward solely monetary ends—more recently they have begun to worry also about decreasing job opportunities for youth. True, automation in business and industry has not reduced the number of available jobs as rapidly as had been anticipated, but a steadily expanding technology inevitably decreases the number of meaningful work experiences. (The relation of education and occupational experience is discussed in Chapter IX.)

If work and leisure have a reciprocal relationship and are to be considered as two parts of a whole, then perhaps a new definition of both work and leisure is necessary. If a sense of personal significance, of a contribution to society as basic as that made by those who hunted the game or harvested the crop or prepared the food for consumption by their immediate group, is a basic human need, then is "paid" work the only means of securing this satisfaction? Assuming that we will have fewer paid jobs in any sense of "necessary" jobs and fewer in which the work involved is meaningful to the individual, perhaps we should expand the concept of "work" to include paid or employed work *and* unpaid or voluntary work. Work satisfactions, those derived from doing something which is meaningful to you or seen as a contribution to your society, can be either paid or unpaid. This means: (1) Not all who work —for themselves or society—will be directly compensated financially. "Income" may come from employment *or* society. (2) Not all who are employed will get their achievement satisfaction from employment. Non-employed work may provide the most direct meaning for their lives. Some will work at a meaningless job but engage in satisfying work for themselves or others during their leisure or nonemployed time. Some will exist economically upon a guaranteed living wage or insurance, but still engage in "work" which is meaningful in terms of self or the needs of others.

The dissent against the value concept of "work as a virtue" does not seem to me to be a denial of the value of work. If it is intended as such a denial, then the dissenter will be going down a blind alley in his attempt to find life satisfactions. To *do* something is highly significant— the question is what you do and for what purposes. Some youths are doing nothing now but do not find it very exciting. They live physically because their parents or someone supports them economically. Their satisfaction comes from seeing their do-nothing existence as a protest, an *active* protest against meaningless life goals. But the prevailing culture cannot appreciate the members of the counterculture who protest against meaningless work. Arthur Miller wrote (and here he was thinking of Willy Loman in *The Death of a Salesman*):

> When a man has spent the best years of his life punishing himself with work he hates, telling himself that in his sacrifice lie honor and decency, it is infuriating to confront young people who think it is stupid to waste a life doing hateful work (italics in the original). It is maddening to hear that work ought to be a pleasure, a creative thing rather than a punishment, and that there is no virtue in submission to the waste of one's precious life. The older generation has an investment in waste and self-denial, and when these are mocked, honor is seemingly soiled and degraded.

> What the young are threatening is the very existence, psychologically and spiritually speaking, of the old. The very idea of self-deprivation for the sake of the hallowed upward climb to success—the most fundamental tenet of America— they deny and are not impressed with. Instead they want to exist now, today, this moment, quite as though it were not more important to arrive at old age in a decent retirement when one can die of inanition or commit suicide. The old are defending precious things. When Biff Loman tried to convince his father, Willy, that he had a right to want only to live an ordinary life, perhaps even a worker's life in the open air, this was like a man's spitting on the Bible. It was to deny the virtue and value of Willy's life of striving and foregoing and accom-

plishment. It was a patricidal attack, for if you take from Willy his self-punish-
ment and his sacrifice for success, you have very little Willy left—except the best
part of him, the part he has been taught is contemptible: his real joy in lying on
the cement stoop in the sun, his simple curiosity about strangers, his love, for
which there is no acceptable expression. (Arthur Miller, "The War Between
Young and Old," *McCall's,* July 1970.)

Work and leisure—can we still live with these two words? Robert Lee
suggests the work-leisure relationship could be viewed as a rhythm in
life, not as opposed segments of time. ". . .Giving need not be confined
to work and receiving to leisure, nor serious requirements to work and
fun to leisure. . . . To give oneself to time (all of it) and to let the events
of life 'happen' is to open oneself to the meaning contained there."
(Robert Lee, *Religion and Leisure in America,* 1964.)

IMPLICATIONS FOR THE COUNSELOR

Women

Throughout the section on women, my aim has been to place the
feminist movement within the mainstream of Humanism. Like Birgitta
Linner ("What Does Equality Imply?" in the November, 1971 issue of
The Journal of Orthopsychiatry), I am interested in seeing individuals
freed from the strictures of sex-role stereotypes so that they can focus
on what it means to be truly human. I have stated that a great deal of the
work must be done by women in terms of changing their own self-perception. They must learn to overthrow their image of themselves as
second-class citizens and as mere appendages. The "consciousness raising"
efforts of the Women's Liberation movement have been most effective
here. However, I do want to be clear on one point. When I say that a
great deal of the work must be done by women, I do not mean to imply
that men are exempt from any effort on women's behalf. As a counselor,
I am well aware of the effects of feedback. The problems women have
with self-image are almost entirely the result of the feedback they have
received. It will be almost impossible for women to reconstruct their
self-image unless the men in their lives change the feedback which they
give to women.

What I have said is my own attempt at consciousness raising for counselors of young women. What follows are questions I think counselors
might do well to ask themselves prior to beginning counseling (vocational
or personal) with any young woman.

1. When counseling with a young woman, am I equally concerned that

she develop all her potential and talents, or do I tend to see her fulfillment as deriving solely from being a wife and mother?

2. Am I willing to take a young woman's career goals and aspirations as seriously as I do a young man's? Or do I tend to show less enthusiasm, concern, and interest in the aspiring female engineer, lawyer, doctor, etc.? Do I inevitably tag on questions such as, "And after college, then what?" with a strong implication that marriage must follow and rule out a career?

3. Do I find it easier to accept career plans from a young woman who lacks physical attractiveness? When a capable, cute, and vivacious counselee tells me she wants a career and not marriage, is my first thought "What a waste" or "What a pity"?

4. Do I convey this message to the counselee? Do I indicate in some way that I consider her career choice somehow "deviant," that I see her as less acceptable than I would if she were planning on marriage as her vocation?

5. Do I tend to view the more independent and assertive young woman as "less well-adjusted" than her conforming counterpart? In my private thoughts do I characterize her as a "castrating female" and silently heave a sigh and prayer for "that poor boy who will have to put up with her"?

6. Do I thus tend to reinforce subtly more docile, dependent behaviors in my female counselees while negatively reinforcing more independent and assertive behaviors?

The counselor needs to be fully aware of his power as a feedback agent. A great deal of the disservice and injustice that has been done to women has been through the "phallocentric" bias of psychiatry and psychology. Counselors are in a position to do much to correct these injustices.

Work

I am hopeful about the changes taking place in work-leisure assumptions. There is much more meaning to life than work (even though I may be a poor personal example of this principle!). On the other hand, there is real danger that "work" will lose its dignity unless we change the meaning of the term. Work does not have to be restricted to paid employment in which the size of the pay check is more significant than what is produced. *Work can mean something done, achievement whether paid for or not, whether accomplished during employed hours or "after hours."* Work can mean a sense of achievement, a reason for being, a fulfillment of a moral objective. Work is very satisfying to me, because I like working in the realm of people and ideas. Both are endlessly varying and stimulating. So when I say "work is satisfying to me," I know it is a blend of my kind of work and of habit. Is it more than this? Is work in its best sense satisfying to many? I really don't know—I don't know how "normal" I am!

The counselor has had the implications of the changing work scene pointed out by many writers. The concern of earlier writers about occupations as paid employment has shifted somewhat to a concern about work—who wants it, how much of it is there, and what about the leisure time which one is unprepared to use effectively? As I read the prophecies made about work and leisure in the future of our society, I am impressed with the specious simplicity and the sweeping generalizations of the solutions that are proposed. For one writer, the solution is a *guaranteed annual wage* so that no one is required to work at tasks not meaningful to him. For another writer, the answer is *guaranteed full employment* so that everyone has a job and gets psychological satisfaction from working. For another, a *shorter work week* for all so that everyone has some days of work each week. Others propose more active and more frequent *recreational opportunities.*

I see no one solution, but a combination of several. Working for pay will not appeal to everyone—perhaps because the authority of the employer is resented, perhaps because there is little satisfaction for some individuals in a pay check. Differences in patterns of motivation and satisfaction will continue, and work will continue to have different meanings for different people. Leisure, in the sense of freedom from any requirement, will continue to appeal to some and not to others.

Perhaps "work" and "leisure" as separate and opposed terms will disappear and be replaced by the term "new work." This could be defined as demanding activity, even strenuous activity, that is satisfying because it is self-fulfilling. "New work" could become the common element in both occupation and nonoccupation. The machine that substitutes for muscle and the computer that does repetitive and demanding brain work will continue to grow in influence. But unless men and women change markedly in the satisfactions they find in achievement for its own sake and in creativity for its excitement, they will continue to need work.

One perception of work that might make sense to youth would present a blend of employed and nonemployed work in a commitment to a responsible whole in which one works for self-fulfillment and the fulfillment of others. This is the concept of *vocation, of a commitment to life, of a sense of purpose in life.* Youth have difficulty in finding a sense of commitment to industrialized, organized, fragmented work. But they want commitment—why not commitment to life, commitment to "vocation," of which paid occupation is but a part? Some adults have this now, of course, for they work in occupations which permit the contribution of self as well as of time in service to others or in creative self-involvement.

Some occupations become vocations more easily than others. I am tempted to name some of the healing and helping occupations here—physician, nurse, teacher, social worker. But this doesn't tell the story. Some workers in these occupations see only the pay check; their job is routine and not self-involved. Workers in many other occupations *make* that occupation a vocation, a commitment to self and others. A secretary to an executive can do this, as can a man who builds houses which become homes, or a woman who sells life insurance to protect those left after death, or a janitor who cares for a building and all of the people in it. Can counselors help youth gain this creative perspective on work?

In the next chapter we deal with two value areas—sex and drugs—where youth appear to be in marked conflict with their elders. These are areas which youth think are their thing: "Don't tell me what to do here!" They are wrong, of course—sex and drugs belong to the prevailing culture also; they are not the prerogative of youth. "We" and "they" are both involved. Developments in one of these areas makes me thoughtful and hopeful, while the other makes me feel depressed.

References for Exploration

"The American Woman" *trans*action, November-December 1970.

Clark, Dennis. *Work and the Human Spirit.* Sheed & Ward, 1967. (A thoroughly delightful book of depth and humor.)

DeGrazia, Sebastian. *Of Time, Work and Leisure.* The Twentieth Century Fund, 1962.

Figes, Eva. *Patriarchal Attitudes.* Stein & Day, 1970.

Goldberg, Lucianne, and Jeannie Sakol. *Purr, Baby, Purr.* Pinnacle Books, New York, 1972. (At times bitter, at times humorous, this publication of The Pussycat League is an articulate denunciation of the Women's Lib movement. It is as intolerant in treatment as the movement which it criticizes but it shows clearly the other side of the coin. Some of the chapter titles suggest the direct nature of the content: "Femininity Under Fire," "The 'Myth of the Vaginal Orgasm' Myth," "Sex and the Single Pussycat," "Mar.ied is Better," "Labor Pains and the 'Equality Game.' ")

Greer, Germaine. *The Female Eunuch.* MacGibbon and Kee, 1970.

Holter, Harriet. *Sex Roles and Social Structure.* Universitetsforlaget (Oslo), 1970.

"How We Live and With Whom" *Women: A Journal of Liberation,* Special Issue, Winter 1971.

Kraus, Richard. *Recreation and Leisure in Modern Society.* (Parts III and IV.) Appleton-Century-Crofts, 1971.

Lepman-Blumen, Jean. "How Ideology Shapes Women's Lives" *Scientific American,* Jan. 1972.

Linder, Staffar Burenstam. *The Harried Leisure Class.* Columbia University Press, 1970.

McDermott, Sandra. *Female Sexuality: Its Nature and Conflicts.* Simon and Schuster, 1971.

Montague, Ashley. *The Natural Superiority of Women.* Macmillan Co., rev. ed., 1968.

Moore, G. H., and J. N. Hedges. "Trends in Labor and Leisure" *The Monthly Labor Review,* Feb. 1971.

Oates, Wayne. *Confessions of a Workaholic.* World Publishing Co., 1970.

"On the Women's Movement" *The American Journal of Orthopsychiatry,* Special Section, Oct. 1971.

Poor, Riva (ed.) *4 Days, 40 Hours.* Barsk and Poor, 1970.

Skolnick, Arlene, and Jerome H. Skolnick. *Family in Transition.* Little, Brown and Co., 1971.

Time, Special Issue, March 20, 1972. (An issue giving comprehensive coverage of the situation of women in America with special attention to their position in the areas of religion, politics, the world of work, law, and education. Consideration is also given to the average woman's acceptance of Women's Lib. Includes a current bibliography of Women's Lib literature.)

"Women at Work" *The Monthly Labor Review,* Special Issue, June 1970.

Of Time, Work and Leisure (film.) 29 minutes. Indiana University, Audio Visual Center, Bloomington, Indiana. (A contemporary analysis —what would our clock-conditioned people do with more leisure?)

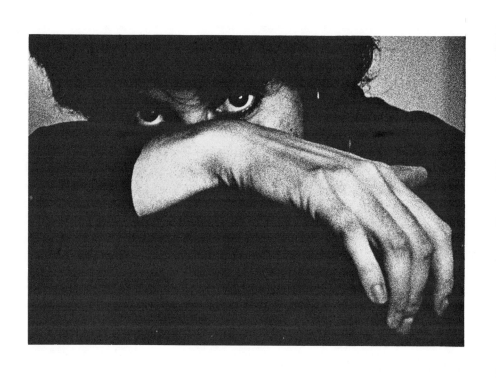

CHAPTER IV

Changing Values 3:
Sex, Drugs

ADULT ASSUMPTIONS REGARDING THE MAJOR FUNCTIONS OF SEX IN OUR LIVES

The values associated with sex attitudes and behaviors have long been more sensitive and emotion-laden than those associated with any other value area, with the possible exception of religion. Every culture has its own pattern of sex taboos and rituals. America is no exception, having most in common, of course, with the countries of Western Europe. Until recently, in fact, we have been one of the most conventionally regulated of all of our neighbors in this area of behavior. Even now we are more conventional than many Western European countries.

That sexual behaviors have changed markedly during even the past two decades would be acknowleged by most adults. Recent follow-up studies by the Kinsey Sex Institute (University of Indiana) conclude that sexual behavior has changed a great deal over this period of time. Whatever the reality accepted by those of the prevailing culture, a great debate still rages over whether such attitudes and behaviors *should* have changed. Of course this is a useless approach. In the main, the middle-aged and older generations argue among themselves or throw down the gauntlet before the young. The young seldom pick up the gauntlet or enter the debate. Rather they simply go their own way being conventional or unconventional as a matter of their right to be themselves.

In a curious fashion, sexual freedom has brought a new kind of anxiety. For people of the prevailing culture, sexual behavior or even erotic thoughts frequently brought feelings of guilt about having done what they thought they should not have done. The new sexual freedom has brought a different anxiety. Instead of worrying about having had pre-marital sexual experiences, people sometimes feel guilt about *not* having had experiences, and anxiety lest they *cannot* have them. Under current conditions many people feel concerned if they do not exercise their full sexual freedom or if they cannot fully experience the sexual act. This has led Rollo May (in Chapter 1 of *Love and Will*) to say that we have now a new Puritanism, a concern if one has not "had sex." This results too frequently in a depersonalization of the sexual experience—sex without love, without feeling. When a person is anxious about whether he has had a sexual experience or can have it, the full meaning of the sex act (the culmination of intensified feelings of intimacy and closeness between two people) is lost. The sex act then becomes a mere travesty of this full reality. A satire titled "Sex As Work," is found in Skolnick and Skolnick's book of readings, *Family in Transition* (see Chapter 3 References).

Factors Influencing Changes in Sex Attitudes and Behaviors

That sexual behaviors and attitudes toward sex have changed is the result of a number of factors, some more obvious than others. For example, the presence of many more youths in our country than ever before gives each young person a greater degree of peer support in behaving on his or her own terms rather than in response to adult mores. To consider a specific age level, during the early 1960's the number of 18-year-olds was growing four times as fast as the rest of the population. Beyond this, more young people are going to college, where they are responsive to peer relationships and peer standards. This is particularly true for an increasing proportion of hitherto sheltered women who are now in colleges. Year by year their proportion has increased, until now about 40 percent of the students enrolled in colleges are women.

The above are broad demographic factors. More specifically, certain technological developments have vitally affected the amount and kind of sexual behavior of young people. There are, for example, numerous and far more effective contraceptives than ever before in our history, particularly oral contraceptives. Whether or not these should be used by the unmarried is a moral point, but the fact that they are used—and used widely—is indisputable. The availability of such contraceptives coupled with the wide use of the automobile for dating and sexual exploration are technological developments of significance in understanding changed sex mores.

The concept of home and family has also changed. The home is no longer a place of drudgery for women in many classes of society. They have more household conveniences and more free time for themselves. By this token many more women can work outside the home if they wish. In 1970 something like 12 million married mothers worked outside the home. Some of these, of course, were heads of families who worked because of necessity. Others worked because they desired to do so, because it lent something to the enjoyment of living. The father also has a new role in the home. With the development of the baby bottle and lessened dependence of the child upon the mother as a food provider, the father came into the picture in a more complete sense of the word as a provider of emotional warmth. It seems evident that the whole feeling of both young men and women about sexual life and home life is one of greater sharing and more equalitarianism. This factor may affect the ease with which young people enter into sexual relationships and early marriage.

The increased mobility of families (more comment on this in Chapter IX) is another sociological factor leading to a loosening of common inhibitions in the field of sexual behavior. This greater mobility of the family has exposed many young people to a wider variety of peer life and behaviors as well as to a wider variety of parental expectations through these peers. The choice between two lifestyles—their parents' way or its exact opposite—is no longer the only alternative known to them. Mobility not only increases exposure to varying ideas in the field of boy-girl relationships but is also a factor in the changing nature of family influence. Families that move about as frequently as do American families seldom grow very deep roots in a community. Children who live in homes that are always temporary are less likely to be influenced by stable family mores than were children in previous generations. There is too little time in any one location to develop mores which are consistent over the total period of one's childhood. Under these conditions it becomes easy for young people to develop their own sexual attitudes and behavior and not depend upon family approval.

The increased amount of erotic stimulation available in this country also contributes to more sophisticated sexual attitudes. Erotic scenes and suggestions are visible everywhere—in movies, on the newsstands, even on the TV. On the bookstands in almost any drugstore in America are to be found paperback book covers which are designed to sell books. Covers exhibiting a substantial amount of near nudity or sexual suggestions are thought to sell more copies than would an emphasis on the title or on the content. Vance Packard in his classic *The Sexual Wilderness* (see References) has one chapter entitled "The Bombardment of Sexual Stimuli." In this he gives descriptions of the particular television scenes, movies, books, types of dress, and so forth that are sexually stimulating. This proves rather shocking reading to a person (like me) who is not too familiar with trends in TV and the movies, but who is certainly aware of the seductiveness of paperback covers and the attractiveness of miniskirts!

There is probably no area of behavior in American life besides sex in which there are so many taboos and no area in which the taboos are being more seriously challenged by the younger generation. This does not mean that the older people have not also violated the taboos but rather that they have felt guilty about doing so and are consequently critical of others who do the same thing. (A sense of guilt is often accompanied by severe criticism of behavior similar to what brought on the guilt feeling—this is the psychological mechanism of "projection.") Young people, on the other hand, behave as they do without much sense of guilt. They simply ignore the taboos.

Certainly all of this has led to a change of value concepts, accompanied in turn or followed by the change in behaviors. Rules in this field, which have frequently been established and enforced by organized religion, now are less effective. In a large part this is because churches play less of a role in young people's lives than they have in previous generations. Perhaps the values of all organized bodies are less effective now than formerly. There is, in general, a greater sense of hedonism among the young people of today in which the enjoyment of "now" is an important factor in the business of living.

A somber note needs to be introduced at this point. With greater sexual freedom there has been concomitant increase in venereal disease. During the past five years the VD rate in the United States has doubled. The November 1970 report of the American Social Health Association declared that venereal disease had become pandemic (an epidemic of unusual extent geographically and of unusual severity). Only twice before during this century has a pandemic condition of venereal disease been reported. It is estimated that at any one time in the United States today, 14 million people suffer either from gonorrhea or syphilis. Nor is this situation confined to America. The World Health Organization, assessing the VD increase in the United States, Scandinavia, and Great Britain, says that "gonorrhea is out of control."

People who oppose sex education (there is strident opposition, well supported by such conservative groups as the John Birch Society) could not be aware of these realities and still be against sex education. Of course, the critics focus upon the placement of sex education in the schools rather than in the church or the home. It requires but little knowledge, however, of the freedom of male-female relations today to conclude that sex education in all three institutions is probably still too little if the sexual behavior of young people is to become more intelligent and responsible.

It may be surprising to some that churches are becoming more courageous in assuming responsibility in this area. A recent announcement described a curriculum entitled "About Your Sexuality," produced by the Unitarian Church for use in the religion classes of that church. Consisting of both printed materials and explicitly clear illustrations on film strips, the curriculum covers topics such as anatomy, intercourse, contraception, masturbation, petting, and homosexuality. "Its purpose is to help 'children grow up to be caring, loving people' who are 'non-exploitative' in their attitudes and decisions about sex," writes a *National Observer* reviewer. This same reviewer pointed out that Herder and Herder, a New York City publisher of books of Roman Catholic interest, has recently published *The Sex Book,* a thoroughly illustrated encyclopedia of human sexuality. The author, Erwin Haeberle, comments that "sex is 5 percent biology and the rest is cultural attitudes." *(National Observer, August 23, 1971, page 1.)*

Some Contemporary Concepts of Sex and Sexuality

For many adults the major *legitimate* function of the sex act is to reproduce and propagate the species. For those individuals, pleasure in the sexual experience is incidental, accidental, and almost surreptitious. For those in the counterculture and for those who are younger rather than older, the major function of sex is to contribute to the enjoyment of living. Reproduction is a planned, and for some a secondary, by-product. Not all of this is selfish and sensual. Young people today have seen many signs of unwanted children. Sometimes they themselves are legitimate but unwanted children.They see an overpopulated planet smothering in its own wastes—all of which makes them more reluctant than ever to bring more children into the world. With the availability of contraceptives and with concern about the millions of children who are, even in this country, undernourished and ill-treated, it seems reasonable to them to think of the reproductive feature of sex as secondary.

There are those who believe that the whole concept of sexuality in human life is coming into better perspective. Someone has said that at some time in the past "sexuality got separated from the rest of life." As a consequence certain features of the total pattern have become abnormally exaggerated. Those who believe that human sexuality is an important dimension of one's lifetime behavior think of sexuality in far broader terms than the sex act itself. Rather, sexuality is seen in terms of all the relationships between men and women, all of the uniqueness of the male and female, all of the ways in which they can contribute to each other.

Marshall McLuhan and George Leonard predict that the former compartmentalization of sex will become a less significant factor in the future of human sexuality. They recall that men and women have become so compartmentalized in their concepts of distinctive sex functions that they have different occupational lives, different ways of dress, etc. Such a distinctiveness of functions resulted in an actual splitting of life between the two sexes. These authors say that in the future there will be less distinction between the sexes and, therefore, more honest enjoyment of each other as people not as sex objects. Their proposal is that as sexual behaviors become more common and less frowned upon, the physical side of sex will become less significant, and the emotional and intellectual dimensions of man-woman relationships will become more significant. By the same token, we will care less about whether men and women dress in the old compartmentalized fashion. The idea of men wishing to dress more like women and women wishing to dress more like men seems to them a healthy attitude. Through their freedom of choice, men and women break out of defined sex roles to become full human beings ("The Seventies," *Look,* January 13, 1970).

In this coming together of the two sexes, there will be less dependence upon the secondary sex characteristics (distinctively male and female physical features) as a full sexuality emerges involving the total personality of the individuals. Part of this new sexuality will develop men who can feel as deeply as women are supposed to feel, and women who can trust their own logic rather than depending on that of men. Associated with this may be the emergence of larger "families," the extended family in a broad sense, one that consists of friends and neighbors who are able to share with each other as do the present members of an immediate family.

An illustration of the healthy impact of this broader concept of sex is found in recent evaluations of coeducational housing on college and university campuses. I can recall two surveys of coeducational housing reported in 1970 in such popular magazines as the *Reader's Digest* and *Good Housekeeping.* Both reporters testified that they undertook the assignment with a negative attitude but discovered many positive benefits in coeducational housing. Their reports agree that college men and women in coeducational housing are able to accept each other as people rather than as sex objects. They behave responsibly, with few exceptions. The exceptions, of course, may well be publicized, but the general body of experience involves healthy human relationships. There is actually far less sexual behavior by students in coeducational housing than by residents in single-sex housing.

In a study conducted at Stanford University, where coeducational housing has existed since 1967, the evidence suggests that men-women relationships are more natural and unaffected when they live in the same house. The students themselves say that they want to know each other as friends and companions rather than as dating objects. They study as much as students in single-sex residences, but more often with members of the opposite sex. In addition, they participate more in cultural and community activities .

The research workers reported that there was very little sexual activity among men and women living in the same residence, and the smaller the residence, the less sexual behavior. This is apparently because they see each other as members of a kind of family and there is a reluctance to exploit the sexual nature of a person who has become a regular companion. One male sophomore student at Stanford put it this way, "You get to know girls as people, not just as sex objects. A sort of brother-sister relationship often develops that makes it possible for us to have close friendships in which sex just is not a factor." Another young man from Washington State University said that he had not had intercourse and did not think he would have until after marriage. But, "I find the knowledge that I can make up my own mind exciting. For myself, I would have to feel that a sex relationship is totally good, that it involved a serious romantic attachment at least, and more than likely that marriage was intended. But those are my standards for myself. I would not want to say that they are the only correct ones for others." This suggestion of naturalness, a feeling of choice, and a tolerance for others all seem to be healthy qualities growing out of the change in sex values.

The openness of verbal dialogue about sexual matters, the frequency of physical sex relations, and the ease of preventing unwanted pregnancies make it more possible than ever for sex values to change and the major function of sex to be seen as that of enjoyment and enrichment of living. It is easier now to separate the pleasure and procreative functions of sex. Whether or not all of this will lead to the future of sex as envisioned by McLuhan and Leonard remains to be seen. But it is obvious that values in this area will continue to change in relation to what seemed "right" only a generation or two ago.

Changing Attitudes Toward Homosexuality.   One illustration of changing values is the greater openness of consideration given to the so-called homosexuals, persons whose sex partner is a member of the same sex. Whether male or female, such individuals are most often just like any other person except for their sex lives. A person is not a "homosexual" or a "heterosexual," he is a person who has homosexual or heterosexual feelings, is attracted to the same sex or the opposite sex. It is a mistake to use the term as a noun, to *label* the person. It is more accurate to use it as an adjective to describe a kind of feeling or a type of sexual response.

Recently I reviewed the manuscript of a simply written book for young people, part of the Youth Forum series (Clinton R. Jones, *What About Homosexuality?* Nashville, Tenn: Thomas Nelson Inc., 1972). The author, an experienced counselor of persons with homosexual feelings, points out that a person may have both homosexual and heterosexual feelings and relations. Many persons with some homosexual feelings also have enough heterosexual feelings to be married and have a family. Marriage to one of the opposite sex may be the result of pressure that claims one "ought" to be married. We are approaching the time when that pressure will be lessened, when one can live with and love the person of his or her choice. Even now some wives and some husbands have learned to appreciate the ambivalent sexual feeling of their spouses and to permit a close relationship with another person of the same sex.

Clinton Jones writes that many established church denominations have broadened their perception of the right of a person to choose the individual he or she can love—the Lutheran Church in America (1971), the United Church in Christ (1969), and the Unitarian Universalist Association (1970) being the latest. The law has been slower—particularly in the United States. Illinois and Connecticut are two states which have enacted recent laws that remove from the list of criminal offenses homosexual acts with consenting partners. Of all branches of society, the military changes most slowly, perhaps with some justification, and still treats homosexual behavior unequivocally as an offense to be punished. (Make no mistake, the lurking child molester or the adult who forces child or youth into a sex act repulsive to him is still seen as a criminal. He is still reprehensible to all, but someday he will be seen more as a psychological deviate to be restrained but given therapy. Unfortunately, now all we can do is to punish.)

There is no millenium as yet; persons who love members of the same sex are discriminated against and ostracized in many segments of our society. Yet in our country there are millions of such men and women in every walk of life, both those with homosexual feelings and those loving homosexually. Many live in fear of discovery, and are made to feel shame for an interest which seems entirely normal and satisfying to them. We have a long way to go, but even this area of sexual experience is being considered more humanely. The Homophile Movement with its many member organizations and the Gay Liberation movement are expressions of a growing willingness of people with homosexual feelings to stand up and be counted.

A thoughtful word to those of us who are older is found in an article on sex, presented in *Life,* June 13, 1969, as an adaptation of Albert Rosenfeld's *Second Genesis.* These particular excerpts suggest that "whatever our attitudes, a more liberalized sexuality does seem to be here to stay. It finally seems to be established, even among many churchmen, that sex is, or ought to be, a good and joyous thing. . . . It looks very much that we will have to abandon the old habit of insisting that sex must serve the same purpose for everyone, or even for the same person at different times in his life. . . . A good many authorities have suggested that it might help too, if we stopped thinking of sex as consisting only of intercourse, if we thought, instead, of sex as something a person *is*, rather than something he *does,* as something incidental to his or her sexuality—that is, to all of the experiences and all of the thoughts, from childhood to old age, that have contributed to his or her maleness or femaleness."

None of us should assume that American young people are more sex-ually active and unconventional than are the young people of other countries. The reverse may be true. Opinions gathered by Vance Packard, which are analyzed in an article by Luckey and Nass, indicate that American young men and women are more conservative in their sexual behaviors and attitudes than the young people in England, Germany, Canada, and Norway whose opinions were sampled. For example, in response to the question of whether young men think young women are willing to "go all the way" or women think men want this behavior on their part, the following figures are instructive. Among college men in the United States, only 14.9 percent thought their female companions wanted to have sexual intercourse, and women believed 16 percent of their partners wished that same behavior. The corresponding figures for England were 34.1 percent and 44.4 percent, for Germany 37 percent and 24.1 percent, for Canada 24.7 percent and 12.8 percent, and for Norway 40.8 percent and 31 percent. (Eleanor B. Luckey and Gilbert D. Nass, *Human Sexuality,* January 1972.) We are far from being a "sex-mad" nation. I believe that a majority of our young men and women, boys and girls, have a feeling of responsibility about sex, even though they may not behave in ways approved by the older generation.

ADULT ASSUMPTIONS REGARDING DRUGS, LEGAL AND ILLEGAL

It is currently fashionable to talk in terms of the shocking "illicit" drug problem among the youth of today while ignoring the extent of the equally shocking "legal" drug problem among older segments of the population. Because people of the prevailing culture are unwilling to examine and acknowledge their own drug problem, the young charge them with "hypocrisy."

The Scope of the Legal Drug Problem

Young people defending their drug culture point to the adult usage of alcohol, prescription drugs, and tobacco—all legal, but which have mind-altering qualities and may be a serious health menace. Their criticism is just. It appears indefensible to ignore the frightening scope of the *total* drug culture of our country, while damning the abuses engaged in by part of that culture. In 1969 there were estimated to be 80 million Americans who were users of alcoholic beverages and 50 million who were users of tobacco. There are at least 6 million confirmed alcohol addicts in the United States. Legal alcohol is an addictive drug, whereas illegal marijuana is not. "Speed kills," but so does tobacco, and in far larger numbers. Ironies such as these cause the counterculture with its illicit drug problem to wonder at the complacency in the prevailing culture about the use of legal but even more lethal drugs. Bill Mauldin's recent political cartoon satirizes this hypocrisy. The cartoon shows a well-dressed drunk in a bar with a glass in one hand and a tear trickling down his cheek as he explains to the bartender, "Itsh my damn kidsh and their dope problem."

It is legal, also, to become addicted to prescription drugs. In 1970, physicians wrote 260 million prescriptions for mind-altering drugs including sedatives, stimulants, and tranquilizers—twice the number written in 1960. Pharmaceutical companies (1968 figures) manufactured 10 billion dosage units of sedatives and 8 billion dosage units of amphetamines; by weight we have such figures as 1 million pounds of barbiturates and 20 million pounds of aspirin! It is estimated that the average American family's medicine chest contains 30 medicinal agents. The errors of physicians in casually prescribing psychotropic drugs, and of drug companies in blatantly advertising them, are carefully analyzed by J. Maurice Rogers in "Drug Abuse—Just What the Doctor Ordered" (*Psychology Today*, 1971, September, pages 16–24). It is not comfortable reading.

These data lead one to question the validity of such terms as "user" and "abuser." The prevailing culture labels as a drug "abuser" anyone, especially anyone under 30 years of age, who takes illicit drugs, however seldom. Responsible adults, on the other hand, who wake up with amphetamines, calm down with tranquilizers on their coffee breaks, imbibe martinis at lunch, "pep up" with more amphetamines during the afternoon, relax with a "couple of tall ones" before dinner, and put themselves to sleep with barbiturates at bedtime, merely "use" drugs. Apparently, application of the term "abuse" is not based on the way in which a drug is used, but whether or not it is legally manufactured and purchased.

Recently I read an article in a national health magazine on "drug abuse," particularly drug usage among the young. In this same issue there was another article proclaiming the magical effects of a new drug discovery which cured the effects of alcohol hangover. The new "hangover" drug, however, occasionally produced nausea, so another drug was developed to cure the effects of the "hangover cure." It sounds humorous, but it isn't. In another magazine containing an article on young peoples' drug abuse, I counted eight advertisements for tranquilizers, sedatives, amphetamines.

It appears that one drug culture is crying "abuse" at another drug culture, while it merely "uses" its own equally powerful drugs. At issue here is the presumption that legality is synonymous with morality. Such a conflict of values is of considerable social significance, if for no other reason than that such a large proportion of both youth and adults are involved.

It would be a mistake, of course, to label drug usage as an "older generation" phenomenon. Young people are also significant users of alcohol, for example. The December 1970 Gallup Report (to be detailed later) reports an incidence of alcohol usage among the college students studied as follows: "Had used within the last 30 days: wine 74 percent, beer 72 percent, hard liquor 58 percent."

The Scope of the Illicit Drug Problem

No one questions the probable magnitude and seriousness of the use of the various hallucinogens (illegal) and the amphetamines (legal, but *most* are illicitly procured and used). The bind is that the seriousness of the problem (how much people are injured by each drug) is not supported by enough research, and the magnitude of the problem (number of people using such drugs) is very hard to determine with any degree of accuracy. In any study of the extent of use, it is almost impossible to ascertain the nature of those who do not respond to a survey. Many who receive questionnaires or who are interviewed are reluctant to admit using illicit drugs. There is always an incomplete response in any such study and, among those who do not answer, there is probably an undue proportion of drug users. Most studies carefully protect the identity of the respondent, but distrust of the research worker still inhibits a portion of any population sampled.

Incidence Among College Students.   Two of the more carefully done studies of college students give different results about marijuana usage. The first, a study of 10,000 randomly selected college freshmen and juniors, presented early in 1971 by the National Institute of Mental Health, reports that only 31 percent of college students "have ever" smoked pot and 14 percent use it "regularly." The second is a December 1970 Gallup Report of 1,000 students on 61 campuses. Of these, 42 percent "had used" marijuana at least once, 28 percent having used it "within the preceding 30 days." For amphetamines the corresponding percentages were 16 and 6 percent and for hallucinogens 14 and 6 percent. The use of "hard drugs" (narcotics such as heroin and stimulants such as cocaine) is rare on college campuses. The NIMH study gave 1 percent and a *Playboy* magazine study of 300 colleges gave 3 percent. *Playboy* indicates that recently the use of cocaine, a drug which is fast rising in popularity, has gone up to 7 percent according to a number of studies.

Although the Gallup Report comparison of the 1967 and 1969 figures with those of 1970 may not be valid (different college populations may have been sampled), the indicated increase in usage is startling. Students reporting they "have used" marijuana were 5 percent of the college population in 1967; in 1969 it was 22 percent; and 1970 it was 42 percent. Students using hallucinogens were 1 percent of the college population in 1967, 4 percent in 1969, and 14 percent in 1970. A University of Minnesota study found that use of alcohol by freshmen had jumped from 58 to 88 percent between the years 1967 and 1970; during the same time "the use of" (whatever degree or frequency that means) the illicit drugs had moved from 8 to 46 percent. A 1971 University of Maryland study showed that 41 percent of the freshman class "had used" marijuana in high school. (The *Playboy,* Minnesota, and Maryland studies are reported in the *Chronicle of Higher Education,* January 24, 1972.)

I am sure that this array of figures is bewildering, but they are safer as facts than the glittering generalities so often heard. The variation of percentages among studies may not mean differences among institutions or areas of the country, but rather, differences in the representativeness of the sample used and differences in the time the study was made. Drug usage fluctuates, according to the surveys, but it is generally increasing.

Several conclusions (subjective, to be sure) might be drawn about the college drug scene, based upon a study of the available research and many random conversations with college students:

(1) It is obvious that the 1970 study reported above represents a considerably higher rate of usage than was the practice in 1967–68, when various college studies suggested an average 15–25 percent use of marijuana, for example.

(2) The incidence of marijuana usage will probably increase during the next few years; the use of "acid" (LSD) and "speed" (amphetamines) will level off at close to their present rate or will decrease; and the greater use of hard drugs off campus will slowly raise the rate of use on campus. Use of hard drugs will still be found, however, on only a very small percentage of college campuses, most often those located in large cities.

(3) A given college may actually have a much higher rate of marijuana usage than the average reported. For example, one prestigious liberal arts college found in 1970 that 73 percent of its students had "experimented with" marijuana. A substantial majority of this number, however, had had their first (and perhaps only) experience in high school. Each year

more college freshmen arrive on campus with their first experience of pot behind them. Some never use it in college, some only occasionally, some use it often—once or twice a week or more.

(4) One of the hazards in estimating incidence of usage for any of these drugs is the failure to distinguish between the implication of asking a question such as "Have you *ever* used marijuana?" as opposed to asking, "Do you use it now?" or "How often?" Estimates of drug usage in college and high school often do not make this distinction. Because the Gallup Report does make this distinction, it is of unusual value. The 42 percent who answer "yes" to "have you ever used" shrink to 28 percent for "recently used"—and there is the even more drastic drop of 16 to 6 percent in the case of hallucinogens. In the 1971 NIMH reported study, the marijuana drop from "have you ever used" to "recently used" is from 31 to 14 percent.

It is important to keep in mind that youthful drug users fall into three categories. Kenneth Keniston (*The American Scholar*, 1968–69, 38: 97–112) labels the groups in terms of both motivation and amount of use: "tasters" (who try it once or twice and then quit); "seekers" (occasional users, dabbling); and "heads" (chronic, consistent users). Keniston believed that when the "tasters" are omitted, less than 5 percent of the college population is left in the drug-using group. That estimate was made in late 1968. We have already seen that the reality of late 1970 is closer to 25 percent for marijuana "users" although much lower for hallucinogens and amphetamines. To be remembered, of course, is that "tasters" are still in the significant majority and "users" in the minority. It should be remembered also that several sources have reported a decrease in the hospitalization of drug cases, meaning fewer overdosages. It may be that college students use drugs more moderately now because they are more aware of the possibility of overdosages and unusual physiological reactions. Some students do report that young people are more cautious than before in their use of drugs.

Incidence Among High School Students.   Careful studies of high school students are rare. The most recent carefully done studies with which I am familiar are those carried out in 1967 and 1968 by Richard Blum (see References). His 1968 study of an upper-middle-class suburban high school provides incidence figures that are from two to four times as great as those reported in 1967. His questions on "marijuana use" turned up 55 percent who have tried it and 39 percent who continue to use it. Corresponding figures for amphetamines were 18 percent and 2 percent, for hallucinogens 20 and 11 percent. Comparisons of studies are hazardous, but one cannot help noting the higher incidence in the Blum 1968 high school study than in the previously reported

1970 college study. This is undoubtedly a sampling factor. If all of the 1970 college students responding had come from "upper-class suburban high schools," I have no doubt but that the college figures would be substantially greater. All of the evidence points to the conclusion that many youthful drug users come from middle-class and upper-middle-class homes.

To prove the point of sampling differences and to confuse the issue further I am including the figures from a 1971 two-year follow-up study of drug usage among junior and senior high school students in Tucson, Arizona. A 6 percent sample of students throughout the city indicates a frightening increase but a still relatively low percentage of regular use:

DRUG	EXPERIMENTAL (OCCASIONAL OR ONE-TIME) USE		REGULAR USE	
	1969	1971	1969	1971
Marijuana	12	28	8	19
Hallucinogens	6	12	3	8
Narcotics	2	11	1	7
Alcohol	60	73	37	50

The Effects of Different Drugs

It may be sufficient here to say that we know a great deal about some drugs and little about others. The hard drugs (heroin, cocaine, etc.) and alcohol are known to be physically addictive, whereas many others—including drugs that affect one's sense of mental and emotional well-being—are psychologically habituating. An "addictive drug" is generally thought of as one which has created a physiological dependence so that the withdrawal symptoms are severe and often agonizing—sweating, nausea, convulsions, muscle twitching and cramps, intense itching and crawling of the skin, insatiable cravings, severe depression, etc. But "psychological addiction" or habituation is also very real for those who have come to depend upon a mind-relieving or pain-relieving drug.

There are some curious anomalies in any categorization such as I have suggested above. Alcohol is both an addictive and a habituating drug. Two drug categories that have the most agonizing and severe withdrawal symptoms are prescription (legal) drugs—barbiturates (Seconal, Nembutal, etc.) and the amphetamines (Benzedrine, Dexedrine, Methedrine, etc.) Abrupt withdrawal by a habitual user of barbiturates is more agonizing, but withdrawal from either may be fatal.

Marijuana. As far as the small amount of research now available can show, marijuana is not addictive. It is probably habituating, and it may become the stimulus to try other more potent mind-altering drugs. The evidence is not firm at this point. Many who use hard drugs started with marijuana or alcohol, but also many more who have used pot do *not* go on to hard drugs. The 1970 Federal Drug Act classified it as a hallucinogen because it may produce euphoria with time and space distortion—a so-called psychedelic effect. Some other authorities classify it as a sedative. Support for this claim is found in the fact that marijuana achieves its effects by depressing the central nervous system thereby releasing lower centers from their chronic inhibitory influences. Alcohol, a true sedative, works its effect in the same manner. The "dreamy" state that is achieved during marijuana intoxication can be achieved with any sedative and again is well known to users of alcohol. Physical dependence on marijuana has been overestimated because, in fact, too little research is available. As with all true sedatives, however, abrupt withdrawal after continued use can produce hyperexcitability.

Despite the high incidence of marijuana usage in that area, of the 5,000 acute drug intoxications treated at San Francisco General Hospital in 1967 no "marijuana psychoses" were encountered. On the other hand, with high dosages acute anxiety and feelings of panic can occur in the marijuana user. These reactions often accompany the feelings of depersonalization which sometimes result from use of a high dosage by an individual with an emotionally unstable pre-drug personality. Such reactions may also occur in an individual who has had experience with more potent psychoactive drugs. For instance, marijuana has been the triggering agent in many LSD "flashbacks."

In another study by Blum of "benefits" and "bad outcomes" of different drugs reported by college student users, a relatively substantial incidence of "bad effects" (46 percent) was reported for marijuana, while 77 percent report "benefits." (It is obvious that what is reported upon is a total of experiences over months or years by any one person for whom one experience resulted in benefits and another had bad outcomes.) A much higher incidence of "bad outcomes" was reported for opiates (72 percent), for alcohol (63 percent), and for amphetamines (61 percent). The lowest incidence of bad effects was reported in the use use of sedatives (23 percent) and tranquilizers (17 percent).

Ernest Barratt (University of Texas) has spent three years on a study financed by the U. S. Department of Justice to determine the long-range effects of marijuana. As reported in a 1972 newspaper account, he is still cautious about any generalizations but suggests that the long-term effect may mean a personality change similar to that found in the "high" state of a single trip. This apparently is a kind of depersonalization in which the user feels himself floating around the room or in another world where he is not in contact with the world about him or even his own physical being. *If* there is a personality change after long-term usage, this change should not be labeled "good" or "bad," because that involves a value judgment. The newspaper quoted Barratt as saying:

> If the drug produces a long-term personality change—you can't say exactly how it's going to change—but if it does, then you have to say will these changes be consistent with the kind of society you want to live in.
> Our society is a very competitive, aggressive society. Do you want to live in a competitive, aggressive society? A lot of the young people say no. A lot of the people who use marijuana as far as I can see apparently say no and I have a feeling that this may be one characteristic that is related to the physiological behavioral changes from long-term usages.

Lester Grinspoon (Massachusetts Mental Health Center) in *Marijuana Reconsidered* reports upon his two years of study. He is convinced of the relatively harmless nature of the drug, less harmful in terms of tissue damage than is alcohol or tobacco. Any commonly used psychotropic drug, whether legal or illegal, may well be harmful when used heavily and consistently. A team of British research workers reported in *The Lancet* that 10 habitual marijuana users suffered from cerebral atrophy (shrinkage of brain tissue). But these patients had also taken other drugs during these same years—were they or marijuana responsible? Here again there is a suspected effect but a lack of certainty.

The National Institute on Mental Health, which in 1971 spent $700,000 in research on marijuana alone and $1,500,000 on marijuana and other drugs, issued an early report entitled *Marijuana and Health.* The report dispels some myths and establishes some general principles: (1) Death attributable to marijuana is extremely rare. (2) Marijuana does not "necessarily" lead directly to other drugs. (3) Marijuana is a minor contributor to violence and crime. (4) At the usual level of social usage, physiological effects are relatively few, but the psychological effects are "alteration of time and space perception, sense of euphoria, relaxation, well-being and dis-inhibition; dulling of attention, fragmentation of thought, impaired immediate memory, an altered sense of identity, exaggerated laughter, an increased suggestibility." (5) When eaten, rather than smoked, its effects are less predictable and often stronger. Although marijuana is one of the "safer" of the widely used drugs, the NIMH Report concludes that until more is known "we certainly cannot give it a clean bill of health." It is a "pleasant" drug with some unpleasant and unpredictable side effects. Its "dangers" simply are not known as yet.

A Few Conclusions

What has been said here briefly about specific drugs will be unsatisfying to many. It is an incomplete statement in a very real sense of the
word. Counselors, parents, or teachers to whom any of this information
is new or surprising should certainly read more in order to be more helpful to those using specific drugs or considering such use. I have written
this much only to suggest that: (1) Drugs vary widely in their potency
and effects and in their potentiality for addiction. (2) Common
knowledge about specific drugs is often dangerously in error. (3) Drugs,
particularly the hallucinogens, have distinctly different effects on different people. (4) The effect may vary widely with a given person
because of differences in his physiological and emotional state at the
time of use. (5) Many illicit drugs vary widely in their potency because
of "cutting" (adulteration), as in the case of acid cut with strychnine, or
because of the variety in geographical source, as in the case of marijuana,
so that any one dose has dangerously unpredictable effects. (6) Of the
illicit nonopiate drugs, LSD and the amphetamines are the most dangerous because of unpredictability and possible damage to vital organs and
cell tissue. (7) The latest estimates of the effects of marijuana are that
although in small doses it is similar in effect to alcohol, it disturbs behavior less than alcohol and is definitely less toxic than alcohol. The use
of other drugs may follow the use of marijuana, but usually only for
those who are generally "drug prone." The long-term effects of heavy
usage of this drug are not known. (8) There is currently a steady increase
in the use of the illicit drugs (remember that the uses of legal drugs,
alcohol, tobacco, etc., already have such high incidence rates that they
are likely to increase much more slowly).

There is no "generation gap" in the use of tobacco, alcohol, the
amphetamines, and the barbiturates. In fact, the young often learn from
their elders in these areas and have access to them only because their
elders use them. The *motivation* for use may be different, however, with
the younger often (but not always!) using drugs to increase feeling and
sensation and elders using them to escape anxiety and tension. One 19-
year-old put it this way: "My mother, who yells at me all of the time, is
taking so much Nembutal and Darvon that she's practically an addict.
I'm expanding my mind when I take drugs. She's trying to turn hers off."

Value Conflicts

One value conflict has already been mentioned—alcohol and tobacco
are not even acknowledged as "drugs" by the tens of millions of both
young and old who use them. They are "relaxing agents" defended

vigorously as harmless or brushed aside with "I could quit any time I really wanted to" by those who use them. Both are built into our culture and can be purchased in any supermarket (in many states) just like meat, eggs, and milk.

The counterculture sees as hypocritical anyone who denies the addictive potential of these drugs, because he is defensive against criticism of his own practices. The young use tobacco and alcohol also, but are more open in admitting that they take a risk in doing so.

Another value conflict is seen in the prevailing culture's condemnation of all illegal drugs *because* they are illegal (although not equally harmful) and *because* they have never experienced them (and are likely to be ignorant of their "benefits"). Many young people consider marijuana, for example, as less harmful and more pleasant than alcohol. They— often unwisely perhaps—are willing to take the legal risks involved in its use.

The striking thing about the profile of the youthful user of illicit drugs is that it is so "respectable." The parents are likely to be economically secure, substantial users or abusers of legal drugs, economically mobile, either very permissive with regard to their children's social behavior or in sharp opposition to their children's point of view. The youth himself is often keenly interested in matters of the mind, aesthetics, and social philosophy. He or she reports having received secondary gains from childhood illness and having been dissatisfied with school. With a bit of uniqueness here and there, the profile very much resembles the profile of an attractive, alert, socially acceptable "boy or girl next door." The soft drug culture is not predominantly that of the disadvantaged but of the advantaged, middle-class youth and adults.

REFLECTION AGAIN

Remember that I said I felt hopeful about the one area and depressed about the other?

Sex Is a Plus For Me.   The reader may not agree that my analysis of the changing assumptions about the function of sex in our lives is a hopeful one. It is not that the sexual *behavior* seen today is necessarily hopeful or attractive: to see a boy fondling a girl in public is likely to be more degrading than inspiring with reference to the dignity and beauty of life. Rather, the movement toward openness and honesty about sex, even though it may currently seem excessive, may lead to more naturalness as to the place of sexual behavior in the total dimension of sexuality. I can see "planned parenthood" as representing a concern for those brought into the world, a concern for the rights and dignity of those yet to be born. In the use of contraceptives and a different attitude toward early abortion, I can see fewer unwanted and rejected children born into an unhappy world—unhappy for them and for the world. I also sense the right of the woman to determine *when* she wishes to carry a baby within her body for nine months, knowing that she is to love and care for it over additional years. It is equally her right to have a strong voice in determining *how many* children there will be for which she will have a large measure of parental responsibility. It seems to me that the total direction of the new values of human sexuality build much more dignity and self-determination into the lives of women and create a better environment for healthy and creative male-female relationships.

As I reflect on these statements I can see that what I say may disturb some of you who think differently. This is a sensitive area but one which is more open to discussion than only a few years ago. I present my comments only as observations of what I think is happening in the area of sexual attitudes and behavior, and my conclusion is that the chances appear to be good that strength and wholesomeness will be the outcome.

Drugs—a Minus.   The widespread use of illicit drugs is fairly recent and is, therefore, unusually threatening. We—meaning society as well as the individual counselor—simply do not know how to cope. There is a great rash of misinformation and exaggeration about drugs. Gemeralizations are made pro and con that are disturbingly erroneous and misleading. On the other hand, a large amount of valid information about drugs is discounted or ignored. To counteract the myths and to face up squarely to the realities about drugs takes some thought upon the part of the counselor—and some character.

I've been involved in writing about drugs, here and in other books, but find that increasing my knowledge about the subject does not make me more hopeful. I am depressed about the total dimension of drugs in our lives. Whereas changed sex attitudes *could* lead to a richer appreciation of life, I see drugs as used chiefly to limit life's richness, not enhance it. The claims of those who consistently use psychedelic drugs that they are "expanding their consciousness" are not denied. This may be true, but the risks involved disturb me greatly. Some specialists in the field of drugs do not label LSD, for example, as a "mind-expander," a psychedelic drug. They describe it as a "mind-dissolver," a psycholytic drug. There are not only the risks involved in the unknown strengths of drugs purchased illicitly, but risks involved in the tremendous variation among human beings in their response to a given drug. Nor can I be hopeful about the sedatives—alcohol and the rest—that merely take us out of the mainstream of life, not into it.

Yet the reality that faces us as counselors is that the drug scene is with us. We cannot wish it out of existence. I believe deeply that the way to meet reality is to *admit it* rather than to pretend that it isn't there. Even worse is to indulge in the childish superstition that "it shouldn't be" and therefore, miraculously, it isn't! The realness of reality does not depend upon its pleasantness or unpleasantness. Nor is it true that to admit reality implies that we like it or approve of it. I am not "lowering my personal standards" to admit the reality of rapists or drug pushers.

We have known for some time that the use of legal drugs is not "a passing fad," and so it is with illicit drugs. They will be with us for at least quite a period ahead. Educators, counselors, and parents who have learned to live with sex and alcohol will have to learn to live with illicit drugs as well. I repeat: "live with" or "deal with" does not mean "agree with."

IMPLICATIONS FOR THE COUNSELOR

Drugs

A good "set" is of paramount importance in counseling with the student who uses drugs, particularly illicit drugs, or the student who is considering experimentation with them. This is possible if one realizes that the problem young people are attempting to solve through their use of drugs is not restricted to youth alone. The problem seems to be the shallowness or quality of life in the era in which we live. All of us are coping with the problem of discovering meaning in our lives, of creating meaning for ourselves, of questioning the validity of current social institutions. It is the drug user's choice of coping mechanism that seems atypical, not the problem he is struggling with.

Old and young alike use various inadequate problem-solving methods. Many are prone to (1) regard objects and things outside ourselves as a source for fulfillment, depend on external resources—TVs, swimming pools, cars—to overcome discontent (this is our "marketing" orientation); (2) depend on mind-altering or mind-relieving chemicals to "fix" what is wrong—alcohol, prescription or patented stimulants and sedatives, etc. The names for the "fixes" used by youth are a bit esoteric— "yellow jackets" and "red devils" (barbiturates), "lid poppers" and "hearts" (amphetamines), and "joints," "acid," and many others.

When a counselor has a set which allows him to perceive that the youthful drug user is not so different after all from the rest of society, he will be much less inclined to take a punitive and judgmental approach with him. Young people are excellent at spotlighting problems in our

society. The counselor's task is to help the young to find viable alternatives to the destructive life styles to which some have turned and perhaps
to learn how to change the social institutions and mores to which they
are responding.

Some Suggestions.   From my study of the counterculture, I can make
these recommendations:

(1) Counselors need to have appreciation for the circumstances in
which youth are likely to turn to them for help. The young user of illicit
drugs might be having an acute drug reaction which includes extreme
anxiety. In such a case, a nonpunitive and nonjudgmental attitude is
crucial. Such a person needs a calm and accepting counselor, not a pan-
icked and punitive one. He may also need specific medical attention.
Other youthful drug users have tried drugs as a solution to their problems, and drugs have failed them, too. In such a situation they are often
hopeless to the point of being self-destructive. Still other youth are able
to take a pretty rational approach to their problems. "There has to be
some other way than drugs," they seem to say. "Help me find it!"

(2) It is probably desirable that the counselor familiarize himself with
the vocabulary of the youthful drug culture. Such knowledge facilitates
communication, and it is of crucial importance in cases where overdose
is suspected. The counselee might be unable to do no more than mumble
that he's been on "rainbows" for two months, and the counselor had
better know that "rainbows" are barbiturates and that this client may
need the immediate attention of medical personnel. An excellent glos-
sary of drug terms is available from the Network for Continuing Medical
Education, in care of the New York City Chamber of Commerce, and in
several books intended for student reading: R. Lingeman, *Drugs from A
to Z: A Dictionary,* McGraw-Hill Book Co., New York, 1969; S. Cohen,
The Drug Dilemma, McGraw-Hill Book Co., New York, 1969; Helen H.
Nowlis, *Drugs on the College Campus,* Anchor Books, Doubleday & Co.,
Garden City, New York, 1969; C. Gilbert Wrenn and Shirley Schwartz-
rock, *Facts and Fantasies about Drugs* or *The Mind Benders,* American
Guidance Service, Circle Pines, Minn. (see References).

(3) At the very least the counselor should have available the advice and
services of qualified medical personnel to whom he can refer students
who need medical attention for overdose, withdrawal, and acute anxiety
or depression. A rough rule of thumb is that medical assistance should
be advised for known users of amphetamines, barbiturates, and "hard"
drugs such as cocaine and heroin. These medical personnel need to be
personally known to the counselor so that he can provide the student
with the reassurance that there will be no legal repercussions. If such
reassurance cannot be given, the counselor had best be forthright and

say so. Often the younger medical personnel are more accepting and nonpunitive with regard to drug use.

(4) The counselor could well become informed about two types of resources that are available in the larger communities. One of these is a rehabilitation house or center for drug addicts who are attempting to "kick the habit," usually manned by ex-addicts operating under the supervision of medical and/or psychological professionals. These are often places to learn about the drug traffic in one's community and about the addicts' struggles to break loose. The other is a telephone service manned 24 hours a day by dedicated volunteers for all kinds of calls for help—just someone to listen, to reassure, to refer (sometimes called YES—Youth Emergency Service). This may be accompanied by "walk-in" kinds of face-to-face listening counsel. Generally manned by young people, it is nonthreatening and widely used for youth in any kind of trouble.

Here the counselor can learn of many pertinent "counseling" activities. Some people in such settings are doing what the counselor wishes he had the chance to do. Some "beautiful" things are being done for drug users by youth using various kinds of group situations and by pastoral counselors and other religious leaders using group settings to provide "a trip without drugs." Some, in the "Jesus Movement" tradition and using Alcoholics Anonymous concepts, have used direct religious conversion to provide the turnaround for the addict. Even the armed services, which have seen 522 investigations of marijuana use in 1965 skyrocket to 19,000 cases four years later, have now become somewhat more rehabilitative than punitive in their attitude.

(5) It is taken for granted that the school counselor is faced with a problem for which he often feels emotionally and intellectually unprepared. He is likely to be poorly informed about the nature and effects of the illicit drugs which young people today are taking. This situation is understandable. When the majority of counselors received their training, this particular form of drug abuse was not the problem that it is today. Catching up on information is no new situation for the counselor, of course, for the effective counselor has never been able to "rest easy" with the knowledge he acquired during his formal training.

In addition to reading what is written by authors who seem to evidence both a research and a clinical background, counselors will find attendance at drug workshops to be helpful. Always, one should ascertain the reliability of those conducting the workshops.

The counselor hears, of course, a good bit of discussion of drug treatment and drug education in the public press and popular magazines as well as in professional journals. *All* treatment is still experimental with much research to be done. *Behavior Today* (January 17, 1972) reports the dismay of sociologist John Ball that there is so little record keeping in treatment centers and that research there is almost nonexistent.

Methadone treatment is an exception. There are almost 300 methadone treatment centers fairly widely distributed and all are experimental. Methadone is a synthetic form of morphine which reduces or stays the desire for heroin. It is used only with confirmed heroin addicts and under careful supervision, for it is as addictive as heroin. The difference is that the methadone addict functions normally in society— returns to his family, holds a job, etc. Its use is widely praised by some and widely feared by others. Substituting one lifelong addiction for another is a serious responsibility even though the second addiction permits normal work and family interaction. LSD is now being experimented with in the treatment of acute alcoholism. Marijuana is used to reduce the agony of terminal cancer patients. Although few counselors will be directly active in drug treatment or research, the drug culture is one area where he should be "keeping up" because illicit drug use is a part of the world of so many of the young people with whom he works.

(6) One final point must be made—how does a counselor deal with the ethics of having knowledge about individuals who use illicit drugs? The counselor is likely to find himself in a bind between an expectation by his or her employer that all drug users be reported to the proper authorities and the counselor's own desire to be effective as a counselor. This bind is further complicated if the counselor is of two minds regarding his legal duty in the area of drug use.

The counselor should think through his position prior to being confronted with a young drug user. Careful thought beforehand can eliminate panic which could lead the counselor to make a decision that he might find difficult to live with later. The counselor's dilemma can be stated in question form.

1. If I cooperate with society's and the administration's expectation that I report drug users, what will this do to my effectiveness as a counselor?

2. If I choose *not* to report drug users: (a) how will I cope with that decision should one of my counselees suffer serious effects from his drug use or cause harm to someone else while under the influence of drugs? (b) how will I square myself with my own conscience in holding moral principle above legal principle?

Whatever the answers to these questions, it would seem advisable that the counselor "spell them out" clearly to his employer and to students alike. Any subsequent revisions in the counselor's policy on drugs should likewise be "spelled out."

This is but one highly sensitive dimension of the large issue of counselor-client confidentiality. The reader may have already come to grips with this and determined that his responsibility to his client is more immediate than his responsibility to his institution or to society—unless there is imminent harm to another person. In the event that this is his conclusion, he should expect that in dealing with the use of illicit drugs the personal risk may be somewhat greater although the principle may be seen by him as the same.

Sex

I haven't as much to say about the counselor's relationship to changing sexual behaviors and concepts as I have about his relationship to drug users because the implications seem more obvious. The need to listen to another's worries about sex and to accounts of his or her sexual behavior *without judgment* has been presented by dozens of writers. Perhaps even more than in the use of drugs, there is need for frequent recall of Jesus' admonition to the accusers of the woman taken in adultery, "Let him who is without sin (without fault) among you cast the first stone."

What must be recalled, however, is that the counselor's formal education or his (or her) own sexual experiences may not have given him (or her) an adequate background for dealing with today's young people. Many more counselors have personal sex hangups (rigidities, rejections, lack of deep relationships with the other sex) than have drug hangups. Sexual experience is common to us all, illicit drug experience to relatively few. So the counselor's personal feelings may intrude excessively into the client-counselor relationship. Is he powerless to control this? He may have conflicting feelings about some topics, and it would seem wise to *admit* them when they appear to be affecting a counseling relationship. This kind of honesty is helpful because the client often senses the counselor's discomfort, and the admission of it may break down a barrier between them. By this I do not mean a "confession" of any sort, for no personal experiences of the counselor need to be related. The counselor's personal life is his own to share at his discretion. But to admit that personal feelings are interfering with a counselor's objectivity and helpfulness is both honest and professional. If the client is describing a personal homosexual experience and the counselor feels very uncomfortable, he doesn't have to say, "Yes, I have experimented in that area but have always felt very guilty about it." He can say instead, "This kind of sexual activity which may seem so natural to you, makes some people very uncomfortable, including me. If you sense my feelings, they are not because of you, but really because of me."

I think that here, as with drugs, the counselor needs to read thoughtfully in the literature—this time the literature on human sexuality and on marital and premarital counseling. Contraceptives and abortion techniques may be either mysterious or repugnant to the counselor, and he might well confer with a family-planning agency or a knowledgeable and trusted physician. If personal sex feelings are too threatening or disturbing for him to be effective in working with youth in this area, personal counseling or therapy may be indicated for the counselor. Group counseling or even encounter groups under responsible leadership could be very helpful.

References for Exploration

Blum, Richard H. *Society and Drugs,* Vol. 1; *Students and Drugs,* Vol. 2. Jossey-Bass, San Francisco, 1969. (An encyclopedia of knowledge covering a wide range of drug cultures throughout the world. A great deal of research on both high school and college student drug usage is reported in Volume 2. This is a standard work of great value.)

Fort, Joel. *The Pleasure Seekers: The Drug Crisis, Youth and Society.* Bobbs-Merrill Co., 1969. (A distinguished scholar in the field of drugs writes simply and clearly on various drugs, their effects, and society's reaction to them.)

Karlen, Arno. *Sexuality and Homosexuality.* W. W. Norton, 1971.

Louria, Donald B. *Overcoming Drugs.* McGraw-Hill, 1971.

Mailer, Norman. *The Prisoner of Sex.* Signet Paperback, 1971. (Unbelievably strong and perhaps distasteful language and yet an unbelievably free discussion of women and Women's Lib. Those working for Women's Liberation see Mailer's emphasis as very negative.)

"Marijuana Issues" *Journal of Psychedelic Drugs,* Special Issue, Fall 1968.

McClelland, David. *Alcohol and Human Motivation.* Free Press, 1971.

Otto, Herbert. *The New Sexuality.* Science and Behavior Books, 1971. (A symposium by experts writing on what they consider the normal, healthy aspects of sex developments in our society.)

Packard, Vance. *The Sexual Wilderness.* David McKay Co., Inc., New York, 1968. (This widely quoted book is the outcome of four years of study in various parts of the world. The book is journalistic in style, with comments and quotations interspersed with statistics on sex practices and attitudes, both premarital and marital, American and worldwide.)

Rosenfeld, Albert. *Second Genesis.* Prentice-Hall, 1969.

Sagarin, Edward, ed. "Sex and the Contemporary Scene" Special issue of *The*

Annals of the American Academy of Political and Social Science, March 1968. (Fourteen articles on sex and family life, sex education, sexual deviations in America, prostitution, abortion, sexual patterns in three ethnic subcultures, etc.)

Sexual Behavior (Any issue of this journal).

Wrenn, C. Gilbert, and Shirley Schwartzrock. *The Mind Benders* (for high school and early college years), *Facts and Fantasies about Drugs* (for students in upper elementary grades). American Guidance Service, Circle Pines, Minn., 1971.

The Drag (film). 9 minutes. Contemporary Films, McGraw-Hill, 267 W. 25th St., New York, N.Y., 10001, 1966. (Cigarettes—a biting commentary.)

The Summer We Moved to Elm Street (film). 29 minutes. Contemporary Films, McGraw Hill, 267 W. 25th St., New York, N.Y., 10001, 1967. (A gentle film—bittersweet views of Doreen's new home, and alcoholism.)

CHAPTER V

Changing Values 4:
Some Dimensions of
a Philosophy of Life

AN INTRODUCTION TO SOME CHANGING ASSUMPTIONS ABOUT THE MEANING OF LIFE

It should be apparent at once that this discussion of values has arrived at a kind of integrative climax. All of the earlier discussions of value assumptions concerning past experience, authority, responsibility, women's status, work-leisure, sex, and drugs have had their philosophic implications but now you and I must dig in a little. We must ask, "What are our changing assumptions about Life itself, its meaning, its evolution?"

This question plagues people of all ages—it is not a query of youth only. It is the concern, from the cradle to the grave, of all mankind. But the assumptions held (or questioned) vary with each generation. Perhaps assumptions vary within a shorter time period than the 20-year span of one generation; perhaps assumptions are seriously questioned now within each 10-year period of life. What life means may vary almost as much from 30 to 40 years of age as it does from 10 to 20. This short-ening of the span of changed meanings is influenced by the rapid rate of change in our technology. It is reflected also in the social pressures that predominate, in the personal problems that present themselves with reference to one's identity, one's future, one's relations with others. Only recently, for example, have we seen that the self-identity crisis is as crucial for the old as for the young. A psychiatrist recently suggested that when a person's self-identity is maintained through old age, "I con-sider it an ominous sign. . . . I suggest that a continuing life-long identity crisis is a sign of good health."

There is certainly a restlessness in America about life's meaning, and perhaps this is hopeful. (Both here and at other points in the analyses pursued in this book, I could hazard semi-educated guesses about what is occurring in other cultures, but I will refrain. I am taking enough of a risk in generalizing about North America!) Life increasingly is not seen as a once-structured, forever-secure experience. In psychological jargon, life is open-ended. The answers to life are to be answered as an open-ended sentence-completion test would be answered. When, for example, the stem "Truth is . . .," is presented, each person must provide the answer from within himself and his generation. He does not now, as was so frequently done in earlier times, adopt the response provided by his teacher or parent, his church or government.

From this open-ended stance I further assume that my answer will not remain constant, that it will change as I change. It will change as I learn more about myself, the world in which I live, the responses given by others to what I say, do, and am. So for "Truth is . . .," there is no final answer. No two people necessarily give the same response, and no one person is necessarily consistent over periods of time in the responses that he gives.

Thus an open-ended attitude assumes a world which is dynamic rather than static in terms of meanings and values. This assumption is also true for knowledge and technology, since neither of these ever stands still. Values change in response to a changing technology and a changing social order. They change for other reasons, too. They may change because I, the observer, experience changes in both my external and my internal environment, and these may modify drastically what I perceive to be important or true.

The discussion in which we are now engaging is strongly dominated by my own subjectivity. I find it hard to advance "facts" as the major source of my conclusions. It would help but little if I did, for my selection of facts and the inferences I draw from them would be almost wholly subjective. True, I see myself as being aware of many factors in our society which can be validated by recourse to facts. I think of myself as being very respectful of facts, respectful of observable and verifiable realities. Nevertheless, when I speak of meaning, when I speak of my definition of an abstract concept (truth, for example), my answers are inevitably colored by how I perceive myself and my world. It could not be otherwise.

Such a statement classifies me at once as being something other than a positivist in my philosophy (see page 99). Rather, I could probably be classified as an experimentalist or an existentialist for whom knowledge can never be isolated from the knower because the knower and the known are one. It should be said here parenthetically that one who follows this line of philosophical thinking is strongly influenced by the psychology called phenomenology (which originated as a philosophy). It is perhaps pedantic to explain the obvious, but let me state here that philosophy contributes to an *understanding of the nature of existence,* of truth, purpose, and values, while psychology is designed to contribute to an *understanding of human behavior.* Philosophy necessarily deals in speculation about meanings, while psychology entails the observation of behavior. It seems fair to say that existentialism depends to a considerable degree upon "observations" of an introspective nature and that phenomenology "speculates" about the meaning of its observations of behavior. From this particular teaming up of philosophy and psychology, it is clear that both are person-oriented and present-oriented. To me it seems almost impossible to consider myself philosophically as an

existentialist unless I also consider myself psychologically to be
a phenomenologist.

From these points of view to pretend objectivity or universality is
ridiculous, and leads only to what is often futile argument. I say, "Truth
is . . ." and here follows a statement which is immediately challenged by
the other person in the dialogue, who quickly says, "Oh no, truth really
is . . ." Of course, both are right but neither has completed the statement by saying "Truth *for me* is . . ." The meaning of any event lies
within oneself and is more appropriate than any definition given by the
other person.

The thrust toward an open-ended, subjective, and uniquely personal
derivation of values is a "growing-edge" type of movement, not a universal movement in any sense of the word. Restlessness and discomfort
about fixed values characterize perhaps the majority of Americans, but
many take strong positions against accepting dynamic open-endedness
as a solution.

What someone has called "an emptiness of the heart" may signify
the collapse of communication between our Western tradition of technology and organization and the inner world of the individual. This may
be apparent to all, but there are "easier" ways out than the ones described in the preceding paragraphs. One way out is to *rely upon
technology* and to assume that all our machine-computer world has
done for us brings with it a commensurate improvement in values. The
nature of this improvement is not very clear, but surely better houses,
cars, communications, gadgets, military hardware, and a higher standard
of living must be good for us. We have more options open to us, more
choices about what to buy, where to go, what to do. We have more of
everything. We live longer; that must be good! This kind of reasoning—
bigger and better, more and longer—provides a surface kind of satisfaction until one begins to wonder "more things for what, more years
for why?"

A second way out is to *identify some well-established values* and preserve them in blocks of incorruptible marble. These become the rock
upon which we can stand forever. They are beautiful values; there is no
doubt about that. One has named his value blocks "the pillars of self-
hood and democracy—intelligence, creativity, conscience, and reverence."
Another lists "the sources of moral values" as recognition of the importance of persons, sharing, duty, work, good workmanship, economy,
honesty, dedication, solitude, faith, etc. Earlier, in Chapter I, I cited
Life's obverse values—its contemporary list of "Seven Deadly Sins,"
selfishness, intolerance, etc.

Making such lists is an intriguing and perhaps useful activity. If one can accept them as universal or accept them as unchanging, much of the agony of decision making is assuaged. The trouble is that one can make neither assumption. Every value area is a battleground, not a museum filled with beautiful inscriptions laid upon marble. A choice of values today is personal, is meaningful in unique ways to each person. The very words used to describe fundamental values have meanings unique to each person—reverence, dedication, love, duty, work, faith. So when I puzzle out the meaning of this value for *me,* I have created a new statement of value which may or may not be acceptable to anyone else. If someone accepts my value as having meaning for him, I rejoice for we can reach each other freely and gladly at this point, but I cannot count upon this happening.

When I attempt to select the areas of life's meanings in which the prevailing culture and the counterculture (remember, not "the two generations" this time) are in most obvious conflict, I at once face a dilemma. Shall I try to be objective or be frankly subjective? It appears to me that however I cut this cake the results that I obtain will be "me," not "it." I cannot make an objective selection no matter how versed I become in the literature of values and cultural change. When I get into an area, I will try very hard to be influenced by all of the "signs and portents" that other and often more scholarly people have provided. But my selection is me.

One or two personal attributes will certainly influence my choice. I have already suggested that I am existentialist in my philosophy. (A few years ago Carlton Beck in *Foundations of Guidance,* pp. 88–93, wrote that I was a *Daseinanalyst,* and that frightened me until I found out that he identified me as a phenomenological-existentialist in my perception of reality. That sounds almost equally formidable!) I am influenced also by seeing myself as a human relations kind of person. How people see themselves and relate to others means more to me than their vocation, education, or the labels they use.

I think the next few decades will see an overriding emphasis upon human relationships. The courageous former nun who has served as President of Webster College and of Hunter College, Jacqueline Grennan, gave this perspective on the person when she wrote: "The last half of this century . . . is going to be the age of the person . . . as the center of society. No longer is the person the possession of the tribe. No longer is he owned by the company town. No longer is he owned by a denominational church. No longer is he owned by his family. No longer is he even owned by his nation, because the student of today sees the United States of America in an open world, interacting with all kinds of other states." Each person "is his own man" or woman and must in turn concede that integrity to every other person. We certainly have not passed the stage of "pushing each other around" but we are more worried than formerly about what we are doing in this connection.

The five areas of movement in our contemporary philosophy which I consider to be the most crucial are, therefore, areas in which I feel the personal integrity of the individual is at stake. They are areas in which the individual considers his own internal relations, his relations to others, and his relations to the Infinite. These are intensely human relations of ordinary persons like you and me. They are somewhat tersely stated here as issues that will be examined as broad areas of conflict or movement. The five are:

1. Science as a means, not an end.

2. Truth as forever emerging, never fully seen.

3. The present as reality, not preparation for the future.

4. Religion as evolving, not changeless.

5. Ambiguity as more certain than certainty.

SCIENCE AS A MEANS, NOT AN END

It is unpopular and even dangerous to one's reputation to question science, just as one never questions the virtues of Motherhood or approves of Sin. But questioning science doesn't mean condemning it. Questioning it means attempting to see it in perspective, insisting that it be realistic in its assumptions. Some of the "antiscience" attitudes expressed by the observant younger generation are believed by the physicist Glenn Seaborg to be an outgrowth of its own success. Science has fostered changes in our society faster than our social and political institutions can understand and absorb them. It has become the proverbial tail that wags the dog.

Science, and its application through technology, has certainly given us almost all that we have in the way of living comforts, transportation, communication, health, our data bank of knowledge. Science may be seen as the body of knowledge gained by observational methods, but operationally science *is* the method, a method of ordering observations, analyzing data, and drawing inferences. In the statement of hypotheses it can be as creative as poetry. On the other hand, it is not a way of life although some people have made it so. Starting out as a new way of interpreting nature, it was soon proposed that science was the only way to apprehend reality. Only those things examined by science were real.

This perception of science is increasingly challenged today, for science was never meant to be a philosophy, an explanation of life. It is a method used to provide a description of nature and only to some degree an understanding of nature. Over the past century the method has become vastly complex and highly respected. It is a powerful method indeed. Thus the means subtly became transformed into the ends. Scientific reality became total reality. What science could not prove was not so. It then followed (since science dealt best with physical, observable things) that the only part of man that was real was his physical, observable self. This became the philosophy of positivism, more popularly known as materialism. Only the material, even with regard to man, is real. No man can ever know his inner self, if indeed he has one. He hasn't one really, because it cannot be proved—scientifically proved. Barfield, an English writer, says that such a philosophy makes life meaningless. One can never see meaning in oneself or the world about one because science doesn't provide meaning. If, as positivists assert, science is the only way, and if science cannot provide meaning, then there is no meaning. Life and nature are meaningless accidents of creation, and their continuation is again accidental and without purpose or goal.

If Barfield objected to positivism as limiting, he would most certainly not agree with Leech, an English anthropologist. Leech draws a hard, positivist conclusion from the fact that science is achieving results in what was formerly known as the supernatural—flying in space, creating living tissue, communicating over vast distances, "making the dead live" with organ transplants—and destroying on a global basis. Because of these new powers, Leech proposes that science must replace God in assuming the resulting moral responsibility. He says: "God was only credited with the authority to establish and enforce moral rules because he was also credited with supernatural powers of creation and destruction. These powers have now been usurped by man and he (the scientist) must take on the moral responsibility that goes with them." And again, "We must now learn to play God in a moral as well as in a creative or destructive sense" (*Saturday Evening Post,* Nov. 16, 1968). Many other dedicated scientists have worried about this issue, with most assuming that in the last analysis science must truly "play God."

These assumptions and presumptions are unacceptable to many people. Science is not the only way to Truth; imagination and artistry and intuition are other ways open to man. Different facets of existence need to be approached by different means. Who is to say that the poet is not seeking truth, or enlightenment at least, as is the composer, the painter, the seer? The need to dream is as real as the need to prove.

It is true that science has stepped far beyond the dogma and super-stition of a few centuries ago. It has offered a clean, creative way of thinking, unfettered by the dogma of Aristotle and the fierce intolerances of the medieval Church. Observation has become more important than authority or belief. A story is told of a school boy in the Middle Ages who heard a monk read Aristotle's description of a lion. The description did not ring true and the boy said, "Sir, that isn't what a lion looks like. I've been to Africa and I've *seen* a lion." The monk replied, "If the lion you saw doesn't look like Aristotle's lion, then your lion was mistaken." Scientific observation was a great improvement over such dogma.

Then that method itself became a dogma—and therein lies the value conflict. Life consists of more than things. Dreams are seen by many to be as important as things. You may not be able to prove human relation-ships but you can experience them. Faith is also real, for much of life today is based upon faith, the faith of the scientist no less than that of the artist. Indeed, every man lives by faith as he deals with checks representing money, stocks and bonds representing factories. In our financially and industrially complex society, one must have faith in those who write the checks and issue the bonds—or leave that society.

Living today requires one *to believe* as well as to know, *to experience* as well as to think, *to seek meaning* for oneself which no science can prove—and to encourage the poet and the artist as we have been encour-aging the scientist.

TRUTH AS FOREVER EMERGING, NEVER FULLY FOUND

There is nothing particularly startling about the statement of truth as always tentative. "Forever emerging, never fully found" is a bit more extreme, but seems to harmonize with this present world in which new knowledge is replacing old knowledge at a rapid rate and in which there is a constant flow of new insights and meanings. If you, the reader, respond this way then you *are* a modern. You are in harmony with the assumption that we constantly are changing our understanding of the meaning of the universe, the world, and man. You are receptive to new truth even though this deposes cherished old truth.

Those who accept this view find themselves in harmony with a philos-ophy called experimentalism (sometimes called instrumentalism). In this approach to truth, to the way in which knowledge is gained, the key concept is continuity of known and unknown, of object and observer. Truth (with a small *t* since it is individual and specific, not universal) is forever tentative because man is forever changing and knowledge and the knower cannot be separated. As the knower changes so does know-ledge. Knowledge can be neither discovery nor disclosure of a predeter-mined existence, for knowing depends upon a joint achievement of knower and environment. Knowing is operational, not just a beholding.

I am writing upon something which I call a "table." What is a table? It is *for me* what I make it to be. It is a combination of the object and the meaning of the object to me. I cannot separate the object from me, from its meaning for me. Apart from its meaning for me, it is nothing to me, it doesn't exist for me. The theologian Sören Kierkegaard once put it this way, "Truth exists for the individual only as he himself pro-duces it in action."

Experimentalism does not begin with universal truths (rationalism and idealism) nor restrict itself to observable phenomena (realism). It begins with specific and particular experience. It is allergic to generalizations. The present and emerging future are stressed, not the past. The past becomes a humble servant of the present.

In saying all of this we are not defining truth in terms of its content, but describing one dimension of truth regardless of content, the dimen-sion of tentativeness. Perhaps even more we are describing the manner in which truth is sought as new knowledge modifies old truth. Experi-mentalists use the empirical method but are under no illusion that observed facts are important in themselves. They are important only as they become a part of the experience of the observer and have meaning for him. Their importance also depends upon their usefulness, their con-tribution to desirable ends. "Is it true?" coupled with, "Does it work?"

In some earlier writing I said, "For the experimentalist, values have no existence in themselves; they are individual to the observer, an attribute of a particular experienced by that observer. Values are the results of human choices made in a transaction involving a person and his environ-ment. Their character must be found in that context and may not be imposed from outside. Intentions and actions should both be appropri-ate to the situation, with each situation perceived as a new one. The experimentalist has no fixed and final values. Truth is dynamic in a world which is constantly changing."

This approach to the meaning of truth is not one which many people can accept with ease. They may want to accept it but find that in their formal (school) education different assumptions were made about reality, about the nature of knowledge. They may assume universal truths (rationalism) if they studied in the humanities or assume that true reality lies in the objective, observable world (realism) if they studied in the sciences. So many who would agree that truth is tentative and for-ever emerging find themselves immediately resorting to qualifiers. They say, "All truth is tentative *except* for a few universal Truths," or, "Values are relative to a given situation *except* for a few things," or, "Knowledge is personal and affected by the knower's interpretation *except*, of course, for the physical, observable phenomena of the world which are real in themselves."

I said earlier in this chapter that truth is individual to each person and that there is no universal or final answer to "Truth is . . .," that no two people necessarily give the same response, nor does a given person's response necessarily remain unchanged throughout his lifetime. I said also that this individualized meaning of any phenomenon, or of one's answer to any question, is the heart of a theory of behavior called phenomenology. The term derives from the assumption that the meaning of each phenomenon, each event, each fact, is unique to each person. This meaning is determined by each person's pattern of experiences, which cumulatively becomes his "frame of reference," his reference point for meaning. Further, since this framework of meanings changes with experience, the phenomenal world in which he lives changes. Hence, truth is not only individual, but tentative and subject to change.

If one then makes philosophical assumptions which are experimentalist or existentialist in nature (one differs from the other only in the greater focus of existentialism upon man and its greater insistence upon continuing uncertainty) and makes behavior assumptions which are phenomenological, then I propose that meanings in the present world are easier to come by. It is not in keeping with the times, however, to use ridiculously long words—"experimentalism, existentialism, and phenomenology" even though they may be impressive. I suggest substituting the simpler terms "specific," "tentative," and "personal," with perhaps an overall term "dynamic." It is a question of being clothed in high fashion as opposed to a simple miniskirt-blouse, pants suit, or jeans-jacket outfit for the woman and the inevitable shirt and pants for the man!

It is obvious that my biases are showing, that my personal convictions have been spread before you. I have been describing the world of knowledge and truth as I see them. These approaches to an understanding of truth are helpful to me and so I share them with you. It would be inconsistent indeed, however, if I failed to state that if other approaches to truth are more meaningful to you, then these may be best for you even though they may not be for me. I think we have outgrown a good many of the assumptions of the older philosophies; they are no longer appropriate to the contemporary intellectual and social world. But you may not agree, and so I must say in complete sincerity, "What is best for me may not be best for you."

When proposing a personalized and highly subjective approach to psychological meanings, I realize that there is an "opposing" and equally contemporary theory called behaviorism. Its assumptions about behavior and how it can be modified are seen by many to be radically different from the assumptions of phenomenology. Certainly they are worthy of your respect. I do not see these two modern systems as opposed, however, because each has relevance for a different dimension of our contemporary need. Carl Rogers has helped us with one kind of understanding, B. F. Skinner with another. What needs to be made clear, however, is that there are individual approaches to the meaning of truth that are different from the ones that I espouse, and they may have real significance for you.

Tentativeness and Commitment

The tentativeness of truth bothers some thoughtful people. They might say: "If truth is specific in nature and transitory in time, then we have little solid rock to stand up on. All is shifting sand. What *can* I believe in deeply enough to make a difference in my life, or in the lives of my students and clients?" This is a rough question, and one is tempted to fall back upon some ultimate values or some observable realities just to get enough security to continue living a life that has meaning.

The concept of tentativeness is coupled, however, with the significance of living in the present, the reality of the "now." What I believe or know to be true may be transitory, true only for now, but then "now" is all I have. My living is in the present and in my present I have some beliefs, some truths. What is true for now is my reality—and a sufficient reality to give me a basis for action. Gordon Allport proposed some years ago, in a statement which has influenced my life ever since, "Tentativeness must be coupled with commitment." What I now believe in, I can be committed to, can act upon, can fight for. It is not necessary that my present beliefs be eternal, unchanging. That is too simplistic, anyway, for life is not unchanging, nor am I. But if I have some present truth, I must act upon that, not wait for new or more permanent truth. Science consistently utilizes present truth in searching for and proving new truth. But until new truth is found and validated, present truth is real.

Tentativeness and commitment can be meaningful to a life of service and of searching. One thinks, "Until I discover something else, I must act as though what I now know is adequate—and it is adequate for now. And now is all that I have." Let me illustrate.

You choose a vocation. It may not be the one you will follow all of your life (indeed, this probably won't be possible), but you prepare for that vocation as carefully as if you *were* to spend a lifetime in the same field. Unless you do, you cannot be fair to the vocation. You enter the vocation with gusto, give it your full commitment, give to it and get from it all that you can. But you are aware of yourself changing—and your society changing—and your commitment may change to another vocation or to another interpretation of that same vocation. The prospect of possible change need not alter the depth of your present commitment. Indeed you can retain your self-respect only if you remain committed. Committed but observant.

Commitment applies to one's beliefs also. What I believe in I must act upon as though my belief were final truth. It won't be and I know it. But it is "final" for my "now" and that is all I can live in. For example, I believe in a particular "truth" about human nature—that if I show another person that I trust him, he is more likely than not to trust me in return and to exhibit behavior which is in keeping with my expectation of him. Now I cannot prove that this belief will last forever, but I must act upon it now or it is no real belief. Of course, not everyone will reciprocate trust with trust; some will betray me. But this reality is part of my belief that "not everyone acts alike." So my belief becomes validated upon a batting average basis—I hope for an average of over .500, but I may not get it. How well I bat depends upon both the particular society in which I operate and the sincerity of my trust. Yet if I bat only .200 and strike out the rest of the time, perhaps the .200 is adequate validation. The .200 average involves significant and irreplaceable *people*, not cowhide-covered pellets. The point is that my belief—or my vocation—may not be perfect but I act upon it, I am committed to it.

Any statement of "fact" is of a tentative fact, yet one acts upon it. The garage man states as a fact that your car is in good running order, and so you start your trip acting as though the fact were true. My wife calls me to dinner—it may or may not be on the table, for she may count upon my having to finish the chapter I am reading—but I act as though the statement were a fact and go to the table. I lend a man some money upon the assumption that he can repay me in six months. The present fact is that he can, but it is also a tentative fact, for sudden illness eats up his reserve and he cannot repay me in six months. Let me assume that I was aware of this possibility, yet not to act upon the fact of present truth is to render oneself immobile.

Counselors can help students in a significant way if the reality of both "tentativeness" and "commitment" can be established. In too much of the school tradition facts are presented as "forever" facts, although all thinking adults know that this is not so. Students should be helped to accept the reality of tentativeness without allowing this to cripple their sense of commitment—to a life purpose, a value, a course of action. Pascal, the French philosopher, wrote that "a commitment is a wager." It is a gamble, we take a risk. No commitment is worthwhile unless risk is involved—and by the very nature of the tentativeness of truth, risk is assured. I would hope that a counselor could *bet his life* on what he believes to be important and in the betting encourage students both to examine what is basically important and to risk a commitment.

EXPERIENCING THE PRESENT IS THE MOST SIGNIFICANT REALITY

For many people of the world the future has little significance. Only today, with its wants and its resources, is meaningful. This is true for some of the world's simpler, underdeveloped cultures, particularly those found in the tropical regions of the world. For such people the supplying of food for the day, with little energy left over, is existence itself. Living only for today is also common among such people as the American Indian, for whom it has not been the enervating climate but a simple trust in and relationship with nature that has made tomorrow something not to be apprehended and prepared for. And this is the way of life also for the chronically poor in any part of the world whose possessions are few and whose livelihood is assured only on a daily or even an hourly basis.

On the other hand, preparing for the future, being provident, taking thought for the morrow, is essential for those who live in the temperate zones of the world where climate variations are severe. In such locations a person plans ahead or perishes. The grasshopper dies and the ant survives. It has come to be a mark of civilization to plan and to store up today what one must have for a less benign tomorrow. Your forefathers and mine did this or we would not be here today.

So what is wrong with preparing for the future? Nothing, of course, except that perhaps in America we are doing too good a job of it. Why are Americans preparing for tomorrow? So that we can be free to enjoy it. Yes, but if tomorrow we miss the enjoyment of *that* day because we are busy preparing for a new tomorrow—then the means begin to assume the proportion of ends. Those living comfortably or even affluently seem to have overlooked the fact that they have reached a level of production, storing, and distribution of the necessities of life where not all of today must be taken up with preparing for tomorrow. We have developed cooperative sharing in anticipating the needs of tomorrow and the accidents of today—social security, health insurance, unemployment insurance, profit sharing of various sorts. Do we then need to prepare for tomorrow as though it were more important than today? (See later section on "From Scarcity and Competition to Abundance and Belonging," in Chapter VII.) Here, of course, I speak of each person's zeal for insuring his personal economic security. But the very people who struggle hardest for their individual futures have little zeal indeed for considering the steps that must be taken to insure the future of our race. When it comes to matters of population and pollution control, most of us act as though today would be extended indefinitely and tomorrow would never come.

Many children see their parents preparing so intensely for future security that all of the enjoyment of today—and of tomorrow when it becomes today—is neglected and ignored. They see parents working for the future when there is little need to do so, when their future is not insecure, because such work is all that the parents know. They are in a lifelong "work bind" which dims the beauty of all the rest of life for them.

In their distaste for such a work-bound, future-oriented life, some young people disdain all such preparation, live hedonistically and for the moment. This is overreaction to be sure. Without acknowledging it, they live upon what others have worked to produce. This is going as far in one extreme as their parents may have gone in the other. Each side accuses the other of "wasting time," but what one side means by the term is the exact opposite of what is meant by the other. A balance is much needed. Might teachers and counselors, as well as parents, present a model which provides this balance, a model in whom there is enjoyment of today without tomorrow's being ignored? The development of a balanced picture seems essential, for we now have only a strident clash between the warriors of work and those who would make a travesty of toil. Often the clash is between (1) the hardworking parent who has not forgotten the depression of the 1930's and to whom Social Security is still new and untried, and (2) the child who is very uncertain about there being a future, let alone a personal future in which his problems will be solved by having money in the bank.

Existentialism

There is a basic philosophical issue involved also, an issue which is only tangentially related to the two-generation question. Existentialism, briefly referred to earlier, is strongly favored by the young, to be sure,

but it is in no sense restricted to youth. This is a "modern" philosophical system, less than a century old, which became prominent only within the past 30 to 40 years. Existentialism means centering upon the
immediately *existing* person, upon the person as he is emerging, becoming. This emphasis upon existence is seen in contrast to understanding
man in terms of essence, which consists of immutable principles and
laws standing above any given existence. The key phrase of existentialism, that "existence precedes essence," signifies that only as we
experience our existence, our being, do we have any essence. For the
existentialist, I exist (am real) only within the now. All that is "real" is
what I personally experience. The only full reality is me—and me in this
instant of existence. I know others only through inference, I cannot
experience them as I experience me. I know time only in the present.
This instant is real, the preceding one is now only memory, and the next
one is only a prediction. Indeed, the next instant may never arrive. So
"now" is the significant dimension; experience it to the full, says the
existentialist; it contains all of the meaning of life.

There is no attempt here to describe existentialism as a philosophy, a
system of thought. Indeed, existentialism is several systems of thought;
it is an umbrella term as inclusive as a circus tent. The dimension of time
is, however, a crucial element in all versions of the philosophy. It stresses
the importance of the present, the present as the only true reality.
Earlier I suggested that perhaps I was an existentialist. I have wondered
whether this would, in the eyes of some, damn me as allying myself with
"a left-wing, atheistic movement," "a Left Bank movement" (referring
to the Bohemian student and artist population of Paris which is scattered along the left bank of the Seine River). It is true that Jean-Paul
Sartre is a Parisian and an atheist, but it is also true that the basic concepts of this philosophy have their origin with Sören Kierkegaard, a
native of Denmark and a theologian. This system of thinking embraces
both theists and atheists. The late Paul Tillich, a leading American theologian, was a major contributor to American existentialism. It has
always amused and sometimes angered me to hear simplistic definitions
of this field of thought. Here, for example, is Anders Osterling in his
1957 Nobel Prize Presentation address to Albert Camus, saying, "Camus
represents also the philosophical movement called Existentialism, which
characterizes man's situation in the Universe by denying it all personal
significance, seeing in it only absurdity." Had Osterling never heard of
Martin Buber, or Paul Tillich? Apparently not.

In many ways existentialism has a close affinity with American character and thought. Quite appropriately, I believe, Rollo May in his
Existential Psychology (see References) cites William James and John

Dewey as being existential in outlook. These two most influential twentieth-century American thinkers were pragmatists (that which works is real) who believed that man could be understood only in terms of his immediate experience, that this *was* his existence.

A Personal Statement—Skip If You Like.   Earlier I also confessed to being a work addict. Is this consistent with calling myself an existentialist? The joy of this system of thought is that you can develop your own personal philosophy underneath the umbrella, and your philosophy can be as inconsistent as you are! In fact, my existentialism may be unique to me for all I know. What I see in this system for me can be condensed into three phrases: (1) The only reality that I am sure of is me. (2) The only time that is real for me is now. (3) My major and perhaps only purpose in life is seeking for new truth, new meaning, new understanding. Me—now—seeking. The fact that I work hard means that I do not ignore the future, but I must *live* in the present, strive to enjoy each moment as though it were the last. Else I miss the whole meaning of life.

In my personal existentialism I can also believe in a Supreme Being, can believe that I am a part of that Being, and that IT (perhaps He or She?) is a part of me. This still leaves me responsible for me—in the now —and forever seeking.

So this is the philosophy of one who is far from being a youth—but for whom the importance of "me" and of the present is as real as they are for youth. There is a large difference between me and the young, however. I believe that you and I cannot understand or improve the Present unless we have recourse to the perspective of the Past. Many of the young would not agree. That which is most "new" about the present revolution of the young is that they would divorce themselves from all commitments to the past and not build upon it at all. They contend that change comes too slowly in this fashion. They would build a new world by building new, not improved, institutions. Not all of the "rebelling" young, I should say, are rebelling by destroying. They do not destroy; they merely ignore the past and the institutions developed out of it. They ignore them as much as possible—school, court, bank, the military. These aren't seen as "real" within the system of need in the contemporary world. So new standards, new institutions, new goals must be established.

I sympathize with youth's impatience over how slowly institutions change to meet new conditions. Youth may be right, maybe we haven't so much time. Though the speed and drastic nature of change from moment to moment within the present is very vivid to me also, I need perspective. I need a little looking back to get a reference point or two in order to tell better the *slope* of the curve of change: how steep is the slope, how irregular, what variables are contributing? So, youthful existentialist, I am with you but not all the way! I guess I could not be all the way anyway, for I cannot be you, I can only be me and in my present—which has a perspective. When it comes to *seeking,* then perhaps we have more in common, for we may be seeking common goals in a future which is as unknown to me as it is to you. The only difference is that you have more of the future than I have.

RELIGION AS EVOLVING, NOT CHANGELESS

One of my most vivid memories of several years of conducting a graduate course on "Theories and Philosophies of Counseling" was the tear stains on some of the term papers. The students were generally mature professionals working on their doctorate degrees, who had never before faced a paper assignment which said, "What Are Your Personal Assumptions about the Meaning of Existence?" In attempting to articulate his philosophical assumptions, a student often got into troublesome waters where his "philosophy" came in contact with his "religion." Frequently the philosophy was contemporary and the religion was not. It was an agonizing experience for some students to find that their religious faith was still based upon the concepts established in childhood while their intellectual, emotional, and perhaps even "spiritual" selves were decades ahead. Because there was often a loyalty to the childhood faith, there was guilt in even examining it, to say nothing of changing it. Hence the tears. Over and over in the papers and in class discussion came the plaintive query, "How can I ever reconcile my grown-up, graduate-school-level concepts of authority, truth, tolerance with what I learned was *right* when I was a child?"

This dilemma is a crucial one for young adults such as my graduate students and for many who are somewhere between the older students and youth. Many older adults appear satisfied with their relatively unchanged faith, while others have been disturbed enough to cut their ties with organized religion. Some see no conflict because they have never been required to examine this faith as to whether or not it is as contemporary as they are. Some young people have remained faithful to what they learned in childhood, while others have dropped away from the church entirely. But many young people who may not miss what they never really had are in contrast to their elders who thought they had something but now run the risk of losing it.

There must be a significant distinction in our discussion between religion and church. I doubt that as many people "lose their religion" as lose their belief in and loyalty to a given church or denomination. I think that one's "religion," or the quest for the values of an ideal life in which one feels a relationship with the Infinite, is hard to dispense with. In former times (speaking now of America and perhaps of our larger Western world), one felt an upward pull to Heaven and a second-story God. Now one feels the inward pull; although the focus is upon me and the Divine within me, the pull is still present. On the other hand, there is little doubt that there is substantial disillusionment with the organization of religious beliefs and religious practices in a given church or a given denomination. Some people, out of habit or fear, stick with a church that they find relatively meaningless. They don't know where else to turn for a greater satisfaction, and so they maintain an uninspired status quo. Others get out of the church, but their religious needs must often remain unsatisfied because they have no substitute. The tragedy is that people who think they are critical of religion may be basically critical only of the church, of religion expressed in a certain way. They are critical of the vessel, but not necessarily of the contents—the legitimate need to feel a kinship with the Infinite, with God.

"One's religion." The phrase conjures up images and associations that vary widely from America to Europe, from Europe to Asia, and so on around the world. Some religions appear superstitious and selfish, immature perhaps, as do many current governments of the world. Yet if every people has a government so does every people have a religious faith, or several of them. When one thinks of another's faith—Islam or Buddhism for example—it is difficult not to be critical, easy to conclude that that faith is inferior to one's own. Such relegation of the other's religion to an inferior status is partly the result of ignorance (few have ever *experienced* any faith but their own) and partly defensive. Every organized religion carries within itself the assumption that it is the true religion, to be defended against any other. The sad part of this ubiquitous and overwhelming intolerance is that it applies also to subdivisions within a religion, such as the various denominations of the Christian faith. This is not unique to Christianity, for other religions have competing sects, but we know our own divergencies best. The bitterness growing out of these intolerances tears away at one in a most personal fashion.

I find that as I am writing I am becoming defensive, the very attitude that I want to avoid! My defensiveness is not of my faith (it is the best for me, in part because it is the only one which I have experienced), not of my denomination (an accident, but a fortunate one for me, since it is tolerant of a wide diversity of beliefs and is people-oriented), not of the

particular church that I attend (right for me with its experimental program of worship and its warm but nonconventional outlook, but wrong
for many others). No, I am defensive about the distortion of religion by
many rigid and uncompromising defenders and its equally rigid rejection
by many critics. Perhaps it is the intolerance of both defenders and
rejecters that disturbs me most.

The failure to see that religion as a dimension of life is evolving, that it
is changing in many ways, deprives many people of this resource. A
crisis occurs when a person sees the gap between his life orientation and
present intellectual understandings and the faith he has kept unchanged
since childhood. All too ofen the crisis results not only in the rejection
of his childhood faith but a rejection of religion in toto. This leaves him
swinging helplessly in midair as he searches for life's meaning and purpose. He searches in other areas, of course, and he should—in truth as
evidenced by science, in beauty of nature, in art and music, in political
and social action designed to reduce injustice and human want.

What the person in this quandary needs to know is that there are a
great many changes taking place in both the churches themselves and in
the manner in which people are seeking God. I have tried to find a less
conventional phrase than "seeking God," but I believe that this is the
phrase that many seekers would use. There is no need for me to be
apologetic and indirect about the word "God," for the concept and the
reality are highly personal. It can and should mean something different
for you from what it does for me.

Changes in the churches of our country are taking place, but to many
the changes come very slowly. What must not be forgotten is that the
church is a social institution, and social institutions change slowly. Perhaps the church as an institution changes more slowly than some institutions because its gaze is turned backward rather than forward, focused
upon past events more than upon present and future demands. The
church is not the only institutional laggard. Law is another social institution, for example, that is based upon precedent and changes slowly.
A law professor colleague recently commented to me that probate law
is being practiced in 1970 almost exactly as it was practiced in 1850.
Some critic has said that the church is living on memories, but whatever
one says about "the church," it would be wise not to attempt a generalization. One cannot even generalize about theology, for "the new
theologies conceive of a developing world where man is continually
changing and his concept of God is changing with him."

Most noticeable, however, are the individual churches and church
groups that are on the move, providing new programs and new ways of
worship. They are trying to carry God into the everyday life of society

and to make Him more relevant. The shaking up that the churches are getting makes some of them emphasize even more rigorously "the faith of their fathers," while other churches are trying to develop a "faith for their children." If one has courage enough to visit widely among the churches of his community, one can be hopeful of finding a church whose members worship God and experience life in a manner that will be congenial. Such a discovery may well aid one in the search for meaning and purpose.

In addition to the changes in the churches, there have been changes among people who are not basically a part of any church congregation. This decade is seeing many unconventional and unorganized approaches to religious meaning. Some movements are devotional—breakfast prayer groups—and some are actively seeking social change in areas of ethnic and poverty discrimination such as nonprofit housing developments that emphasize nondiscrimination. Other movements stress the appeal of religious mysticism. Some drug users have a strong mystical feeling about their hallucinations and/or feelings of peace and love. Others seek meaning through meditation and the practice of Zen.

The year 1971 brought the excitement of a burgeoning religious youth movement called the "Jesus Movement," which had first become apparent as recently as 1967. Those involved are called "Jesus people" or "street Christians." These are often earnest young people inspired by a concept of Jesus as a personal savior. They testify constantly that Jesus is the best "trip," superior to any drug. They should know, for many of them formerly sought their highs on drugs. Their dress is often hippie-style, but their actions are different in several ways: They use no drugs; they cluster in communes often called Christian Houses (some 600 of these are scattered across the country with at least 200 in California alone); they testify to their faith openly and in an obvious effort to attract others to their vision and their faith. Their youthful evangelism involves fundamentalist concepts of religion which they see as relevant to the spirit and language of their day.

This spirit has invaded the rock music world with many new pieces that are openly evangelistic. Some disc jockeys spin only religious platters; Christian Rock Festivals are appearing; and religious singing groups—both independent and church sponsored—appear in coffee houses, street rallies, school assemblies, night clubs, and wherever people are, even churches! The dramatic rock opera, *Jesus Christ, Superstar,* although written for youth, has been received enthusiastically by many who are not youthful in years. I believe that by mid-1971 something like two million copies of the recording of the opera had been sold. I saw the show advertised as a "coming attraction" on the Strip in Las

Vegas, to be presented by a Canadian rock group. It originated in England and has a wide intercultural appeal. The sweeping nature of the Jesus Movement is further indicated by the publication of some 50 free (literally) Jesus newspapers across the country.

Some people would not have written as friendly a report of the movement as I have just done. They are unconvinced of the sincerity of the Jesus People. They feel that much of it is a "put on." I am sure that there *are* rotten apples in the barrel, but I am not inclined to empty all of the barrel into the garbage can.

I have commented on changes in the church and on the youth movements as though they were completely separate. They may not always remain so. Some churches are being changed by youth. In my church recently I saw a statement of this change by its minister, Edwin Grant. It is a youthful statement, but it meant something to this congregation composed of all ages. The statement reads:

There is a new goal—*relationship, not religion.*

There is a new strategy—*people, not programs.*

There is a new style—*vulnerability, not defensiveness.*

There is a new stance—*involvement, not pronouncements.*

There is a new vision—the *future, not the past.*

There is a new church—*the strength to love.*

Beliefs change with difficulty, and religious beliefs are often deeply rooted in childhood associations with parents and the family. If this early religion was what Gordon Allport has called *extrinsic* in orientation—utilitarian, self-centered, formal, other-directed—then dogmatism is almost an assured outcome. Such a faith may have made the young believer so dependent that when he questions the particular creed and dogma he was taught, he is cruelly threatened. In consequence, he may cling to the familiar all the more tightly—or he may rebel completely by throwing that dogma and all religion out of the window. He has been taught that "this is the only way" and when "this" is no longer viable for him, then no faith seems tenable.

What Allport calls *intrinsic* orientation, in contrast, includes trust in others, compassion toward others, dogma tempered with humility, tolerance toward other points of view. These beliefs are people-oriented rather than creed-oriented. They will weather questioning with less pain and are more capable of changing with the times.

It is my assumption, first, that man has no choice about being "religious." The choice is with regard to the object of his religious loyalties and acts, the things which he believes in and to which he is committed. My second assumption is that religion is not changeless. It changes with time, or it becomes sterile and is no longer religion. For religion, to me, means both devotion and action. My method and spirit of devotion change with increasing experience and wisdom, my service to others changes with the needs that appear and the methods developed to meet these needs. I probably do not need to say that my concept of God changes. This does not mean changing God, merely my perception of Him. At least, this has happened to me. I go further, for I find that I may not need a changeless God. Why not a God who changes also, changes in a dynamic union with the changes of His Universe? This is what is meant by being vulnerable rather than defensive. *I do not know,* I know only in part and forever will.

AMBIGUITY AS MORE CERTAIN THAN CERTAINTY

Recently a colleague told me of an unpleasant conclusion that he had reached. In examining the transcript of a trial case, he found witnesses had given sworn testimony in court that was contradictory to evidence given in an earlier but equally legal deposition. He said, with resignation and sorrow in his voice, "This shakes my confidence in sworn evidence. It is no longer clear to me, but is gray, not black or white." My friend must recall what he certainly knows, that people change within themselves during the time period between deposition and trial so that what happened "certain white" to them once now appears "uncertain gray." Beyond this, I think he must accept the principle that ambiguity is a far more common reality than certainty. Few things are *only* what they first appear to be, few people mean *only* what their words convey. This does not mean that one needs to become suspicious of hidden meanings, see deceitfulness in people and situations. It means, rather, that a common property of most situations, ideas, and perceptions is that they have more than one meaning. Seeing black or white in a situation is simpler and involves less effort, but is less realistic and involves more risk.

Thinking in terms of dichotomies is a very common practice. Something is "wrong" or "right," this is "true" or "not true," I am a "failure" or a "success." Several kinds of error characterize such thinking. *Making a generalization from a specific instance* is a type of error which science constantly cautions us to avoid. As a matter of fact, "do not generalize" is a basic axiom of the scientific method. This happened once, but will it always happen again or even happen once again? If wrong for one situation, is it wrong for every other situation?

Animals generalize very rapidly from specific situations: a dog once beaten avoids all men with anything long in their hands; a cat which singed its paws on a hot stove is not expected to sort out the heat of the stove. It simply avoids all stoves, hot or cold, black or red. People fall into this kind of thinking all too readily. "I'll never trust men again." "You can't depend upon parents to follow through; it only took one experience to teach me *that* lesson." "After *that* experience, I'll never ride in an airplane again." "I don't see anything hazardous about skiing; I had a fine time last weekend." "You can trust an Englishman; I had a very good experience with an English business man." "All principals are cheats—one certainly played me a dirty trick." Such conclusions are not only lazy and superficial in the extreme, they are hazardous to one's safety and limiting to one's future experience.

People get themselves into frightful boxes by generalizing about themselves. A girl came to a counselor one day in a state of extreme depression: she was "no good," no one cared for her, she was "fat and ugly," etc. This was clearly a call for help, but rather than offering sympathy or glib assurances, the counselor helped by particularizing. She neither admitted nor denied the validity of the girl's statements, but realized that back of these gross generalizations were some particular stimuli or situations, and that perhaps these, not the generalizations, could be handled. So she questioned gently, "When did you start feeling this way?" (This morning as I was dressing.) "When, during your dressing, did your depression begin to be felt?" (When I looked in the mirror and saw my stringy hair, my greasy complexion, my fat ugly body—oh, I'm a mess!) "Are you depressed about you as a person, or about the way you look?" (I guess—it's about the way I look. I get along in school all right.) "Can you do anything about how you look?" (Well, I guess so. I do need a shampoo—and I've got to lose some weight.) "Would you feel better about yourself if you looked better?" (I sure would!)

This is an oversimplification of the interview, of course, but the method used offsets some of the damage done by generalizing. People who damn themselves by generalizing can be helped by particularizing. "All teachers hate me" might boil down to one teacher who gave what was seen as an unfair grade. "Nobody likes me" particularizes down to one friend who gave a snub or seemed to do so. "I'm no good" could mean, "I haven't finished that term paper that is due tomorrow."

A second error in "black-white" thinking is *failing to see that few situations or experiences can be neatly placed in one of two categories;* that each possesses a given characteristic to a degree, rather than its being totally present or absent. A familiar example of this type of error is found in any discussion of freedom. "Free will" and "determinism" in the absolute have little meaning for anyone's life. Almost every situation in which you find yourself contains "a degree of freedom," seldom ever total freedom or its antithesis. I have heard class discussions by the hour and read papers by the score on freedom. Almost invariably in the discussion of whether or not one has "freedom to act," there was an assumption that freedom was either present or absent, and was similar from situation to situation.

The use of the term freedom without qualifiers can be very misleading. The implication is that if one has "freedom" or "free choice" then the choice is completely free, without being influenced by past successful or unsuccessful experience, by social mores and expectations, etc. Such a conclusion is totally unrealistic. It bears a close relationship to the "either-or" fallacy.

Not only must the degree of freedom be specified, but it must be specified for a given person in a given situation. "Am I free to write what I wish to write in this book?" And the answer is "yes—and no!" I am partly free and partly restricted. I am free to choose topics—but only within the boundaries of what has meaning for me and what I think will have meaning for the reader. I am bound by my experience, by the canons of good taste, by my limited vocabulary, by time-and-space pressures, etc. I am more free on some topics than on others, more free on some days than on others. "Am I free?" represents a question to which there is no answer! I am free, yes—and no. I am free to a degree. ("Human Freedom and the Counselor" by Wayne Maes carries these thoughts a bit further: *Personnel and Guidance Journal,* 1968, 46; 777–781.)

A third type of error in this simplistic type of thinking has been already introduced in our discussion of phenomenology: *falsely believing that the meaning of a situation is the same for everyone, rather than understanding that its meaning is unique to each person.* There are accidental overlaps of meaning between two people, of course, but the situation possesses meaning for me within my world, not your world or the world at large. Beyond this, its meaning may be relatively clear to me but not to you. The ambiguity of a situation to me (uncertainty of meaning or double meaning) may seem to arise from the impact of the situation upon me, or reciprocally, it may be the impact of me and my particular set of meanings upon the situation. In the first instance, the situation may be ambiguous to anyone; in the second it is obvious that the problem may be mine alone.

A friend senior in years to me from whom I wanted to ask a favor recently canceled a luncheon date with me. The reason given seemed a possible one. But could it have been that he sensed the purpose of my visit and wanted to save me the embarrassment of hearing him say "no" to me? Later, a pleasant card came saying that he was sorry about the canceled date. He did not suggest another one. Was the card an apology, or was it a suggestion that I could ask for another date if the need still existed, that it was up to me? Was he trying to tell me something, and if so, what? A second card came, expressing appreciation for some help I had given him earlier in the year. Now what was the message—encouragement to me to seek a date or was he winding up the year's business? If you have ever been in a similar situation, then you will understand the meaning of ambiguity. (In the situation cited, that particular ambiguity has not yet been resolved. I must live with it a while longer—or forever.)

Even more difficult for some people is the acceptance of ambivalence —the coexistence of conflicting and opposed feelings about some person or object. Can one both like and dislike a person or object simultaneously? Yes, because you respond positively to some characteristics of the person or object and negatively to others. If getting to a football game through heavy traffic and parking my car is part of the game, then I like part of the game and dislike another part. Some people I both like and dislike; I have conflicting feelings about them. A child may both love and hate his mother or father; both emotions are real. Feelings are more freely admitted by this generation than by some earlier ones. The ambivalence that is admitted by today's children would have been denied by their parents. In the parents' culture one *should* love one's mother. To admit hate was to violate both moral and social canons.

The fact of ambiguity is certainly not new. What appears more recent is the greater degree to which ambiguity is accepted, is seen as something to be reckoned with. If science is not the only approach to meaning, if new truth is forever emerging, if religion is evolving and not fixed—then it must follow that ambiguity characterizes many situations. There will be fewer permanent certainties and less neat placing of people and events into categories of good or bad, true or not true, fewer decisions that "I clearly should" or "I should not."

I am not sure of the extent to which ambiguity is admitted as a trend in all parts of our culture. The rapidity of technological and social change threatens most people, but people react differently to threat. Some admit to being confused, less certain than before, more open to what is new. Others refuse to admit confusion, adjust their perception of the situation in a manner designed to reduce the threat, lean increasingly upon their certainties, and become more dogmatic about them. In general, newness "turns on" some people and opens them to risk the advantages of newness. Others tighten their defenses against change, deny it or damn it, and increase their tendency to dichotomize and generalize. "The Communists are the cause of it all." "Once we get a new administration, everything will be all right." "If they would just break up those big labor unions, we'd put a stop to inflation." "It's the Establishment." "America is like all other imperialist nations." "If you can't prove it, it isn't so."

For me, then, ambiguity is more certain than certainty; ambiguous situations have a higher frequency than those with a clear unequivocal meaning. It is safe to be "sure" about one's wife, car, favorite team. ("My wife is the best cook in our neighborhood." "The Rambler is the best car in America." "The Giants will win the pennant race this year.") Dogmatism of this sort harms no one and is likely to lead only to pleasant arguments. Other issues, however, are inherently ambiguous: arbitrary rejection of birth control in the face of increasing numbers of rejected and starving children; the killing of men and women in war in order to insure a peaceful world; the policy of steadily increasing our consumption of goods as a protection of our industrial economy; protecting the rights of the criminally accused without further protecting the rights of the victims of crime. Such social and economic issues as these bristle with ambiguity. Dogmatism here is of a different order; it represents superficial and often irresponsible thinking in an attempt to find an easy and final solution to a situation that defies simplistic solutions. So I am willing to admit my confusion, and to follow poet John Ciardi in saying that "I prefer the larger confusions to the smaller certainties." Contemporary man in general faces more uncertainties than certainties. Nor should you or I feel any hesitancy in admitting this— it is only by admitting that there is more than one interpretation or more than one solution that we are freed to consider alternatives and to choose the most meaningful one.

IMPLICATIONS FOR THE COUNSELOR

The implications of this chapter—science and dreams, truth and tentativeness, the enrichment of the present, religion as dynamic, and ambiguity as always present—are perhaps more for the counselor in his personal life than for the counselor as he deals with the client's questions about life. What are the implications for you, the reader, of these fluid fields of thought?

Consider it a good sign of mental health if you lack full assurance about life's meaning and purpose! There is an old Chinese saying, "It is easy to paint a goblin but hard to paint a horse." We know so many variations of life that it is hard even to see the outlines. One can become so uncertain and confused as to become immobilized, but a degree of confusion is an asset. This concept is related to a characteristic of anxiety—too much of it and you are too preoccupied to be effective, too tense about yourself to relate to others; too little of it and you are too contented to be sensitive to the world around you. A contented cow, chewing its cud, is impervious to both the destruction of the storm and the beauty of the sunset. Some anxiety, some degree of confusion, is a stimulus to change and growth.

Some people prefer objective tests to sentence-completion exercises. They are more secure in being "right" or "wrong" than in giving person-ally meaningful responses which might reveal them to others. Teachers have a bad habit of always wanting to be "right," meaning totally right, admitting no degree of error. The reality of much of life is that few answers are totally right except for a very limited area of application or for very simple concepts. "Am I over 25 years of age?" can be answered, "Yes" with no qualifiers. "Am I tolerant?" "Am I truthful?" "Am I free?" call for a totally different kind of answer. The only reasonable answer to any of the above questions is, "To a degree, or in some situ-ations" or, more simply, "I don't know."

Being willing to admit confusion or being able to say, "I don't know," might form a bond between counselor and client. The counselor then appears honest (for an evasive or dogmatic answer will make the other distrustful) and he is seen as having something in common with the client's confusion or uncertainty.

Few of us ever appreciate, except occasionally, the power of a simple "I don't know." This, when given in a spirit of "But I'd like to know" or "Perhaps I—or you and I—can find out," strengthens both you and your client as persons.

Another implication of what I have been writing is that it is "right" to dream, to muse, to be sensitive to truth in forms other than the scien-tific or the logical. To read poetry, to hear music, to see beauty in art and nature may help a person apprehend life's meanings more than will logical thinking or doing. There is merit in just "being" and not always doing. We are such "doers" in America that when we are not active we feel guilty or restless. As a personal reflection, I suppose this is one of my worst faults—I get *too much* satisfaction out of doing! Achieving is supposed to be an admirable American trait, but there is "achievement" also in relaxing and letting life take over for a little while. We manage life so well, some of us, that we get nothing else done but managing.

The quality of living in a person that permits an active experiencing of

Being and Beauty can be quickly sensed by others. One does not have to talk about what he believes in, is sensitive to. The other person becomes aware of it, whether he be friend or client. To fight hard for what one believes in, what one wants to achieve, is highly desirable but only if the fight is less than a 24-hour-a-day business. The beautiful life, to me, is one that has an occasional but deliberate hiatus in the day's fight for achievement, a "coffee break" with one's self, perhaps shared with another. Sometimes truth appears not when we seek it but only when we allow it to find us. Perhaps the hiatus, the break, is all that allows the present to be meaningful.

I have spoken in preceding pages of tentativeness. I think the counselor can afford to be tentative about both the client and himself. We as counselors are taught to withhold "judgment," the firm character- ization of another, when we deal with our clients and friends. He or she is changed from yesterday, at any one time displays only one facet of a complex self, is defensive and shares himself cautiously, is inconsistent in both word and deed. This we know about the other person, so we are tentative and perhaps tolerant.

It is just as important that one not be too severe on oneself. What you now know and are is tentative, not complete, not perfect. Counselors are often severely self-critical, blaming themselves for lack of knowledge, for error, for lack of courage. As was said earlier, *some* degree of concern about oneself is healthy, but teachers and counselors and people in the helping professions generally are overly harsh on them- selves. There is a hazy borderland between being constructively self- demanding and being cruelly self-destructive. No one has committed the unpardonable sin except the person who has lost respect for himself. Such a person has closed the door to the potential of tentativeness, which can be a powerful force in himself for both honesty and growth.

Although it is a sensitive subject, one implication for the counselor is that he should consider clarifying his own religious stance. This means religion in the full sense of commitment to life and relation to the ultimate. In this I find it hard personally to separate my religion from my philosophy. Or I vacillate between subsuming my religion under my philosophy and reversing the order. The fact that I have clearly iden- tified myself as a theistic (possibly pantheistic) existentialist was not done with any intent to influence the reader to adopt my model. Perhaps I could have described other models as well, but had I done so the reader would have sensed their inherent falseness. I can expound with directness and a sense of conviction in this area only in terms of that to which I am committed.

My plea for the counselor is that he: (1) articulate his assumptions about man in the universe, about truth, about values, and (2) distinguish in his own thinking between his religion and the church. The church can be seen as a *fellowship of people*, not a building, a creed, or a minister. If the counselor can focus upon what he wants to be committed to in life and how he hopes to be related to both God and man, then he can find a fellowship called a church that can help him. And if not a church, then a group, or a commune, or a friend.

Finally, there are two overriding implications that I hope are as clear to you as they are to me. One is that ambiguity, uncertainty, and tentativeness are not threats, are not to be feared. They are freeing agents that open us to the new and changing as well as to the slowly firming concepts of assurance and commitment. A counselor who is unafraid can drain some of the fear from a student's life and free him as well.

Then, too, I have advocated pleasuring the present and dallying with dreams. These experiences are as real as those associated with the sober words of compassion and responsibility. To me, a counselor's effectiveness is related to his enjoyment of being, as well as to what he knows and does.

References for Exploration

Axline, Virginia. *Dibs: In Search of Self.* Ballantine Books, 1964.

Bakan, David. "Stimulus: Response: Psychology Can Now Kick the Science Habit." *Psychology Today,* March 1972.

Barnes, Wesley. *The Philosophy and Literature of Existentialism.* Barron's Educational Series, 1968.

Bush, Vannevar. *Science is Not Enough.* William Morrow and Co., New York, 1967.

Cook, Fred. *The Nightmare Decade: The Life and Times of Senator Joe McCarthy.* Random House, 1971.

Fisher, Robert B. *Science, Man and Society.* W. B. Saunders Co., 1971.

Intellectual Digest. Any issue. (Each issue carries sections on Arts and Humanities, Politics and Foreign Affairs, Science, Social Science and Education, Sports, Humor, Books, etc. The March 1972 issue, for example, contains colored photographs of the artist's concept of the Creation, Anne Sexton's contemporary concepts of Grimm's Fairy Tales, Dr. Hans Kung and the Catholic Church, the American Irish, Ode to the Jersey Mosquito, Who Shall Live and Who Shall Die?, The Myth of the Racially Superior Athlete, a review of *Present Past and Past Present* by Jonesco, etc. Ask for it and you're likely to find it in this journal. It is only in its second volume but it will endure.)

"Interview with R. Buckminster Fuller," *Playboy,* Feb. 1972, pp. 59–70, 194–204. (This amazing man "covers the universe" literally in his comments, and the reference could be attached to any of several chapters in this book. He refers so frequently to man, his mission, and his future, that I feel this chapter provides a useful association.)

"Is There a New Man?" a symposium with Alexander Comfort, Hugh Downs, Martin Marty, Stringfellow Barr, et al., as participants. *The Center Magazine,* November–December, 1971.

Laing, R. D. *Knots.* Tavistock Publications, London, 1970. (For the person who needs assurance. In verse form, Laing delineates the psychological Knots with which we place ourselves in bondage to our own fears.)

May, Rollo. *Existential Psychology.* Random House, 2nd ed., 1969. (A classic in brief form. For those who want to go a little further on the philosophy side, read another small classic, William Barrett, *Irrational Man: A Study in Existentialist Philosophy.* Doubleday Anchor Book, 1958.)

Montague, Ashley. *The Ignorance of Certainty.* Harper and Row, 1970.

Reiser, Oliver L. *Cosmic Humanism.* Schenkman Publishers, Cambridge, 1966.

A Unicorn in the Garden (cartoon film). 10 minutes. Contemporary Films, McGraw Hill, 267 W. 25th St., New York, N.Y. 10001, 1953. (Thurber's classic story— who is sane?)

Chinese Firedrill (film). 25 minutes. Canyon Cinema Cooperative, Room 220, Industrial Center Building, Sausalito, Calif. 94965. (Film poetry about a schizophrenic young man. Brilliant and esoteric.)

Nohanni (film). 19 minutes. Contemporary Films, McGraw Hill, 267 W. 25th St., New York, N.Y. 10001. (Story of the indomitable spirit of a man, seen within the beauty of the Canadian Northwest. It is important that it is in color.)

CHAPTER VI

Our Contemporary Universe and World

NEW NOTIONS ABOUT THE UNIVERSE

Moving from personal values to the universe seems a large step indeed, reminding us of Neil Armstrong's "one small step for man" to his "giant leap for mankind." But giant leap or not, the contemporary man must be aware not only of himself and his society but of his world and universe. I speak in part, of course, of the excitement aroused by the space explorations of the past decade and a half. Sputnik jarred us not only because "the competition" was there ahead of us, but also because we suddenly became aware of what science and technology could do to our concepts of space and earth's position in space. With man no longer earthbound, the prospects opened up for a new dimension of existence. David Block wrote that if man was born of creatures emerging from the ocean, then man was now entering a new ocean—the ocean of space. What would emerge from *it*? He likened our reaching out into space to "the first clutch of a tool by man, or the fish straining to be an amphibian."

This is, of course, hyperbole, and there is now a sober awareness of the vast amounts of money and technical creativity needed to achieve our newly awakened dreams. But this decade will surely see us moving from our past adventures on the moon to manned space stations orbiting the earth and on to new adventures on Mars. Beyond that are reaches still dimly apprehended. The counselor *as a person* must be aware of the new vastness and the new nearness of the universe. To do less is to atrophy. Students like people who are enthusiastic, have imagination, think beyond their job, perhaps beyond their world. Part of the contemporary counselor's "world" today is, of course, some visioning of our planet and of its place in space.

If travel in space is part of our contemporary world, so also is the traveling done by the visual and radio telescopes of the earth's astronomers. Their "travels" have revealed a universe so vast that the mind boggles and turns away in fear and fascination from the concepts involved. Who, for example, can comprehend the distance light travels in an earth year (this is called "a lightyear"), roughly 6,000,000,000,000 miles? Or the fact that our most powerful telescopes reach out into space some 2,000,000,000 lightyears. Multiply six trillion by two billion and be reconciled that beyond that number of miles into space we do not know what exists! In a sense we do, however, for out beyond the limits of our visual telescopes, one billion lightyears farther, are the quasars, the sources of radioactivity that can be detected by our radio telescopes. In a universe so vast our perceptions of both science and man are likely not to prevail. We cannot "prove" that Time, Space, Life can be understood in Earth terms, nor of course, can we disprove it. Schiller once said, "The Universe is a thought of God," and perhaps that poetic definition is as comprehensible as our current scientific explanation.

At one time the earth was the center of the universe, with the sun and all of the stars revolving around it. This was Ptolemy's mistaken contribution of about 150 A.D. This theory prevailed until Copernicus about 1500 began his studies that proved the earth revolved around the sun. Some of the Greek astronomers, notably Aristarchus of Samos, antedating Ptolemy by several centuries, had advanced the correct postulation that the sun was the pivot point, but the earth-centric theory proved too popular—it was more ego-satisfying to man!

From thinking of our sun as center of the universe to recognizing the sun as one of more than 100,000,000,000 stars in a galaxy called the Milky Way was a giant step indeed—and one still not known nor accepted as "real" by a majority of the world's inhabitants. And our sun, no longer the center of the universe, is not even at the center of the Milky Way. It is four-fifths of the way out to the edge of this one galaxy. Are you up to traveling with me still farther into the vastness of space? Well, then, know now that our galaxy, 100,000 lightyears in diameter, is only one galaxy among an estimated 100 trillion galaxies that lie within the scope of the earth's telescopes. Within the bowl of the Big Dipper alone can be seen a cluster of some 300 galaxies, most of them larger than our own.

So man exists on one of the nine planets revolving around our sun, and the sun in turn is a tiny member of a galaxy of more than 100 billion stars, and this galaxy in turn—I'll go no further.

The vast number of stars within this universe and the similarity of the elements within the different solar systems have suggested to scientific and lay minds alike that other stars have planets, and that some of them, as in our solar system, provide conditions favorable for life. The fact that planets are not seen revolving around other stars is no deterrent to this line of reasoning because the planets would have only dim, reflected light and at the distances involved they would be invisible. (From evidence other than the visual, however, it is known that seven of our near stars have planets, even though they are not visible.) Harrison Brown of the California Institute of Technology believes that every star has from forty to sixty bodies of various sizes and degrees of density revolving around it. Since two of the most important elements of our solar system—helium and hydrogen—are the most abundant elements in the universe, Brown sees no reason why some of any sun's planets might not be similar to the planet earth and hence contain the elements that make life possible. He sees *logically* every reason to postulate many millions of planets with life. Three percent of our solar system possesses a "life zone" which is neither too hot nor too cold and is of the right density for chemical development. If this proportion prevailed in other solar systems, Brown reasons that each star similar to ours in chemical composition would have one or two planets suitable for life. And if one accepts the possibility of life forms different from our own, then every star has the possibility of having a life-bearing planet. Hermann Muller, Nobel Prize-winning geneticist, has stated that *of course* there is life in other parts of the universe, but that we must anticipate different life forms from our own, since our particular sequence of evolutionary developments may be unique to this earth.

Harlow Shapley, Harvard astronomer, estimates that 100 million stars may possess planets with the potential of development of life. Ronald Bracewell, Stanford radio astronomer, reasons that there may be only 10,000 technologically developed planets within our galaxy—planets that are from 1,000 to 100,000 lightyears distant.

One constantly hears the assumption that planets throughout the universe may be at different levels of technological development and that some may be far in advance of earth. Our solar system is only five billion years old; there are doubtless other worlds that are a billion years older than we are. This prompts the assumption that their technology may have led them to the use of space probes a million or a hundred million years ago. Radio astronomers listen constantly for beams that may carry messages across the lightyears. Will we recognize them as messages?

Few scientists indeed will go firmly on record as saying that UFOs (unidentified flying objects) are space probes from other solar systems. On the other hand, there are some who say that too many observations of such objects remain unexplained to rule out the hypothesis that some UFOs may have an extraterrestrial origin. The National Investigating Committee on Aerial Phenomena (NICAP), an organization with a membership of some 10,000 scientists and laymen, has on record several hundred carefully authenticated observations for which there is no explanation within the limits of our present principles of science. Another line of evidence is suggested from a chemical analysis of the Murchison (Australia) meteorite of 1969. It was found to contain seventeen amino acids of which six are important elements in our life-sustaining proteins. The meteorite is four and one-half billion years old, having originated somewhere in the universe at about the time our earth was developing conditions favorable for life. A meteorite that fell in Kentucky in 1950 provided similar evidence of the presence of organic matter attested to by separate analyses at NASA (National Aeronautics and Space Administration) and at the University of Arizona.

The reader may ask, "Fascinating stuff perhaps, but why pertinent to the counselor?" I'm not sure that I can make a case for this except to explain what it means to me. I believe that we are a part of a universe that has for this generation more scope and pertinent meaning than it has had for any other generation. Man is probing space itself—gently to be sure—but probing. And space is coming to man via telescopes, spectrum analyses, "celestial" radio receivers, discussions of UFOs, and even the chemical analyses of meteorites. The universe, then, must become a part of each man's existence. Beyond this, *observational proof* might come at any moment that life exists elsewhere in the universe. It may come tomorrow, it may be a hundred years from now, but come it will. And it will more likely be brought to man before he is able to seek and find it.

The assumption that life exists elsewhere, in many "somewheres," is part of our complex change in value assumptions. Man is not alone in the universe. How will we treat such proof of life on other planets when it comes? Will it be with suspicion and distrust, as we now treat so many of our earthly neighbors? If knowledge of life elsewhere in the universe is regarded not as a strange thought but as an expected occurrence, we are much less likely to feel threatened by it and, in our fear, provoke hostilities. Beyond the issue of rationality in how we react, there is this exciting source of new learnings about the universe and the life that surely exists within it. It adds a new dimension to our being. Barbara Hubbard, in an issue of *The Futurist* (April, 1971) tells of her excitement when she first conceived of a universe that might be teeming with life: "The lid had gone off the top of my life. It was open-ended. . . . It was to seek my destiny in the Universe: to find the greater meaning of man. . . . We have a birth to announce: the birth of mankind into the Universe." Out of this excitement came the book, *The Search Is On,* with another by her husband, Earl Hubbard, *The Need for New Worlds,* soon to appear. This team heads up a national Committee for the Future, Inc., and publishes a journal, *New Worlds,* at Lakeville, Connecticut. The February 1972 issue carries an article by Barbara Hubbard, "New Worlds and the Human Potential," a treatment based upon Abraham Maslow's hierarchy of needs.

Heady stuff this, but to conceive of other life in the universe is to expand the meaning of one's life in truly "universal" terms.

GUESSING ABOUT WORLD TRENDS

As the title of this section suggests, I find it easier to write about the universe (so far from us) or the United States (so close to me) than about the world. The world is in between—some of it close and some of it very far away. Perhaps that is the key to my distress; there is little that I can say about the world as a whole. Almost anything one could say about what is happening in one part of the world is not true for some other part. The newer developing nations of Africa are most unlike the long-established countries of Europe, although they may pattern themselves after the Europeans. North America faces many issues that are not found in South America. Asia must be subdivided into areas (Japan or India for example) before discussion. Then there is Oceania, so different from the United States, both geographically and culturally, as to appear to be on a different planet.

What is common to most of the world scene? I make three guesses.

A Smaller World through Increased Communication and Travel

Increased radio availability and coverage has influenced all parts of the world. For many countries television is the more influential. The advent of the communications satellites has made it possible to project images or voices almost instantly to all parts of the planet. The most recent Com Sat to be orbited could carry 23 times as many messages simultaneously (6,000) as did Com Sat I. The increase in efficiency and in number of satellites may (within the decade?) literally make obsolescent much of our telephone, radio, and television ground equipment. Astrophysicist Arthur C. Clarke predicts that before the end of this century there will be Central Communications Consoles in as many living rooms as now contain televisions. From this console one could dial for news from any news center in the world, for entertainment programs of all sorts, for any telephone number in the world, for stored information of a million kinds—all through the magic of the Com Sat network. He foresees (as does Marshall McLuhan) that the spoken and viewed word will replace the written word as the major means of education, with enormous benefits to the heavily populated illiterate countries of the world. Several hundred villagers could gather around a television screen each night and learn by "word of mouth" and picture images about birth control, food preparation and preservation, agricultural and technological methods, and not least of all, what is *happening* in other countries and to other peoples. One major outcome may be the development of one language for all via the universal Com Sat medium, with a great reduction in political tensions and crisis situations. A dream of

Arthur Clarke's? It is at least a testable hypothesis and, at the present accelerating rate of technological development, we may see it supported long before the year 2000. A first step toward this development was made early in 1972 with the FCC approval of two-way cable television in the homes of America. This is part of the general surge of development in the communications network—where telephone calls in the United States increased from 125 million a day in 1940 to 450 million a day in 1970 and pieces of mail handled annually increased by 35 billion during that same period (*American Psychologist,* November 1971).

Travel is booming within our country and throughout the world. Any country of the world that is short on travel is long on being visited. (Mainland China was a striking exception to this generalization but that too has changed.) The air lanes and the train routes are crowded with travelers, many on "vacation." Ideas about another culture are often drastically changed as a result of travel. It is true that most trips *originate* with people in the more technologically developed countries—Western Europe, Japan, and the United States. On the other hand, these travelers *visit* the developing countries of Asia, South America, and Africa as well as each other. For every American traveling abroad in 1950 there were seven in 1971 and will be fifteen by 1980. People in every country visited are changed perhaps as much as are the visitors. The impressions gained of each other may be biased and limited—neither tourists nor tourist centers provide a balanced picture of the countries represented. But each year myths are destroyed. With education at the upper levels involving more and more study of countries other than one's own, valid understandings of each other will increase. "One World?" No, a long way from it, but common to every country are the leavening influences of mass communication and travel.

Physiological Survival Problems Such As Hunger and Pollution

It will be readily acknowledged that hunger exists in many parts of the world, but someone says, "Certainly not in the United States or Europe or other civilized countries!" The record is not that clear. In our country hunger arises from poor distribution of food rather than from inadequate production of food. All technologically developed countries (let's abandon this condescending word "civilized") suffer from this deficiency but the United States perhaps most of all. There is certainly a serious poverty problem in the United States, and people die from lack of food or malnutrition in the midst of abundant food. Nor is this because of too many people, as is true in some parts of the world. The United States has the relatively low annual rate of population increase (number of births over number of deaths) of 0.8 percent (as of 1970) as compared with a world growth rate of 2 percent. (In some European countries—for example East Germany, France, Sweden, the United Kingdom, and Hungary—the growth rates of 0.4 to 0.6 percent are still lower.) The U. S. also has a relatively small family size, with 2.4 children compared with a world average size of 4.7.

Some Population Figures.   In the United States the birthrate has dropped sharply from an annual rate of 24 or 25 per thousand in the 1950's to a low of 17.5 in 1968. In 1970, however, it had risen to 18.2, and it may continue to increase because of a 35 percent increase between 1968 and 1975 in the number of women aged 20–29—the most fertile age group. In general, of course, the death rate has been decreasing as the birthrate is increasing. (More arriving and fewer departing!) On the other hand, it may be that the further perfection of contraceptive methods and the desire for smaller families will counteract the trend toward an increase in birthrate.

In the United States there *appears* to be a tendency for young people to plan for small families, a tendency possibly more apparent among white youth than among Black or Chicano youth with whom size of family is apparently perceived as a compensation for minority status (Robert Buckhout, "Toward a Two-Child Norm" in *American Psychologist,* January 1972). The 15 percent decrease during the 1960's of those under 5 years of age, by far the largest decrease of any decade of the last century, has drawn a good bit of comment. It will certainly affect school attendance figures during the 1970's but may have nothing to do with birthrate during that time! Much population prediction must be seen as population guessing. This has been a pastime for 200 years at least—in 1775 the Reverend Ebenezer Baldwin of Danbury, Connecticut, projected an America of 192,000,000 people by 1975. This was considered a wild statement at that time but he came very close. Anyone projecting America's population for 2175 is likely to be off by more than 20 million!

The trend is therefore uncertain, but at the *present* rate of growth (an average of about 2.4 children per family) the United States will have in the year 2000 a population of about 300 million (currently increasing about 2,000,000 a year), an increase over 1970 of almost 100 million mouths to feed. Our problem even then will not be lack of food but inadequate distribution. Now we have the curious anomaly of people suffering from hunger in the United States while the government subsidizes land owners *not* to grow more food. In 1968 the government distributed $185 million in food stamps to the poor, but that same year the government distributed $4.5 *billion* to the farmers so that they would not grow food. Incidentally the food stamps went to only 5.8 million of the 25.5 million who are classified as poor. Hunger has some curious twists in our economy. We have ample food for all, but our distribution is tragically inadequate. Overall, of course, the U. S. is a terrifically profligate nation. With only 6 percent of the world's population, we devour 40 percent of the world's resources (*Time,* September 13, 1971).

The kind of hunger that exists in other parts of the world is a more desperate one, with sizable proportions of national populations dying from lack of food or from diseases caused by malnutrition. (It is estimated that two out of every three people in the world go to bed hungry.) Part of this hunger results from the unimpeded increase of population, with such annual national increase rates as 3.5 percent in Mexico, 3.1 percent in Brazil, 2.7 percent in Nigeria, 2.5 to 3.0 percent in India. The average growth rate for the *developing* countries in general is 2.2 percent. The base of the hunger problem in such areas, of course, is inadequate food production for the number to be fed. In these critical areas of the world, then, the population growth rate is high and the food produced per capita is low. These are the areas which are technologically underdeveloped, including the technology of food production and food processing.

The desirability of achieving Zero Population Growth (ZPG) is widely discussed. In the United States it is ordinarily considered that the replacement size family would have to drop from its present average of 2.4 children to an average of 2.1 children. Census Director George Hay Brown says, however, that if immigration is taken into account, it would have to drop to an average of 1.9 children per family. (Immigration currently accounts for 20 percent of the U. S. population increase.) As stated earlier, the world average family size is almost double that of the U. S. At present growth rates, Brown says, the world population will double to over seven billion by the year 2000. Even though the replacement size family were to become an *immediate* goal (an impossibility, of course, on a world-wide scale), Bernard Berelson, President of the Population Council, states that it would take several decades to achieve ZPG because of the inherent pressures of the age structure. Witness, for example, how the baby boom in the United States in the late 1940's became the young mother boom of the 1970's. The United States took a step toward national population planning with the establishment by the Congress of the Commission on Population Growth and the American Future. This commission submitted its first interim report in March 1971, with its final report due March 16, 1972.

Population growth, large family size, and inadequate food production are threats to existence itself for those large areas of the world that contain 71 percent of the people of the world (all of the world except North America, Europe, Soviet Union, Oceania, and Japan).

Environmental Pollution. In a curious but anticipated paradox, the low-population-rate countries are the high-pollution-rate countries! They are, of course, the most technologically developed countries in which the crucial factors of existence are less those of food and more those of illness and death from air and water pollution. Extensive technological development generally results in high consumption rates, and pollution arises at both production and consumption ends of the process. The exception might be technology for the production of *armaments* rather than for consumption goods, but even so pollution results from armaments testing and fuel consumption. Population control might affect the pollution rate but only if it involved affluent whites. They are the heavy consumers and polluters, with minority people tending to be the victims of pollution rather than the cause (P. B. Ehrlich in *Playboy,* August 1970). Here again, population control will be generally *ineffective* unless there is production and consumption control as well.

In the United States there *appears* to be a tendency for young people to plan for small families, a tendency possibly more apparent among white youth than among Black or Chicano youth with whom size of family is apparently perceived as a compensation for minority status (Robert Buckhout, "Toward a Two-Child Norm" in *American Psychologist,* January 1972). The 15 percent decrease during the 1960's of those under 5 years of age, by far the largest decrease of any decade throughout the day as automobiles, trucks, airplanes, and factories get into full operation and all landmarks across the city or on nearby mountains become blotted out entirely. It becomes personal when the increasing chlorination of drinking water becomes nauseously obvious, or when rivers, streams, and lakes become too polluted for people to swim in or for fish to live in. It becomes personal when one's plane approaches a city which is seen under a pall of gray that almost hides it from sight.

It became very personal indeed when we recently spent some days with our son Robert and his family. Bob, a professor and counselor at the University of Arizona, has a home on the edge of the Catalina Mountains, some 500 feet above the city of Tucson. Upon several occasions I have sat in his living room at three or four in the morning (I am a night prowler!) drinking in the beauty of the clear sparkling lights of the city below—sharp clear lights of gold, red, and white. But by the time breakfast is over, the outlines of the city begin to get fuzzy and by noon all life below is moving about in a haze. Let me hasten to say that Tucson is a very healthy place to live, pollutionwise, but will it be if the pall grows thicker each year?

The reader has heard all the concern expressed about automobile exhausts poisoning the air, industrial wastes and raw sewage pouring into rivers and lakes, the life-endangering radiation from nuclear power plants (greatly exaggerated, according to some ecologists) and wonders "Where is our technology leading us?" Two solutions seem apparent: massive technology efforts turned about to reduce pollution, and fewer people to consume and pollute. Both of these require equally massive changes in attitude. There is no doubt that we could reduce the rate of pollution by these two means if we wanted to badly enough. We probably can never scrub out the accumulated pollution in atmosphere and water sources, but we can reduce or stop increasing it. I am convinced that to survive we must do this. For the oceans and the atmosphere reach all parts of the earth. Continued pollution of these will drastically affect both the health and food supply of the entire world.

The earth's atmosphere contains all of the pollution released into it—and will retain it forever. We can never decrease what has gone into our protective covering of atmosphere—only increase it. The ocean is one of our great hopes for an increase in food supply, yet the offshore waters of more than one continent have seen an alarming decrease in the supply of food fish. DDT, mercury, and oil appear to be the most serious pollutants. Some oceanographers give the world only a decade or two to reverse the process of pollution if we are not to see the oceans totally bereft of life. You are incredulous? You think it impossible? Remember the chain of life in the ocean—plankton feed many of the small forms of animal life, the small are necessary as food for the larger, the larger for the still larger. Decrease the supply of life at any point in the chain and the effects are felt by *all* life above that point.

Have I proved to you that population increase and pollution increase are world survival threats? I have never been classified as an alarmist, but I confess that I am "running a little scared" right now. We will probably make the turnabout in time, but still so slowly as to make appalling the cost in human life and health. It is more than aesthetically saddening to see the green fields around my home town of Tempe replaced by concrete freeways, service stations, and houses, houses, houses. (Why don't people "stay home" in the Midwest or somewhere? Why do they like Arizona as much as I do?) It is also a fact that it takes 25 square feet of grass to regenerate enough oxygen to maintain a person, yet grass and trees and green fields generally are being wiped out at a shocking rate.

As the fields and forests are decimated, something is also happening to us as people—we are losing that feeling of being close to Mother Earth, we are losing our ability to take a deep breath and fling wide our arms in the sheer exuberance of being alive in the wide open spaces of our earth. Can the developing countries of the world, rushing toward industrialization, shortcircuit some of our growing pains and avoid technological pollution? Can they reduce consumers and polluters to a manageable number? I have some hopes for this—some, but a little less for the speed with which we, the "advanced" countries, meet our problems.

For a rather vivid summary of what will happen, either arbitrarily or by plan, let me point up a long-range world view of imposing dimensions as given by Jay W. Forrester, M.I.T. professor, in his 1971 book, *World Dynamics* (see References). This book is Forrester's application of "System Dynamics" to the world, as he has earlier applied it in *Urban Dynamics* and *Industrial Dynamics,* both award-winning books. He believes and proves that the growth concept must give way to an equilibrium concept since the world space is fixed. He states that throughout recorded time there has been a continued focus upon growth in population, capital investment, food consumption, and standard of living. Because the world is limited in space, atmosphere, and food production, limits will be essential for population, pollution, and crowding. These limitations will be imposed upon us arbitrarily, in time, by circumstances involving widespread death by starvation or pollution or agonizing wars between people in their competition for the remaining resources. The question is, can we *plan* for limitation of growth or wait until it is forced upon us? Forrester writes: "Both the developed and the undeveloped countries face the common problem of sharing the natural resources and the pollution-dissipation capacity of the earth. Without effective arbitration only war and violence can settle the competition for a limited earth" (p. 125).

World Dynamics is an impressive, solidly based study, not a "scare" book but one that makes the reader very thoughtful indeed. (A potential reader of the book might want to turn first to Hugh Nash's interesting and rather complete review of it to be found in the Friends of the Earth journal, *Not Man Apart,* February 1972. Another analysis of the concept of continued, exponential growth, this time in relation to energy and power and this time pro (the power companies) as well as con, can be found in *The Scientific American,* September 1971.)

Political Survival Problems Such as National Distrust and Conflict

It seems almost unnecessary to expand on national distrust and conflict since both of these are all too apparent. Since World War II distrust and conflict have not only centered around the two superpowers and their differing ideologies, but have included the distrust of newly independent African and Asian nations for their former European colonial overseers and the distrust of the Latin-American countries for their Big Brother to the North. The fear that the two major atomic powers would engage in open warfare and wipe out most of the human race has greatly subsided during the past twenty years, but the distrust of each other is still there. Each has its supporters. In some of the curious situations that have developed in the United Nations, some relatively insignificant but *uncommitted* nations have held the balance of power.

It is nations rather than people that still exhibit the greatest distrust of each other. People have, through the increased communication and travel mentioned earlier, come to be more tolerant of each other. True, extremists in any country work hard at fanning the flames of hatred, but people are somewhat more resistant than formerly to pompous, demagogic, or even official statements in national policy. Sometimes they have been told so many lies or obvious exaggerations that they have come to disbelieve *all* that is said, which, unfortunately, would include the truth as well as the lies. Who believes any longer in the infamous "body counts" coming out of Vietnam, in which the "enemy" always has greater losses than the side making the report? (I can scarcely use the term "body count" without a sick feeling that man's violence against man could reach so low a point that success is evaluated in terms of men—women and children also—killed, not territory gained or goals reached, but just human beings killed.) Who believes claims made by candidates in political campaigns or, all too frequently, the promises made by these candidates?

The distrust and the conflict are not restricted to nationalistic lines. Civil wars have been in evidence in many parts of the world, in particular Latin America, Africa, and parts of Asia. Here demagogues have done their work and, once emotions are aroused, people slay their brothers by the thousands. Some of the civil wars have formed around the ideologies of Communism versus non-Communism and the support of the Soviet Union or the United States has been sought. A regional conflict involving the same kind of support, support sought from the superpowers, is inherent in the Israel-Arab situation.

It would be presumptuous indeed for me to suggest solutions, even if I had some! I do not believe that man is inherently a warring animal (as a matter of fact, animals do not "war!"), or that the population increase is best kept in balance by war, or that our greatest times of invention and progress are when a nation is united in an effort to "defend itself." (Remember that each nation is always "defending" itself from the other, that the other nation is always the aggressor.) All of these are superficial attempts to justify what has been done in the past or is now being done.

Basically, what must be changed is *attitude,* both of one people toward another, and of each people's attitude toward its political leaders' attempts to guide "people" decisions and determine "people" values. Charles Reich, in *The Greening of America,* writes that in the United States we have moved from Consciousness I, in which man competed against man for survival in an era of assumed or real scarcity, to Consciousness II, in which the corporate state and the industrial corporation are dominant. (There is similarity here to Kohlberg's three levels of morality, see Chapter VII.) Rules and procedures set by government or one's employer determine one's way of life. Not only is the assumption of scarcity no longer a valid motivation, the conflict is no longer a matter of man against man. It is man struggling for psychological integrity against the influence of the corporate state.

It has not been only the forces of technology and psychology which have brought us so far down the road to robotism. Ours has been a society which has operated on the assumption that goods are scarce relative to people. In a scarcity-based society, "success" consists of competing for that which is scarce. The end—the acquisition of goods— is the thing to be considered, and the means do not matter even if they include lying, swindling, stealing, and killing. One does these things to *people* (who aren't scarce) in order to obtain *goods* (which are assumed to be scarce). But for many who were at the stage of Consciousness II, writes Reich, it was no longer possible to believe that competition was really between individuals. For these people the resolution of dissonance between *things* and *people* lay in creating a total dichotomy between their business or work ethics and their private or personal ethic. The fact that work was often no longer a satisfying part of their lives facilitated this ability to dichotomize. Consciousness II thinking totally separates the "dog-eat-dog" ethic of business from the personal ethic of concern for man's rights and dignity.

Thus in Consciousness I we moved toward robotism via a lack of compassion (heart), while in the second stage we moved in the same direction via compartmentalization. This resolution of compartmentalization, used heavily by those at the level of Consciousness II, has been labeled "hypocrisy" by many of their children who are members of Reich's new Consciousness III. These seek to reintegrate or unify the values split asunder by their parents and to eliminate the "survival-of-the-fittest" dogma of their grandparents and great-grandparents.

The development of this new integrative humanistic thinking during the 1960's has been stimulated by both the hope and the despair of the times. In hope lies the promise of a freer, more open life made possible by affluence and the services of technology. But resistance to status quo is also stimulated by the threat of a meaningless vocational life stretching out before one and the horror of the Vietnam or other wars. Reich writes:

> As the new consciousness made you more distinct, the younger generation began discovering itself as a generation. Always before, young people had felt themselves tied more to their families, to their schools, and to their immediate situations than to a generation. But now an entire culture—including music, clothes, and a radical attitude toward certain drugs—began to spring up among the young. As it did, the message of the new consciousness went with it. . . .
>
> The extraordinary thing about this new consciousness is that it has emerged from the machine-made environment of the corporate state like flowers pushing up through a concrete pavement. . . . For those who thought that the world was irretrievably encased in metal and plastic and sterile stone, it seems a veritable greening of America.

Reich's widely quoted book has been criticized, often bitterly, as unrealistically critical of the present, illogical, and very idealistic regarding youth's new postures. (Peter F. Drucker, on the other hand, proposes that Reich's future is really past, that the idealism and rebellion of the sixties is giving away to the conservative realities of job hunting in the seventies.) Many who belong to the prevailing culture, Reich's I and II, see rebellious youth as irresponsible, shallow and non-constructive. Yet they read Reich and often, I think, do so because of the hope expressed in Consciousness III. All of the technological countries of the world face the inadequacies of Reich's I and II and their youth look for III. The dilemma is simply stated but is enormously complex. Can a nation and a people rise high in technology without losing their sensitivity to human rights and dignity?

IMPLICATIONS FOR THE COUNSELOR

I suppose that I have lost some readers in the speculations of this chapter. For speculations they have been—sometimes conjectures, sometimes projections. But they are not wild and aimless speculations. Over the years I have read widely, and I checked the statements of many scientists before I dared to write a chapter such as this. Even then I have written with a light touch and have not said much that I could have said about the implications of such works as *Intelligent Life in the Universe* by I. S. Shklovskii of the Soviet Academy of Sciences and Carl Sagan of Harvard University (see References), or a 1969 NICAP summary, *UFOs: A New Look* (National Investigative Committee on Aerial Phenomena). This report contains, for example, the testimony of the six scientists who appeared before the 1968 House of Representatives UFO hearing—astronomers Hynek and Sagan, professors of engineering Harder and Baker, atmospheric physicist McDonald and social psychologist Hall. Five of the six stated their conviction that life elsewhere in the universe was at least a reasonable hypothesis—and put their reputations as scientists on the line in doing so.

There may be only a limited value to a counselor-as-a-counselor in dreaming about the universe. But the counselor-as-a-person is what comes through to a client. If a counselor is sensitive to "the big scene" as well as thinking carefully on the here-and-now, the client will sense the combination. Some clients will respond to the counselor's imaginative dimensions, others to the practical. A counselor who is concerned with something "far out" (and here I do not mean only far out in space!) is more interesting as a person. It is curious what restricted images student-clients have of counselors—often no more than that of a large ear, a data bank, or a human version of a signature machine.

Revealing a counselor's interests must be indulged with discretion, however, for most often a student has indicated by the act of coming to a counselor that he wants to talk about himself. Occasionally though, I have found that allowing a student to see me as a person enhances his confidence in me as a counselor.

Seeing the world around him in total world terms enables a counselor to see his client, and in particular his client's future, in a more adequate perspective. The young people of today are, or will become, familiar with the world at large via TV, if not by travel. "Thinking worldwide" is one way of touching bases with them.

Many alert and sensitive young people are *concerned* people. They worry about such things as war, starvation, and pollution. They see these as wide-ranging phenomena that will affect the larger environment as well as their personal lives. And, of course, the larger environment becomes their environment. It seems to me that counselors should be no less concerned than their most concerned students about national and world conditions. It is too easy to have one's awareness restricted to school, home, and town.

References for Exploration

Amosoff, Nicolai. *Notes from the Future.* Simon and Schuster, 1970.

The Brothers Čapek. *R. U. R. (Rossum's Universal Robots).* A Play. Oxford University Press, 1961.

Clarke, Arthur C. *Childhood's End.* Ballantine Paperbacks, 1969. (You will not soon forget this story.)

Clarke, Arthur C. *Profiles of the Future.* Harper and Row, 1963. (Science and science-fiction by a master in the art of both.)

Crosby, Harry H., and George R. Bond. *The McLuhan Explosion.* American Book Co., 1968.

Downs, Robert. *Books that Changed the World.* American Library Association, 1956. (Obviously not a recent compilation but still an exciting account of 16 great books—from *Celestial Revolution* (Copernicus) and *The Prince* (Machiavelli) to *Mein Kampf* (Hitler) and *Relativity* (Einstein).)

Forrester, Jay W. *World Dynamics.* Wright Allen Press, Cambridge, Mass., 1971.

Goulet, Denis. *The Cruel Choice: A New Concept in the Theory of Development.* Atheneum Press, 1971. (The choices that must be made by nations and by cultures if they are to survive.)

Heinlein, Robert. *Stranger in a Strange Land.* Medallion Book, 1968. (More than science fiction—philosophy, anthropology, and a fascinating psychology.)

Higbee, E. C. *Question of Priorities.* Morrow, 1970.

Mailer, Norman. *Of a Fire on the Moon.* Signet Paperback, 1969.

Montague, Ashley. *Man: His First Two Million Years.* Columbia University Press, 1969.

Not Man Apart (Friends of the Earth). Western Book Service, 1382 Natoma St., San Francisco, Calif., 94103. (Journal of an active, nationwide, ecology-dedicated association. They get action on many fronts.)

Robinson, Donald. *The 100 Most Important People in the World Today.* G. P. Putnam's Sons, 1970.

Shklovskii, I. S., and Carl Sagan. *Intelligent Life in the Universe.* Holden-Day, San Francisco, 1966. (*The Last Whole Earth Catalog* says that this book will "blow your mind." I can't guarantee that, but you will surely have your concept of the universe stretched until it hurts. Did you know that with 10^{11} stars in our galaxy and 10^9 galaxies in the universe, it is probable that a million new solar systems are formed in the universe each hour? It provides an excellent review of evolutionary astronomy together with a recounting of the most recent discoveries in astronomy. Thus it leads up to speculation on the likelihood of intelligent life in abundant quantity in the universe.)

The Brothers Copek. *R. U. R. (Rossum's Universal Robots).* A Play. Oxford University Press, 1961.

At Home, 2001 (film). 25 minutes. Contemporary Films, McGraw-Hill, 267 W. 25th St., New York, N.Y. 10001, 1967. (Hugh Hefner, Don Fabun, Walter Cronkite—all look to the future. A real "future" film.)

Of Stars and Men (cartoon film). 52 minutes. Brandon Films, Inc., 221 W. 57th St., New York, N.Y. 10019, 1961. (Harvard's Harlow Shapley —the world of time, of matter and energy, and man's response to it.)

This Is Marshall McLuhan: The Medium Is the Massage (film). 53 minutes. Contemporary Films, McGraw-Hill, 267 W. 25th St., New York, N.Y., 10001, 1966. (This is McLuhan, clearer on the film than in words only.)

Universe (film). 28 minutes. Contemporary Films, McGraw-Hill, 267 W. 25th St., New York, N.Y. 10001. (An awesome and exhilarating glimpse into the vastness of our universe.)

CHAPTER VII

Changing American Attitudes About National Life and Human Life

INTRODUCTION

The close of the last section brought us back from the world at large to the United States and to changes to be seen here. A readable and concise summary of some of these changes is found in an article entitled "The Stormy Seventies" (*Changing Times,* August 1972). Commenting that "the soaring sixties" were supposed to be followed by "the surge of the seventies" but that as we entered this decade there was little to cheer about, the article continues:

> Changes ripped at the very fabric of family and community life. Personal and social values were challenged. Traditional institutions were frontally attacked. The youth rebellion, the drug culture, "emancipation" from respected sexual mores, and abandonment of long-established criteria in schools and colleges all compounded to widen the gap between baffled elders and their children. Minorities spoke out in emotional protests, the poor organized themselves into pressure groups, women's lib became more than a gag."

I have selected four areas of change that appear to me to be nation-wide and that round out some of what has been touched upon earlier.

TECHNOLOGY IN SEARCH OF AN ETHIC

Thanks to our technology, America is beginning to realize that a great deal of what happens in the world can be ascribed to man's will rather than to God's will, and it becomes imperative that we in our country develop a new ethic to establish man's responsibility. Someone has suggested that what is needed now is a philosophical technology by which we can examine the ends to which we wish to use our means—our technology. This matter of an ethic to match our technology was expressed in question form by Marshall McLuhan when he inquired, "Can we afford universal *consciousness* without universal *conscience?*" Technology in the form of the media has provided the universal consciousness, but thus far we are still struggling to find a conscience appropriate to our American technology-oriented society. Reich calls the TV set "the riot box," because it parades a continual display of better living before those who will never have it, before the hereditary poor, the discontented, the casualties of our society. He says, "It raises a fury of dissatisfaction and mocks those who watch it." The delayed birth of such a universal conscience is a very painful process as we know from our experience with Birmingham, Watts, and Detroit.

Our technological age is, of course, pragmatic. That is, technicians say, "If it works, it is good." It is means-oriented with the ends only dimly seen or not at all. We ask, "Good for what?" The answer is, "Well, give us time, we'll find out." Technology feeds upon the new. The present good is soon discarded for a different good, and those who learn to cherish the familiar are put down. Last year's model or style is presented as clearly inferior to this year's, no matter how much one has learned to like it. One doesn't dare to become dependent upon a technologically produced possession, for it is soon removed by obsolescence.

In a technological world, great power is available and new means for expressing it are constantly developed. But few means for *controlling* the power are developed because there is little examination of the unseen implications, the ends to which the power is directed. Lewis Mumford in *The Pentagon of Power* (see References) comments that, like the sorcerer's apprentice in Goethe's fable, we are beginning to drown in our own flood, the flood of our technological output. Once an automatic process is begun, one should have the power to stop it or reverse it. If we cannot stop an automatic process, then we come to defend it, to pretend that it conforms to our purposes, that it meets all of our needs. To do this successfully, to justify the automatic process, we abandon any human trait that would "impede the process." It is thus easy to sell our souls for a mess of pottage because the pottage is *there,* and there is no easy way to shut off its production.

Creating an ethic to meet our technology is no easy task. Once a technological development such as the automobile or television has been absorbed into our social and political structure, accompanied by the positive assumptions that led to its acceptance, there is strong resistance to any questioning of these assumptions. The development of a new technological ethic demands a long look at the interrelatedness of the various elements of our society. Often there is neither time nor desire to do this—until crises arise such as riots in our streets, a senseless war, a flood of easily accessible drugs. Consider, for example, the substantial reduction in the time span from the first use of a new technology to its widespread use in our society. Dean Chauncy Starr estimates that the current time span has decreased during the past century by a factor of ten. New crowds upon new and means dominate ends. Things are in the saddle, not man.

Longing for the "good old days" is particularly senseless. They were not necessarily considered "good" at that time, no matter how we idealize them in perspective. "The old oaken bucket, the iron bound bucket, the moss covered bucket that hung in the well" was not a thing of beauty and delight to those who had to use it. Some of my boyhood was spent pulling water from a well and lugging it to house and barn, with aching shoulders and cold water sloshing down my legs! (Sing to me no songs of longing for the past. I prefer indoor plumbing and hot water faucets to any open well!)

Stuart Chase writes (*Saturday Review,* February 20, 1971): "The philosophy of retreat to a simpler era may have had some validity 200 years ago when Rousseau was celebrating the virtues of Cro-Magnon man, but too much water has gone through the turbines. . . . Is it possible to conceive of a civilized society in the 1970's without electric power, motor vehicles, railroads, airplanes, telephones, elevators, flush toilets, central heating, air conditioning, antibiotics, vaccines, and anti-septics?" No, said Chase, we are stuck with our technology and had best come to terms with it, "encourage its good effects on the human condition."

Even though there is little chance that a technological society can retrace its steps, we may look with interest to some parts of the world where the people have a simpler life. They have learned to live *with* their environment rather than master it. We can ignore much of our im-mediate environment—steel and glass shut out the elements, trans-portation brings us materials from all parts of the world. This has marked advantages, but in mastering our environment we also insult it, sometimes damage it beyond repair. Christopher Williams, an industrial design teacher, studied many of the simpler cultures which had "in-digenous designers" and believes that they have something to tell us. Respect for the materials at hand, for example. He writes that if you lack the machinery "to bop a material on the head and make it do what you want it to do," then you learn to listen to the material itself and heed its vernacular. Plastic, for example, would not be used to represent the warmth and naturalness of wood. Williams sees this as dishonest. He also proposes that the indigenous designers, working with simple and local materials, have learned to respect the total economy of an envi-ronment. "Mechanization has not given them the freedom to become dishonest," he says. They use their materials and their environment with respect for both. This is the "ethic" of that society, an ethic that we have not yet learned for our technological society.

In the seventeenth and eighteenth centuries our nation conquered a geographical frontier to move to a frontier of industry and technology in the nineteenth century. A new frontier of human relations now faces us before we have really come to grips with all of the implications of the old. The transition between the two is painful. It is essentially a question of morality.

Lawrence Kohlberg of Harvard has outlined three levels of moral development: (I) Preconventional; (II) Conventional; and (III) Post-conventional. Most of us function within Level II--the Conventional, which contains two stages of development. In the first stage we are concerned about *roles* and our *conformity* to the expectations of others. We expect to be judged by our intentions (our ends) and not by the means we employ. Further along in the Conventional level we *do our duty* and *show respect for authority* and the social order. In Level III, the Postconventional, the basis for moral judgment does not depend on externals such as role expectations or authority. An individual at this level operates either on a contractual basis, *a commitment to another,* or he relies upon his own *internal conscience* and the mutual respect of others (see *Psychology Today* April, 1971).

Historically, the military has inculcated and maintained Level II moral judgments, even though its Military Code has, since 1863, provided for Level III judgments. So how do we account for the controversy which followed Lt. William Calley's conviction of murder in the killing of villagers in Vietnam? It was a matter of universal consciousness (we all knew about the massacre); but this time it revealed not a void but a cleavage in the national conscience. And it is this gulf between Level II and Level III morality that accounts for the furor that followed the conviction.

Kohlberg has stated that an individual cannot comprehend a judgment made at more than one stage above his own. A conformity-conscious person is able to understand the authority-based judgments of another person, but he cannot understand a person's operating at a stage of internal conscience which may entail civil disobedience.

This difference may help us to understand our society's differences over the Calley case. The military court passed judgment on Calley despite his allegation that he was obeying the order of a superior officer. Existence of the order was neither proved nor disproved. Obedience to such an order apparently was not relevant to Calley's defense. The court ruling clearly implied that Calley was guilty of premeditated murder, even if he were obeying a superior's order. It was assumed that he was morally obligated to *disobey* the alleged order to "waste" the villagers of My Lai. This verdict of the court thus called for a Level III decision on Calley's part. If Kohlberg is correct, U. S. citizens operating at Level II cannot comprehend such a judgment. They protest it, while Level III people defend it. (Of course, many people believe that the major guilt lay with those who gave such orders, if orders were truly given. Such people would say that Calley was no more guilty than, if as guilty as, his superiors in command.)

Does the fact that an authoritarian institution, the U. S. Army, had the courage to uphold a position which calls for the disobeying of military orders under certain situations provide a hopeful sign that a universal conscience is being born? It may be wishful thinking to expect it, but I hope that the message of the Calley case is *not* soon forgotten. It has been well said that "a conscience is a wellbred thing and soon leaves off talking to those who do not wish to hear it."

Kohlberg's Level III with its reliance upon personal conscience and respect for others may be the ethic we are seeking. Somehow there must be a counteraction against obeying authority while nullifying internal values, against using means before ends are considered, against things as more important than people, against newness to be preferred to familiarity and usefulness, against mastering one's environment rather than living with it.

FROM SCARCITY AND COMPETITION TO ABUNDANCE AND BELONGING

The history of our country is based upon an assumption that the world's goods, such as land, minerals, food, things, are in relatively scarce supply. This meant that each man (or woman) was in competition with every other person to get his share. At first the "share" meant enough food and other necessities for any man and his family to live; later it meant that he wanted his "share" to be more than the other person's share, whether he needed it or not. Those who take the largest share of the world's resources are even today said to be the most successful. Those assumptions of scarcity and competition are part of a culture which tends to give preference to property rights over person rights (witness the man who, in defending the National Guard action taken at Kent State University, said, "Those kids had to be kept in control by some means—they have just destroyed some very valuable property!"). Such a culture also gives preference to technological requirements over human necessities, concentration and control over distribution, the producer over the consumer, etc.

This assumption of scarcity is no longer valid for a large segment of our population. It is maintained as a kind of myth widely believed but without basis in fact. It is, indeed, a spurious scarcity. Philip Slater (see References) writes that this spurious scarcity is ". . . man-made in the case of bodily gratification and man-allowed or man-maintained in the case of material goods." As spurious scarcity it "now exists only for the purpose of maintaining itself." This maintenance of spurious scarcity is perpetuated via the components of Lewis Mumford's mega-machine, his Pentagon of Power: progress, profit, productivity, property, and publicity (see References).

From Bishop Richard Raines this analogy: There are 4 billion people in the world but that figure is too much to absorb. Let's settle for imagining that a village of 1,000 represents the world. Only 60 of these would be Americans and they would be living in the Country Club area. Of the 1,000, there would be 303 white, 697 nonwhite. The 60 Americans in that village would have 15 times as much to live on as their 940 neighbors. They are also polluting the earth at a rate 50 times greater than are the other 940. They would have an average life span of over 70 years; their neighbors would have less than 40 years to live. Is it any wonder that Americans, who have so much, are not always loved by the rest of the world?

Some see this as a movement into an Aquarian Age of Abundance. But perhaps the young who are moving us in new directions are operating on a scarcity-based assumption also, but a new type of scarcity. What the young perceive as scarce in our society are the things they are pleading for: *congruence within the individual, mankind in harmony with nature, men at peace with each other.* This counterculture is based on assumptions of abundance of goods rather than scarcity. It asserts that the resources for satisfying human needs are plentiful, that competition is unnecessary, and that the most serious danger to human beings is human aggression.

I write these words with difficulty, for I have belonged all of my life to the "scarcity culture." Competition, as long as the "rules" of fairness were observed, was seen as self-fulfilling. And there *are* many areas of scarcity: if less of food and goods, then more of pure air and water. Not scarcity of food potential perhaps, but great scarcity of distribution resources.

I do not believe that Americans have to opt, however, for a motivation of either scarcity or abundance. For a large segment of our population, Maslow's lower-level physiological, security, and social needs have been fulfilled. These needs no longer motivate many of the young. Their social needs for affiliation and belongingness are met, to whatever degree they are met, within their families or their peer subculture. But the ego needs for achievement, competence, knowledge, and independence are thwarted in our society. In this respect, the society operates on a scarcity assumption and feels it cannot afford to grant these young people full membership.

It is Slater again who writes that "possessions actually generate scarcity. . . the more committed to them one becomes the more deprived he feels, like a thirsty man drinking salt water." If there is movement from an assumption of scarcity (of goods and organizations) to abundance, then relationship needs move from competition to belonging. For if you take "things" for granted (rather than allowing them to absorb you), then your need for people is allowed to surface.

There is a massive movement in the United States toward people's experiencing themselves and each other in small groups. Some of this is faddish in nature and extreme in expression. But for the majority it demonstrates a concern for human values rather than thing values. Loneliness is accepted as real and as something to be combatted. Things are not enough; people and emotional warmth are new goals. From an addiction to goods, the mark of our society could become an addiction to people! If so, the results would be emotionally rewarding, for people respond more fully to people than to things.

Chapter VI contained some discussion of the world pollution phenomenon, and in particular the implications of the continuous growth concept (Forrester). A steady increase in the Gross National Product appears still to be central in the American Dream. Yet increased production, with consequently increased consumption, is now dangerously close to a collision course with environmental pollution. The course can be changed, for survival dictates that, yet that is not enough. We must recognize that the postindustrial age that America is now entering places an overriding emphasis upon people and their relatedness. If in the industrial age we have (and still do?) loved things and used people, the future calls for reversal—to love people and use things. This is necessary for *psychological* survival far and beyond physiological survival. To decrease economic and social distances between people and to increase our systems of sharing among people are the essential moves forward. Even if the pollution threat is checked, the loneliness threat is present today and promises to increase. Privatism or separatism leaves the individual exposed in a crisis, with no one caring. One can die that way as well as by dying physically from pollution. The poison of being alone and unloved can corrode the soul even as chemical poisons destroy the tissues. Caring and sharing are essential to survival in the decades ahead.

THE TRANSIENT NATURE OF LIVING AND LOVING

Life in the United States is highly mobile. The average American family moves fourteen times in the course of its lifetime. Junior executives of corporations may be moved with their families every two or three years. We not only move our homes and our jobs, we move all too rapidly from one new acquaintance to another. Sometimes we take pride in this mobility, of being able to boast about the many places we have lived, the many people we have "known." More often we are frightened by these shifts and question our ability to adapt to them. We are made lonely by knowing so few people, or knowing no one very well.

Between March 1969 and March 1970, a total of 36.5 million Americans over one year of age changed address at least once. This is comparable to the moving of the entire populations of Cambodia, Ghana, Guatemala, Honduras, Iraq, Israel, Mongolia, Nicaragua and Tunisia. What we are less likely to realize is that even our architecture has become disposable to the point of its being called a "Kleenex architecture." Structures built in colonial times had a life expectancy of 100 years. Houses built today average 40 years in duration. In some cities, buildings are toppled after only 10 years.

The young are unruffled by this. Alvin Toffler tells of sending his daughter out to the familiar neighborhood store. She returned saying calmly that it wasn't there anymore—it must have been torn down. Toffler was disturbed but she was not. Paralleling the short life of buildings is an increase in portable buildings. In Los Angeles the Board of Education has decided that 25 percent of the city's classrooms will be temporary structures that can be moved about as needed. New York City talks of 12 portable playgrounds to be installed on vacant lots and to be moved elsewhere when the need arises.

Toffler writes in *Future Shock* that "never in history has distance meant less. Never have man's relationships with space been more numerous, fragile, and temporary." This means that commitments to a community are often shallow or lacking entirely, to the loss of both the person and the community.

The combination of a growing diversity of equipment and goods (from 1950 to 1963 soaps and detergents increased from 65 kinds to 200 kinds; frozen foods from 121 kinds to 350 kinds, etc.) with extreme mobility leads to the forming of many subgroups in society. "Teen-agers" are one subculture, itself subdivided by sex, race, and family position on the economic scale. There are baseball fans, football fans, bowlers, skiers. Movement is frequent from one subgroup to another, with many caught between subgroups and between life styles. A *Life-Change Units Scale* developed by Drs. T. H. Holmes and Richard Rahe enabled them to give to each person they surveyed a life-change score (the death of a spouse, for example, rated 100 points, moving to a new home 20 points, changing line of work 36 points, etc.). A striking finding is that those with high life-change scores are more likely than those with low scores to be ill in the months that follow important shifts. A person's pace of life is apparently closely tied to the state of his health. Toffler suggests balancing the severity of the change sequence so that a stability zone follows a crucial change; for example, a divorce (73 points) should not be too closely followed by a new marriage (50 points).

Many of the moves a person makes today are the result of job changes. In the last three years there has been a 9 percent decrease in the average length of time a person holds a given job. We might learn to speak of *job trajectories,* which take into account the general thrust of a man's work rather than speaking in terms of discrete job titles, which so often change.

Another aspect of transience is the tremendous potential of the number of persons with whom we do or could come in contact. At the time of the American Revolution the average person could not possibly encounter more than 300 individuals in one day. Today in a densely populated city like Chicago and with transportation far advanced beyond the footpower or horsepower of the Revolution, a Chicagoan has a pool of 3,000,000 possible contacts.

As for the press of mobility, people have developed at least two ways of coping with transient friendships. Some decide against making emotional investments in relationships of even medium duration. Emotional investment is reserved for long-term family relationships only.

Others have taken a different approach. They have mastered the ability to make deep relationships within a short time. A young friend recently put it this way: "I used to feel guilty that I didn't have the 'life-long friends' that my parents cherish so. But then I realized that in 33 years they've changed residence only 3 times. In 33 years I've moved 15 times. So I decided that while I might not have the capacity for permanent friends, I could acquire the permanent capacity to make friends quickly. I've grown so adept that I can quickly cut through the periphery of relationships. I can achieve, in a matter of weeks or months, an intimacy and closeness and trust which my parents and their friends have spent a lifetime achieving." Her eyes clouded briefly and then she brightened and continued. "At first the pain of relinquishing these close ties was almost unbearable. I felt cheated. But then I realized that few people can relate deeply to more than three or four others anyway. So, I have to be willing to say 'goodbye' to someone before I can say 'hello' to someone else."

Toffler speaks of the "future shock" incurred when one tries to adjust to a prematurely arrived future. He suggests that about 25 percent of the population of the world live in industrialized societies—they lead "modern lives" and are "the people of the present." This conclusion is much too optimistic. Many "live in the present" at only a superficial level. They use modern gadgets but they think and feel in terms appropriate to 25 years ago. They suffer from "present shock," from lack of the ability to adjust to the realities of the present. They think and feel in the past while living in a social present that they cannot accept as real. It is *the shock of the present* that hurts, of a present that is truly accepted by only a minority, a present that contains:

1. Congested living in cities.

2. Congested traveling on highway or airway.

3. Breathing a polluted atmosphere.

4. Drastically changing family patterns.

5. Uncertainty of one's occupational future.

6. The challenging of authority and the escalation of violence.

7. Concepts of drugs, sex, and moral freedom that are deemed justifiable "if no one else is hurt."

8. Creeping inflation, etc.

The shock of this kind of a present causes many to develop adaptive behavior which is a constant denial of the reality of the present and a constant retreat to the past. The reality of the present often stands as a barrier between parents and their children, with the young accepting a much larger proportion of the present than do their parents. Nor will the severity of the shock be likely to grow less. Some estimate that our technology and the structure of our society will change as much in the next ten years (1970–1980) as it has in the past forty years (1930–1970). There is not likely to be a slowing down of a technology that has as by-products some of the troublesome social and health conditions previously described. Nor are we likely to effect a quick turnabout in the quality of our human relations. "Present shock" will be present for some time to come.

WAR AND THE CHANGING ROLE OF THE UNITED STATES

There is a curious paradox in the belief of some that the United States should be strongly nationalistic (take care of itself) and yet be an active world leader in its opposition to Communism. They want both nationalistic isolation and belligerent involvement. Somewhat contradictory, too, is the proposal of another segment of our society that we provide friendship and aid to the developing countries of the world but stay out of any quarrel between Communists and non-Communists. There, again, sharp conflict between those who see the United States in a leadership role *for* the developing nations and those who see us providing leadership *against* Communism.

One of the major changes of attitude within the United States has been occasioned by growing opposition to a greatly enlarged military organization. Accompanying this opposition is fear of the dependence of a large portion of our economy upon the production of armaments and military equipment. It is possible that no government can ever again marshal the resources of our nation for such an effort. Any future movement toward "involvement," no matter how worthy the cause, will bring a quick recall of the unexpected escalation of the Vietnam "brushfire" engagement, with its loss of life and equipment far in excess of anyone's most pessimistic estimates. Resentment will be rife for some years to come over the extension of Selective Service for more than a decade in the absence of any declared war or of immediate danger to our country. We have yet to see the impact upon our economy of a decided cutback in the production of military supplies.

It seems clear that there is a deeper concern than ever before about the effect of this "war" experience upon the men involved. Hundreds of thousands of civilians who had the normal respect for human life were inducted into a military setting where they were hastily taught how to kill. This has happened before, of course, but never before were draftees given such an immediate opportunity to practice their new skills against people who looked and acted "foreign." (The Korean conflict was different in several respects.) Compounding the problem was the fact that a Vietnamese foe looked like a Vietnamese friend: a Viet Cong enemy could not be distinguished in clothes or appearance from a friendly farmer. To preserve one's life one had to be suspicious of all. In such circumstances as these it seems impossible that one could preserve a strong concept of the sacredness of human life.

Perhaps etched just as deeply upon our consciousness has been an awareness of what has happened to the "civilian" morals of many who lived for a year in Vietnam. In a land where addictive drugs could be procured cheaply and where their use was largely condoned, thousands of Americans became addicts and brought their addiction back with them. We do not yet know the end of this trail. Beyond this, morals generally and honesty in particular are often considered more casually in an Asian environment, and the temptation to be dishonest was frequently present. When one saw an Asian offering stolen American goods on the black market, it could easily be rationalized that one was justified in doing the same sort of thing.

The disclosure of the scandals of brutality, drug usage, and dishonesty has made many Americans ashamed of their part in permitting this "war" to happen. As is often the case, a sense of guilt seeks someone to blame; both "the President" and "the Army" have been targets. Some, perhaps many, Americans have reacted with an attitude of distrust toward both civilian and military leaders (not limited, of course, to the President and the Army). This attitude will affect our "world leadership" role and how active we will make it in the future. Perhaps I am engaging in fanciful thinking; perhaps people will forget quickly, and similar intervention conflicts lie ahead. We are, however, certainly changed as a people by the Vietnam experience, but the residual nature of this change may not be the one that I am suggesting. Much will depend upon two unknown factors. One of these is our perception of the international activity of the two world centers of Communism, Soviet Russia and the People's Republic of China. The other is our commitment to the investment of the time and money necessary to resolve our own internal problems of poverty, education, minority discrimination, drug usage, and violence.

Nicolai Amosoff of Kiev, the surgeon-novelist and widely read author in the Soviet Union and elsewhere (his first book sold 4,000,000 copies), has just published his *Notes from the Future* (see References, Chapter VI). It is a dramatic book, full of both superscience and romance, in which the chief actor, Prokhoroff, puts himself into a frozen state of hibernation. After twenty years he is restored and returns to see the world in 1991. The world is fully automated, of course, but he sets out on a quest to see the two most industrialized countries of the world (and the ones which Amosoff knows best), Japan and the United States. Is the United States any happier than it was two decades earlier? He is not sure. He says: "In the world since my 'departure' the most important change that I have noted is the almost total elimination of war among younger people. The suicidal super-weapons made any large-scale war impossible, and the prolonged induced state of peace seems to have made the very idea of war intellectually unacceptable." Is this our future?

I am aware that in the preceding paragraphs I have expressed a personal conviction on a sensitive subject. My critical reaction to our having entered the Vietnam situation and my interpretation of the outcomes are not, of course, shared by everyone. Even though I am aware of this, I can only say that I could do no less. I cannot pretend to be objective and neutral. Yet I accord you, my disagreeing reader, full respect for your point of view. I am fully familiar with it since it has been well expressed to me by many of my friends. Yet you, I am sure, will admit that the war has made a strong impression upon us as a people and that our role in world leadership will be affected by that experience.

IMPLICATIONS FOR THE COUNSELOR

The "changing attitudes" of this chapter could also be considered areas in which national goals are changing. I propose that we Americans look to the recognition of human values within a technological society. We are witnessing an increasing emphasis upon the need for meaningful relationships rather than an abundance of things. Because of the increasing mobility of people, there is a need for a sense of depth in living. And finally the American's sense of guilt about the war is leading to a recognition that lives and moral living are more important than national pride or fear. The common element in the four areas of possible growth that we have discussed is "people importance."

This is a country with greatness in its history, and pride in it should come naturally to a counselor. I have little patience with those who see only the evils of our society and thus prophesy doom for us all. The attitudes of a counselor toward our society, including an awareness of its virtues as well as its faults, is quickly sensed by students. A counselor needs to ask himself: "How intelligently dedicated to my country am I? How patriotic am I in the sense of Sydney Harris's definition of patriotism (see Chapter II)? Can I, by my attitude, help students to feel both pride and responsibility for our society?"

This chapter has pointed up four areas which can be viewed either positively or negatively, depending upon whether one is looking *only* for assets or only for liabilities. Our present states of technology, of abundance, of mobility, can all be praised for their positive benefits. But the question immediately follows: How can the survival of people and their enhanced welfare be developed within these areas?" One can reflect on the tragic consequences of the Vietnam situation and then say, "What have we learned from this experience that would give us guidelines for the future?" That is what this chapter and much of this book is all about—the need to be thoughtful about conditions of national life in which the value and quality of living need careful examination.

I do not provide a list of techniques to be used by the counselor in helping clients become aware of their national life and their responsibility for it. Such a list would suggest superficiality and would be an insult to the counselor as well. I am sure that if a counselor is both aware and concerned, his feeling is communicated to the client. More specifically, in discussing a client's vocational future, if the counselor is *concerned,* it will be easy to point out many vocations that will contribute to a better quality of living in our industrialized, urbanized, and highly mobile society. For example, there are many vocations that deal with an attempt to make people feel that they are persons of worth. There is merit in pointing out to the client vocations in which he or she can contribute to the national need for a better quality of living. This will also contribute to the client's need for feeling that he as a person is working at something significant. He can accept the virtues of technology and industry if he can see how he can help to humanize the process.

There is merit also, it seems to me, in helping students see the futility of a solely negative attitude. It is easy to protest against a power-hungry establishment, an arbitrary government, and a senseless war. But who is benefited by protest alone? Perhaps protest helps the students to vent their feelings of frustration and resentment, but that is realizing a purely selfish goal—and they are protesting *against* selfishness in business and government! Yes, the counselor can help a student to face up to the question, "What can I do with my life to improve the lives of people in our society, to bring about needed changes in national conditions—not only by some isolated act today, but with my total life?"

Some of this advice goes back to what was said earlier about helping students to develop a sense of responsibility for other people, for our society. Even the conforming ones, who "fit in" all too well, might be helped to ask what they can give as well as what they can get.

I am saying one thing over and over again. If the counselor is concerned, then clients will be affected. If there is trust in the counseling relationship, clients will want to know what seems important to the counselor. The counselor may share with clients, but the question is, *what* does he share?

References for Exploration

Drucker, Peter F. *The Age of Discontinuity: Guidelines to Our Changing Society.* Harper and Row, 1968.

Eisley, Loren. *The Immense Journey.* Random House, 1957.

Eisley, Loren. *The Invisible Pyramid.* Scribner, 1970.

Environment Action Bulletin. 35 E. Minor St., Emmaus, Pa., 18049. (An 8–10 page newssheet on ecology developments and issues.)

Fabun, Don (ed.). "The Markets of Change"
 One: *Ecology: The Man-Made Planet,* 1970.
 Two: *Shelter: The Cave Re-examined,* 1970.
 Three: *Energy: Transactions in Time,* 1970.
 Four: *Food: An Energy Exchange System,* 1970.
 Five: *Mobility: From Here to There,* 1971.
 Six: *Telecommunications: One World-Mind,* 1971.
 Kaiser News, 765 Kaiser Building, Dept. 670, 300 Lakeside Drive, Oakland, Calif., 94604.

Fuller, R. Buckminster. *Utopia or Oblivion.* Bantam Books, 1969.

Galbraith, John K. *The New Industrial State.* A Signet Book, 1967.

Heilbroner, Robert L. *The Future As History.* Grove Press, 1959. (An earlier *Future Shock* which provides a rather frightening analysis of American optimism.)

Hoffer, Eric. *The Temper of Our Time.* Harper and Row, 1967.

Kahn, Herman, and Anthony J. Wiener. *The Year 2000: A Framework for Speculation on the Next Thirty-Three Years.* Macmillan Co., 1967.

The Living Wilderness. The Wilderness Society, 729 25th St., N.W., Washington, D.C., 20005. (A beautifully illustrated publication.)

Mumford, Lewis. *The Myth of the Machine: The Pentagon of Power.* Harcourt Brace Jovanovich, 1970.

"The New Man: A Symposium." *The Center Magazine.* November-December 1971.

Reich, Charles. *The Greening of America.* Random House, 1970.

Slater, Philip E. *The Pursuit of Loneliness: American Culture at the Breaking Point.* Beacon Press, 1970.

Automobiles: The Great Love Affair (film). 57 minutes. Contemporary Films, McGraw-Hill, 267 W. 25th St., New York, N.Y. 10001, 1965. (Automobiles, their impact upon our lives.)

The Detached Americans (film). 33 minutes. Carousel Films, 1501 Broadway, New York, N.Y. 10036. (Explores the causes of the passive uninterest of Americans for one another.)

Have I Told You that I Love You? (film). 16 minutes. University of California, Extension Media Center, 2223 Fulton St., Berkeley, Calif. 94720. (No interpersonal communication, at home or on the job.)

The Inheritance (film). 60 minutes. Contemporary Films, McGraw-Hill, 267 W. 25th St., New York, N.Y. 10001. (Designed to be a documentary of immigrants and the labor movement, it is, in fact, a rather complete history of the United States over the past sixty years.)

Hunger in America (film). 52 minutes. Mass Media Ministries, 2116 N. Charles St., Baltimore, Md., 21218, 1968. (A stark but moving film—"Ten million Americans don't know where their next meal is coming from. Sometimes it doesn't come at all.")

The Sixties (film). 15 minutes. Pyramid Films, Box 1048, Santa Monica, Calif. ("The passion and polarization of a decade still too close for most people to put together; but Braverman has—with irony, compassion and guts." Made for CBS *60 Minutes* program, but only segments of it were used by two other networks. A powerful film in its entirety.)

CHAPTER VIII

Youth and
Attitudes Toward Youth

Is the youth of today "the canary in the coal mine" of this generation? The canary, ultrasensitive to noxious odors, is sometimes used to warn miners of an impending accumulation of lethal fumes. Are young people today warning us of the international involvements, the class and poverty war, the mounting wave of crime and violence, the thickening poisons of pollution that may become lethal for our nation? Adults retort to this generation's criticism by saying: "What's the matter with our society and what have we done? We have developed technologically beyond all of our dreams. We have the finest industrial machine in the world, which has given us better transportation, better homes, and more comfort in living. We are the envy of the world in both industry and military strength. These things are nothing to be ashamed of." "But," youth replies, "the hungry—too many thousands of them— still have empty bellies. Blacks, Chicanos, Indians are still second-class citizens. Cars, jets, and our industrial machine are slowly poisoning our atmosphere beyond recall, and our military strength is a two-edged sword which we have not learned to use judiciously. National pride appears to mean more than human lives."

Is our youth saying that the young sense the urgency, the explosive potential of conditions with which we have lived too long, to which we have adjusted too well? Is this the canary's warning?

Much has been written about youth in the United States, a dozen or so books and hundreds of articles only within the past five or six years. We are undoubtedly giving much attention to youth, but also undoubtedly much of it is negative attention. There is now a different spirit in the land from the mood of just ten years ago, when I wrote *The Counselor in a Changing World.* In that book one will find sentences such as these: "The counselor's role is one of expression of our society's deep concern for the welfare of children and youth. So deep is this concern that families sacrifice themselves for their children in many ways. . . . Youth tends to be for many a cherished period of life, one idealized and held apart. . . . The emphasis on children and youth is a sign of the American tradition of respect for the integrity of each human being."

It is true, of course, that I also wrote: "Other observers view this emphasis with alarm. They consider it an example of overattention to the young. . . . (They believe also) that adults may feel an actual hostility toward youth, that the youthful person becomes the scapegoat for the frustrations and anxieties of the adult. . . . We are harsher toward our young people, less tolerant of their behavior, in a sense more willing to blame them for our society's difficulties than is true in many European countries. We have not allowed them a 'psychological moratorium' during which they can experiment without being called upon to succeed. . . . Many unpleasant outcomes may be attributed to our overindulgence on the one hand and our harsh criticism on the other." (Pp. 3–4.)

So even within the reported spirit of affection and indulgence of a decade ago, the overtones were already uncomfortable. We anticipated difficulty without being at all sure of its nature. During the past ten years we have had dramatic expressions of what has become increasingly explicit. Yet when youth became more articulate, telling us "don't treat us like children, *listen!*" we really became hostile. Youth lost its favored position in our society; youth became suspect instead.

Most that has been written about youth, counselors will know. But parents will not know, at least not with their hearts as well as their heads. In this chapter I hope to pull together a few observations that will not be new to most counselors, but they are ones which the "prevailing culture" as a whole has difficulty in accepting. This book is for counselors—parents may or may not read it. But if parents do not, counselors' understanding of parents' views could lead to counselors' help for parents. The goal would be to help parents accept more gracefully the feelings of their children. I have talked about youth throughout the book, particularly in Chapters II, IV, and V, and I will try to avoid repetition, but there is much yet to say. There are so many myths about youth, myths that many in the prevailing culture not only accept but promote. Counselors should be aware of these misunderstandings and confusions that so often afflict parents.

YOUTH IS DEFINED IN MANY WAYS

The language used in describing youth is often imprecise and overgeneralized. This same difficulty was pointed up in the earlier discussions of "generation gap" and "counterculture" (Chapters I and II). The counterculture contains many young people, but not all by any means. A generation gap to the point of alienation exists for some of the young, but again far from all. Youths not only come in many shapes and colors, they separate into widely different subcultures. On a few points the young think and feel alike, but the spread is wide on many values, beliefs, and behaviors. As I walk along the mall to the library on my university campus, among the people I pass, I see a range of sizes, expressions, clothing, skin color, and national background that is bewildering. How could I ever have been so rash as to attempt a chapter on "youth"! And when I reflect on how often in counseling I have changed from my first impressions as the person revealed himself little by little, I realize that the differences I see in my walk down the mall are outnumbered by the differences not seen. All these people are youth? As a very simple beginning, let us ask, "youth incorporates what age range?" For some it suggests adolescence, another vague term which generally includes ages 12 to 20. For others "youth" means those of college age, 18 to 22. For still others "youth" merges into young adulthood. This could mean up to age 30. Perhaps the answer could be in terms of the age range within which young people are most active in "being themselves" and in speaking out about themselves. With youth of high school age increasingly aware of the social scene and active in asserting independence and with many assertive youths becoming youth leaders in the period after college, I propose that "youth" be defined as those within the 15-to-25-year age range.

This identification of youth in terms of age, however, leaves one dissatisfied. Let us say that youth in the sense of an attitude toward self and life is most frequently found in the 15-to-25-year range, but it is the attitude not the age that is the identifying factor. This "youth attitude" is, of course, complex and difficult to define, because basically it is *an attitude of distrust both of self and of society.* A youth is often well informed through the mass media and perhaps through his parents' grumblings about the many shortcomings of society, and he is certainly aware of all that he would like to be and is not. Kenneth Keniston calls this "a pervasive ambivalence" toward both self and society (see References).

This ambivalence results in alternating periods of assurance and alienation, writes Keniston. Sometimes a youth is exuberant because he is really "with it," sometimes he is lonely and feels deserted by all. The attitude of youth is one of action and includes an aversion to the inaction which adults are inclined to label "patience." Thus, as a psychological stage, youth is characterized by a fanatical need for action—reckless action for high causes—and contempt for those who do not agree.

Of course, describing youth is not so simple. David Bazelon, Professor of Policy Sciences, University of Buffalo ("Notes on the New Youth," *Change,* May–June 1971), adds to this drive for immediacy, "anti-intellectualism" and a craving for "community" at any price. Paul Goodman, who has moved about a bit in his characterization of young people, now sees them as possessing a "metaphysical hunger." Peter Drucker sees them becoming more conventional during the 1970's, if for no other reason than their need for jobs and economic survival.

Scratch any writer with even half a question about youth and you get a different set of adjectives! Some of these are self-projections, some are accurate with regard to a particular sampling of youth, none describe all youth.

If youth is "a state of mind," some people well past the 25-year age limit share concerns similar to those ascribed to youth. These include concern about discrimination whether based on race, age, or sex; an acute sense of responsibility about the Vietnam war; a jealous guarding of the freedom allowed them in which to "do their own thing;" a suspicion of the status quo—whether in school, college, law, or other social institutions. They jointly question the validity of what appears to be severe punishment for damaging property in contrast to less severe punishment when people are damaged.

An even more important limitation of terms describing youth is to note that many young people are *not* members of the counterculture; rather they are passive dependents of the prevailing culture. They care little about change because their present life is comfortable. They do what they are told to do in school and college and will marry and enter the vocational world without a ripple. I do not speak disparagingly of this group of youth although the phrases "passive," "dependent," "do what they are told to do" may carry a negative connotation for some. Nevertheless these words apply.

Related to these comments is the research directed by Brewster Smith in which Kohlberg's three stages of morality, described in Chapter VII, were applied to large populations of student protesters and nonprotesters at Berkeley and San Francisco State College. They found that 85 percent of the *nonprotesting* students were at the "Conventional" stage in which right and wrong are defined in terms of existing conventions and standards. In comparison, only 34 percent of the *protesters* functioned at the Conventional stage. On the other hand, 56 percent of the protesters and only 12 percent of the nonprotesters were at the "Postconventional" stage in which right and wrong are determined by one's internal conscience and concern for others (B. Rubenstein and M. Levitt (eds.), *Rebels and the Campus Revolt,* Prentice-Hall, 1969).

TOO MANY GENERALIZATIONS ABOUT YOUTH

What has just been said underscores the greatest error made in thinking of youth—the assumption that all youth are rebellious. Closely related is another error, that of assuming rebelliousness to be destructive and without social merit. The militants get the headlines, and many militants or activists play to the news media. But the militants constitute a small minority of youth within the age range suggested, perhaps 5 percent of those who are in school. Some of the popular terms used to describe dissenting youth are overgeneralized both as to the numbers involved and the variety of behavior to be observed. Many youths have long hair and wear casual, exotic, or deliberately dirty clothing, but the great majority of these are persisting in school or college. Of those seen on the road or on the streets, there are several subgroups, yet parents or adults generally lump them all together.

Among the subgroups are some road rovers, college students who are out of school for part of a year or an entire year in order to sample the world, both here and abroad. Many of these are frustrated by school and family and seek "to get away from it all for a while"; some are trying out their ability to survive the challenge of the road; some are adventuresome and curious and go with the full knowledge of (reluctant?) parents. These vacationing students are in a class by themselves, since the great majority intend to return and will return to school.

A related subgroup (perhaps the true Flower Children) has roots somewhere also, but its members are running away from that "somewhere" with little intention of returning. They seem vague about themselves, are careless about sanitation, pick up sex and soft drugs easily. On the other hand, they often work for their "bread," and they share a "pad" with others in uncomplaining acceptance. They are not destructive except on rare occasions. This type of youth is most clearly identified, however, by his or her inward search. They are not so much rebelling against the Establishment or society in general as they are seeking something. They are emotionally and spiritually impoverished (Paul Goodman's "metaphysical hunger"). They seek for meaningful experience and assurance in many ways: new sensations (drugs, music); someone to share with them (they may live in communes); perhaps someone to love them *as they are.* They are quietistic and generally harmless to others. On the other hand, they have little sense of service to others; they seldom fight for a social cause. They are unselfish in sharing with their peers, but not with the world. In their seeking they may harm themselves through overuse of drugs, through disease and malnutrition. LSD, mescaline, and the other hallucinogenic drugs are not physically addictive, but dropping acid may become a way of life—a way which removes them almost constantly from the reality around them. Seeking becomes an escape.

The very name, "San Francisco," calls up immediate images of the crowded Haight-Ashbury scene, once full of love children and now more characterized by heavy drugs and violence. A happy "hippie" outgrowth was described in *Time* (April 5, 1971)—the street minstrels. These are often talented youngish musicians who play classical music in groups of three to six—on the street, wandering about at will. They make "an honest living" with appreciative listeners of their uncaptive audience dropping their attendance fees into an open violin case on the sidewalk. These youths are free; they learn new repertory and they have companionship of their kind. The *Time* story quoted them as saying that Mozart and Haydn prove to be the most effective composers for the street.

A still different group comprises the truly alienated, nonresponsible wanderers (sometimes called Street People). These might be called the true cop-outs. They seem more numerous than they are because they are so obvious when on the road or street. It is difficult to determine the exact number because they are thinly scattered and always on the move, but the estimates range between half a million and a million. One could say, "A *million* people, what a waste!" Or one could say, "After all, this is only two percent of the 36,000,000 youth aged 15 to 25 (1970)."

John Pierson, writing in *The National Observer,* calls these wanderers "today's bitter, alienated, apathetic version of yesterday's happy, love-filled, evangelic flower children. . . . Their babyhood 'youth culture' has soured, producing more and more disenchanted youngsters roving the country." Street people seldom work; they panhandle or "crash" another's pad. If these efforts are not effective, they move on. Many are runaways and have been totally rejected by their parents. They in turn have rejected their parents and many social institutions—school, church, law as justice, etc. But the rigors of street life disillusion them. They seek a romantic carefree existence which they do not find. Drug usage is common but seldom entails hard drugs; it is mostly marijuana and LSD. Their sex life is free, but venereal disease is rampant.

These unhappy youths are generally careless but are easily caught up in a demonstration—sometimes only because they are on the street when a demonstration is initiated. Some are destructive, some are openly anarchistic. Most, however, are happy-go-lucky wanderers who "join in" when something happens. The university town of Tucson, Arizona, was the scene of a demonstration in 1971, labeled by the press as a "University demonstration-turned-riot." A total of 150 people were arrested, but only 40 were identified as students. The rest were wanderers.

An offshoot of the causeless hippies and the careless street people are the Jesus People described on page 112. These youths have found a cause—a fundamentalist, mystic religion, to which they invite others. *Time* (June 21, 1971) described two related groups of religious youth: "straight" young people who have developed an interdenominational, evangelical movement, mostly outside of the church, and the Catholic

Pentecostals who remain in the church but worship privately with an evangelistic devotion.

One could name other groups of youth but the names may fade, including the ones that I have used. The subgroups identified are distinguished from the large number of youths who carry the same banner of frustration only by the *means used* to express their discontent. The hippies and street people leave school and family and often permanently cut their ties. The majority of the discontented youths, on the other hand, endure school and family, compromise and adapt, and sometimes grow to achieve more satisfying relationships with themselves and others.

So counselors can perhaps help parents to understand that age-defined youth can be subdivided into the conforming and nonconforming and that psychologically defined youth can be subdivided into the wanderers and the endurers. Some of the discontented in school or college work actively or even violently at changing the present; some merely object, some work at reform. All except the happy, passive ones have counter-culture values in mind. They want change. A lack of good manners seems common to most dissenting youth. This makes them objectionable to many people, both older and younger, who see "manners" as a form of consideration for others—not a superficial nicety. It is a bit sad that this rudeness alienates many people who *need to listen to youth.* Instead they are driven away by the youths themselves.

The August 17, 1970 issue of *Time* carried a comment that is half humorous and wholly believable. Here are some excerpts from advice to youth given by Henry Muller, a 23-year-old *Time* reporter:

> I have never been busted for pot, my hair doesn't brush my shoulders, and you won't catch me nude in the park. I am so straight, in fact, that I actually have a job. Yet despite my failure to display the more flamboyant trademarks of the Aquarian generation, I find myself on the far side of a communications gulf born of the 30-year difference between my parents and myself.

> We spar over My Lai 4 and the Chicago Seven, guaranteed incomes and Women's Lib; our tastes for entertainment have little in common; our views on America's changing mores are worlds apart; and my hair is still longer than my father's. But these differences have not severed the link between us. Disagreement is inevitable, but we are not estranged. For this, credit is due to my parents' patience. Communication, however, remains a two-way street. Here are some tactics that have proved successful in lessening the conflicts:

> Chances are that parents will never like Janis Joplin or Country Joe and the Fish, no matter how many times you insist they're outasight. So save your confrontations for topics that you consider important.

> To someone over 30, "rapping" just means knocking on wood; so steer away from contemporary jargon, a semantic roadblock that can easily alienate those

who don't understand it. N.B.: lay off the word "fascist" unless you're describing Mussolini.

Look for opinions you have in common. Talk about ecology, for example.

When you decide to have it out on an issue, make sure you know what you're talking about. There's no quicker way to lose credibility than to be caught with unresearched facts or specious reasoning. . . .

Parents derive pleasure from reliving their own youth through the experiences of their offspring. Give them this treat by clueing them in on the unimportant things you do. You'll soon find that talking about trivia keeps the gears of communication oiled.

Try seeing it from their point of view, if only occasionally. They've been around for 40 or 50 years and may be having trouble keeping up with the accelerating pace of events. Imagine what *you'll* be like after enduring half a century on this globe. . . .

Give yourself the ultimate test of open-mindedness. If you're 20, see how easily you can talk with someone 15. And if you're 15, try it with a twelve year old.

Counselors might reflect on these comments with some of their younger clients.

THE DANGER OF COUNSELOR BIAS

Counselors are apt to see a self-selected sample of students, including both the independent dissenter and the rejected child. Each, for different reasons, may have negative attitudes toward adults in general and toward parents in particular. Several studies of Free Speech Movement students at Berkeley indicated that such students are likely to be from families where the parents have encouraged analysis, criticism, and free speech. A "healthy" family perhaps, but one that contributes to criticism and even militancy. The children in such a family are likely to be critical of parents even though there is love in the relationship. The rejected child, on the other hand, rejects his parents in turn and there may be no love between them. The counselor often sees only those who seek him, and he may know little of a nameless majority containing students who range in their family life from affectionate acceptance to complete rejection.

I believe that there are many happy families. We hear, either as counselors or through the press, of the unhappy ones. A recent cross-section study of youth revealed that 80 percent were living with both parents. Another study indicated that, all divorce statistics to the contrary, 85 percent of existing families were cohesive and stable. You do not believe this? Remember the sampling factor for both counselor and the mass media. Remember also that students who see the counselor gripe about parents in the same fashion that college authorities expect them to complain about food in the dining halls!

Using the corrective factor just described, one could safely say that, "broadly speaking," youth react to past, present, and future as a "different generation." Philip Slater in a brilliantly written book, *The Pursuit of Loneliness: American Culture at the Breaking Point* (see References, Chapter VII), speaks of "cultures in collision" and assumes that the two generations parallel the old culture and the new. I think it is more accurate (although less dramatic) to speak of "tendencies" for the young to value differently from the way older do. The "old culture" *tends* to believe in an economy of scarcity, postponement of gratification, good taste expressed as restrained behavior, complacency about long-standing injustices, acceptance of injustice as unavoidable, etc. There are marked exceptions to any such statement of trend, and certainly many leaders of the new culture are members of the older generation.

A chart of value changes developed by the Business Environment Study Group of the General Electric Company provides an illustration of these trends. Given as Figure 1, the left-hand column tends to represent the prevailing culture and the right-hand column the counter-culture. The young tend to find themselves in the right-hand column, pulling for a change from the values stated in the left-hand column. Many of these youth trends have been referred to in earlier pages of this book—the emphasis upon the individual, privacy, quality of life, change, immediacy, leisure, participation, pragmatism, situation ethics, social justice, goals.

Kahn and Wiener of the Hudson Institute, in their dramatic and comprehensive survey of the future (*The Year 2000: A Framework for Speculation on the Next Thirty-Three Years,* (see References, Chapter VII), project twelve major movements to take place during the latter part of this century. Summarized in the G. E. study, these cover a wide range of political, technological, and economic changes, but in three of the twelve one hears the voice of youth:

1. Emergence of a "postindustrial" culture—one dominated by learning, service occupations, and attention to the quality of living.

5. Increasing emphasis on "meaning and purpose."

7. Some possibility for sustained "nativist," messianic, or other mass movements.

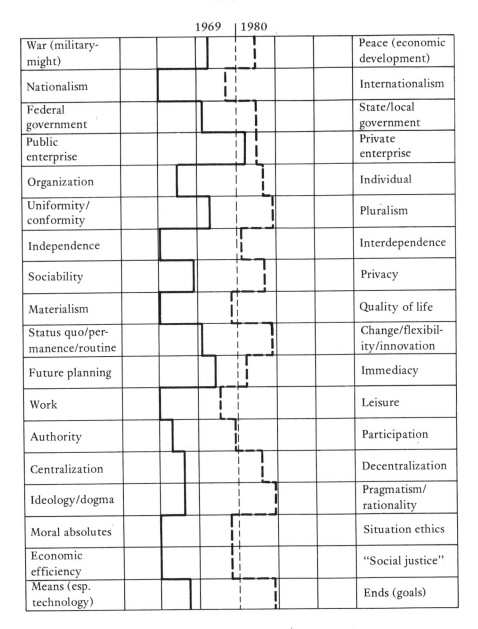

Figure 1. Profile of significant value-system changes: 1969-1980

——————— 1969 Values Profile

— — — — — 1980 Values Profile

An area of difference in attitude not frequently enough identified is the "generation gap" in attitude toward money. The middle-class youths in a so-called affluent society do not have the "respect" for money that their elders have. Money is seen as a means, not an end. The General Electric study concludes that money is not unimportant to youth, "only that, in psychological terms, it is more likely to be a 'dissatisfier' than a 'satisfier,' " that is, its absence is more noticed than its presence.

Here again counselors must be aware. This is an important generation difference but is of course also an economic class attitude. To youth in lower economic circumstances, money as an end may be more important than ever. The lower-class youths see middle-class youths as having more evidences of money than ever before—cars, travel, expensive dating, etc. The class gap in money terms may be as wide as the generation gap is for the affluent.

ADULTS ARE STILL IN THE SADDLE

Little study has been given to adult attitudes toward youth. There have been fulminations, attacks, and diatribes in abundance, but few surveys of parents. It seems reasonable to conjecture, however, that *any* of the moves of youth to change the present will be disapproved by those who control the present. I am prejudiced enough to believe that those who cling to the present, whether they be old or young in age, will do so more obstinately and with greater outcry than will those who seek change. The changers are less certain of what they seek; the clingers have found it and hang on to it. There is a very old story about the youth who played the cello but played only one note, hour upon end. His doting mother could see only virtue in this until she attended a concert and heard another cellist. She reported to her son that this cellist played several notes, up and down the scale. Her son replied, "That's easy to understand, Mother. He is still looking for the right note. I have found it." Many, both older and younger, have found the right note in what they have now, and they will object strenuously to any change which threatens that security. Those playing up and down the scale are less sure of themselves since they are still seeking "the right note."

The major institutions of society or their representatives—law, education, government, business—are supporters of the status quo. Many representatives of these institutions are likely to speak out loudly against dissenters. They attempt to "fit the individual to the group" by indicting the dissenter (law), indoctrinating him (education), controlling him (government), and not hiring him (business). The odds are against those who would change the present scene. Some adults are threatened by the sheer numbers of youth involved—the 36 million aged 15 to 25 in the year 1970 will rise to 40 million in the year 1975. Such a threat could result in more stringent attempts to control youth through repressive measures. (The figures cited for youth are taken from "Population Estimates and Projections," *Current Population Reports,* November 1971.)

It seems safe to say that the attitudes of adults toward youth are more intolerant than the attitudes of youth in general toward adults. Furthermore, the adults have "the law and the prophets" to back them up. Young people often have only themselves and a few courageous, but not always powerful, older change seekers. Young people *are* often intolerant, impatient, arrogant. Adults may be even more so.

YOUTH IN THE SEVENTIES?

The decades have seen marked differences in the prevailing concerns of youth. The 1950's were called the years of complacency and passivity for youth. This was the "silent generation." The 1960's—particularly the latter half of the decade—were characterized by active and open dissent and demonstration. Sometimes constructive change was sought; more often there was only dissent, violent and otherwise. Most visible in the colleges, dissent has also been very present in high schools (see p. 21).

The 1970's may see little diminution of the discontent, but the channeling of energies may be more constructive. Under certain circumstances of resistance to change in schools, colleges, and in government, youth's dissent—sharpened by the experiences of the 1960's—*could* become more vigorous and violent. On the other hand, *Time* in June 1971 reported a general feeling that the 1971 freshman class was "the quietest class in years. In part, they have seen it all in high school; in part, the economic downturn pressures them to do well academically. . . . Some of today's freshmen seem less susceptible to peer group pressure than their predecessors."

Three other views suggest somewhat the same trend. Writer Norman Cousins (*Saturday Review,* February 20, 1971) believes that a reaction has set in against mindless violence. He believes that Buckminster Fuller (see References, Chapters II and VII) may be youth's hero of the 1970's. He "speaks their natural longing for a compassionate society in which technological possibilities are intelligently developed for the human good." Cousins, himself a compassionate intellectual, sees these positive attributes emerging from youth's violent explosiveness of the past few years. Psychologist Julian Rotter (*Psychology Today,* June 1971) sees a quieting down of youth, but as a result of discouragement, not hope. Between 1962 and 1971 administrations of his *Internal Control-External Control Scale,* a large increase in External Control scores was seen. Fewer in 1971 than in 1962 depended upon their own consciences and values (internal control) and more reacted as though outside forces would determine the issues (external control). As earlier mentioned, economist Peter Drucker ("The Surprising Seventies," *Harpers,* July 1971 and *Reader's Digest,* September 1971) sees a flooding of the job market in the 1970's (a population fact) with youth, therefore, becoming conventional and concerned about jobs and a livelihood. All three, idealist, psychologist, and economist agree: youth will be quieter and more submissive in the 1970's. I am not sure. And I don't know whether to laugh or cry if they are right, if we are to have a return to the passive 1950's.

I am hoping that youth will not lessen its concern. Much as to how youth may react depends upon the concern shown by the leaders of the prevailing culture. There is a large question mark as to movement into or out of the majority group by conforming, enduring, unconcerned youth. While not all young people dissent, or ever will, we should keep our eyes upon the considerable number who want to participate in *doing something about* our societal problems. It remains to be seen how seriously our society takes this concern and gives youth a way to serve. The Peace Corps and VISTA have been helpful in the past. Will society offer youth more opportunities and, as well, act vigorously itself? Will schools and colleges channel student energies into "doing something *now*" as well as "learning for the future?"

In all fairness one must say that youth's struggle for recognition and self-identity during the 1960's displayed some characteristics that were neither pleasant nor responsible; youth were seen as obsessed by their own style, displaying little patience and great intolerance of all adults. Youth worshipped relevance at any price and indicated little depth or persistence of effort. But youth learned from the struggle. Youth may be seen in a somewhat different light during the 1970's. Without generalizing in any sense of the word, let me present a few illustrations of the kind of learning that has been taking place.

1. United Press International carried a report in the *Arizona Republic,* November 7, 1971, entitled "Haight-Ashbury Veterans Still Search for Love." Some excerpts follow:

> Today, the original hippies are going from the Haight but many still live what they call "the revolution." In communes all over the country, they till the soil,

seeking harmony, simplicity and love. Marijuana remains their sacrament, but most are as horrified of heroin as any "straight."

A strong religious theme has infused their search for "higher consciousness," and they look upon violent radical politics as immature and self-defeating. Most of them hold more hope for America than for any nation on earth. And some of them, now in their 30s, are even starting to worry about the younger generation.

Thelin's commune, . . . nestles among towering pines in northern California. In the complex there is a lack of enthusiasm for some current causes. No posters of Angela Davis or Che Guevara hang on the walls, although radicalism has everyone's sympathy.

Thelin . . . sees anger against society as a waste of time. Political activism, he says, is infantile. "It's the other guy always being wrong. . . . "

As Thelin puts it, a common theme of Haight-Ashbury veterans is "I can change the world by changing myself. I can't change others."

. . . .

The women think all the emphasis on women's liberation is a mistake. Women's lib, they say, is only a small part of an individual's whole liberation problem.

"We're in a situation where we need men to cut the wood and fix the car," one said. "You don't complain about caring for the children (nine have been born at the commune), the most creative job in the world."

The general attitude of the Haight-Ashbury veterans is that America is to be loved and has a bright future, and, as Lisch put it, "Our mission is to take responsibility for the country and transform it. Then, America will lead the way."

2. *The National Observer* (March 15, 1971) devoted a full page to excerpts from a diary of a University of Oregon freshman coed. The entire account glows with the intelligent alertness of a girl who is struggling to retain her personal autonomy in the midst of peer pressures. She associates with the campus leaders, the dissidents, and the drug abusers—they are friends of hers—without finding it necessary to imitate them. The entry for April 26 follows:

I've made a lot of decisions today. First and foremost, I've decided that drugs just are not my kind of thing. I have a hard enough time grasping reality without making it even more slippery.

I've also decided that the SU (Student Union) crowd is definitely out. I've been trying to "fit in" to their lives. I've made the mistake of conforming and worrying about what they think of me. I don't like to be that way. I don't like their opinions of me and their attempts to make me more like them. . . .

Suddenly, tonight, while I was walking home in the rain from Shakespeare class, I realized how beautiful it was to be a Riki T. . . and alive. The street was shiny, the leaves sparkled, the air was crisp. Everything looked so beautiful through unstoned senses. I began to sing. There weren't many people out, mostly just me, the night, and the rain. I hummed and skipped and soaked my tennis shoes in mud puddles. I ran up to a girl in front of me and asked her if she wanted to share my umbrella. We were both laughing by the time she had to turn off. Then a guy walked by, and I smiled and said "Hi." He looked surprised and broke into a big grin, returning the greeting. When I got home I was feeling awfully good. Then I found an invitation to get stoned waiting for me. No way! I'm a Riki T. . . and alive tonight and the last thing I need is grass!

3. The 24th National Student Congress in 1971 made quite different observations of the social scene from those it had made three years previously. No longer did the Congress assume that youth could "go it alone." Justice in a constructive sense was the emphasis rather than revolution. Their strongly supported declaration stated in its preamble:

In the early sixties we fought for Civil Rights and freedom. . . . In the late sixties we fought for peace and social responsibility.

Now we fight for justice—for a society which maintains a balance between its resources and its needs, for communities which help all citizens determine the best contribution which they can make, for institutions which foster the dignity of every human being.

Justice demands more than a mere effort at solving problems. It demands an effort to work together to pursue the highest social goals which we can imagine.

Justice demands more than an effort to erase specific forms of oppression. It demands that we develop a common morality from which to attack oppression wherever we encounter it.

Justice demands that we move beyond the cloistered walls of the university into the communities where people live and work. It demands that we help build a People's movement to fulfill the dreams which the apostles of profits, power and wealth have tried so hard to destroy.

4. A feature article in *The National Observer* (February 26, 1972) concludes that campus militancy has been replaced by personal activism:

The old militancy depended on mass confrontation: the new activism focuses on one-to-one relationships. The "concerned student" of the late 60's typically was obsessed with the war and other grave national and international issues; his counterpart today, freed of worry of going to war, is most concerned with people, with his own environment.

The reasons for the shift? The *Observer* sees two: the increasing disengagement of American troops in Vietnam and an increasing concern about jobs and personal economic security.

IMPLICATIONS FOR THE COUNSELOR

This chapter simply underscores the general thrust of this book and its emphasis upon attempting to understand contemporary youth. At the risk of belaboring the obvious, I will restate my conviction that the *main responsibility of the school and college counselor is to attempt to understand contemporary youth and the worlds in which they live.* And as was also pointed out in Chapter I, there is a correlative responsibility for the counselor *to attempt to understand himself and his world.*

For example, I as a counselor can never understand you, except in part, just because you are a different person and carry around a different world with you. I can understand you only to the extent that your motivations and your interests resemble mine, the extent to which the boundaries of your "real" world overlap mine. To the difficulty of ever totally understanding anyone else, the added age and "world" difference between counselor and client makes the phrasing "attempt to understand" the only reasonable possibility. No counselor should chide himself for "not understanding" if he is thinking of fully understanding.

So the task is then a challenge that will be with the counselor each day of his or her life that he counsels with others, the struggle to understand in part, to "see through a glass darkly."

If you are a rather typical, over 30, middle-class "Conventional-stage" person yourself, the Conventional-stage students will be easiest to understand. You will feel most comfortable with them, and they will reinforce your need to feel that you are both helpful and respected. There is no "bite" in these words; these students are very important. It is also necessary that you see enough of them to maintain your own feeling of significance.

The unhappy, fumbling, self-preoccupied, dissenting student will be the hardest to touch bases with. He is likely to be suspicious of you because you are an adult and a member of the school Establishment. Not many of them will seek you out; you may have to look for chances to make contact with them. Perhaps just *being* yourself is enough, that is, if this means that you see them as having a full right to a different point of view from yours. Also, if being yourself means that you have as much concern for their happiness and health as you have for the well-being of the more comfortable, conventional student.

I do not want to overemphasize a counselor's responsibility for seeking out the unconventional student. Few of us feel at ease with a prickly militant, or could live for long with the dirt and carelessness of a real "cop-out" on the street. The more comfortable people need your help, too. The real difference is that the comfortable ones have other resources open to them, other people who will consult with them just because they are comfortable. The hurting, rude protester does not have many adults who will listen to him and try to understand. The counselor could be his only concerned, accepting, yet rational resource.

If, on the other hand, you, yourself, happen to be at the discontented, protesting, seeking, "psychological youth" stage (see page 164), then you will find the placid conventionals hard to understand! "How *can* they be so unconcerned in the face of the crucial problems that face their generation?" You will be singing Professor Doolittle's refrain in *My Fair Lady*: "Why can't a woman be like a man?" So you will run the risk of being impatient and rude to them because they are "so hard to understand."

As mentioned earlier, I don't know what the counselor will face in the 1970's. As always he will face a variety of students—different maturities, backgrounds, and stages of content and discontent. Whether he will face much open discontent or an increasingly repressed discontent, I do not know. All I do know is that he (or she) will have to work hard at attempting to understand various kinds of young people and their various worlds. Listening, visiting "other worlds," working with non-school agencies that deal with youth, reading research on the subject, keeping well informed on the world outside the school—these are the counselor's resources for understanding.

References for Exploration

Adolescence for Adults. Blue Cross Association, 840 N. Lake Shore Dr., Chicago, Ill., 60611, 1969. (A *free* 100-page booklet useful for many counselors, for all parents.)

Califero, Joseph A., Jr. *The Student Revolution: A Global Confrontation.* W. W. Norton, 1970.

Erikson, Erik H. *Identity, Youth and Crisis.* W. W. Norton, 1968.

Graves, Wallace. *Trixie.* Bell Books, 1969. (A warm, moving story of a Black girl who lives both in the Black world and in Whitey's world: an idealist and a realist, sexual yet innocent.)

Keniston, Kenneth. *The Uncommitted: Alienated Youth in American Society.* Harcourt, Brace and World, 1965.

——. "Youth: A (New) Stage of Life" *American Scholar,* Autumn 1970.

Michener, James. *The Drifters.* Random House, 1971. (A story of six young people from various parts of the world finding themselves together at Torremolinos, Spain, each escaping from something but each also "seeking." A dramatic account of warm, believable youth.)

Pettitt, George A. *Prisoners of Culture.* Scribners, 1970. (A controversial and provocative look at modern youth in American society by a noted anthropologist.)

Smith, G. Kerry (ed.). *Stress and Campus Response.* Jossey-Bass, San Francisco, 1968.

"Youth and Work" *New Generation,* Fall 1970.

Day after Day (film). 27 minutes. Contemporary Films, McGraw-Hill, 267 W. 25th St., New York, 10001. (The dehumanizing effects of factory life.)

The Game (film). 17 minutes. Cinema 16, care of Grove Press, 80 University Place, New York, 1967. (Rejection of the stranger in any culture.)

Lonely Boy (film). 17 minutes. Contemporary Films, McGraw-Hill, 267 W. 25th St., New York, 10001. (Glimpses into the life of a contemporary singing success, Paul Anka. But is it success?)

Phoebe (film). 28 minutes. Contemporary Films, McGraw-Hill, 267 W. 25th St., New York, 10001. (A pregnant high school girl who cannot communicate with others about her condition, least of all to the boy. The focus is upon "a paralyzing moral failure of our time; the impersonality of our relations with one another.")

CHAPTER IX

Facts and Trends in Three Vital Areas of American Life

INTRODUCTION

This chapter will differ from earlier chapters in the considerable number of figures that are cited. I well realize that many statistics in the three areas, *marriage and the family, urban conditions,* and the *occupational world,* are valid only for a relatively short period, but these are the most recent data that I could locate. It would seem almost dishonest for me to suggest a trend without providing the data on which the trend is presumably based. The reader is then free to accept the trend as a valid possibility or to reject it. Sometimes in these pages no trend is suggested, so that the reader is free to draw his own conclusions.

Some readers will be dismayed at the liberal sprinkling of figures while others may be enough like me to be delighted! I like figures because then I can see the boundaries of any generalization that I make. I use vague terms like "many," "most," and "few," but I distrust them even as I use them unless I know the data on which their usage is based. If it were not so irritatingly repetitious, I would preface each such usage with the phrase "It is my opinion that . . ."

The three areas chosen appear to me to be significant ones for the counselor's consideration—whether or not the most significant is a matter of judgment. Counselors are constantly faced with the impacts upon the student of both family life and community life. Rarely is there an adequate awareness of the student's world outside the school, the world that is almost always more vivid to him than the world of the school. As mentioned later, neither teacher nor counselor can truly sense the realities of these worlds without living in them, yet some cognitive understanding of them is a first step.

Unreal to both student and counselor is the occupational world of which the student will later be a part, but understanding its broad outlines is a small step forward. "Work attitudes" were discussed in Chapter III and "career counseling" will be given attention in Chapter XI; this section describes job opportunities and trends.

It was my original intention to include additional sections on minority groups and economic trends. As I wrote on families, cities, and occupations, some minority problems unfolded themselves within a natural context. I decided that to write more carefully on racial and poverty minorities would unduly lengthen the chapter or require an additional one. Developments concerning minority groups, of course, are of the highest priority in our current society. This is particularly true for those who counsel students from these sectors of our society.

A Little on the Economy

The events of the spring and summer of 1971 made the writing of a section on economic trends too hazardous a task. Economists are certainly not in agreement on the economic impact of crucial political decisions made on the Vietnam war, relations with China, Taiwan, Japan, and Russia, aeronautics, and space exploration, for example. Nor do they agree on the economic impact of a paradoxical paralleling of inflation and unemployment, of labor's increasing aggressiveness, of the wage-price freeze, and the "floating dollar." If this economic combination taxes the best efforts of economists, who am I to make an amateur's attempt?

Even so, a few economic certainties and uncertainties stand out:

1. In 1969 the median *family* income was $9,400, almost 90 percent greater than the 1947 median family income of $4,972, in 1969 dollars ("Consumer Income," *Current Population Reports,* July 1970).

2. Despite the above figures the gap between rich and poor changed scarcely at all. In 1947 the families in the top 20 percent of income received 43 percent of the total national income while those in the lowest 20 percent received 5 percent of the total. In 1969 these figures were 41 percent and 5.6 percent.

3. The economic forecast for 1980 seems very uncertain. Estimates of the Gross National Product range from one trillion dollars to one and one-half trillion dollars. In addition to some of the recent economic and political developments cited in the preceding paragraph, there are some additional trends which make projections a risky business (Charles Silberman, "The U. S. Economy in an Age of Uncertainty," *Fortune,* January, 1971), such as these:

> Productivity rate (output-per-man-hour) did less well than predicted in 1968. Although predicted to increase 2.7 percent annually during the decade, it failed to reach this level by a considerable margin, and between 1966 and 1970 fell to an average of 1.6 percent annual increase—the lowest annual increase in 50 years.

> While productivity failed to increase as expected, the size of the labor force has been increasing since 1965 one-third *more rapidly* than predicted. A smaller increase in productivity and a larger increase in labor force are certainly an unwelcome alliance.

> If federal and local governments intensify pollution control, productivity may drop still farther. Repressive measures used against violence in the cities could

adversely influence new capital investment. So might many other developments.

There are some hopeful possibilities as well. Productivity may increase as we move into a postindustrial society in which work becomes more meaningful and is entered into with more zest. I cannot see how much of this will develop in the 1970's for we still have a substantial industrial America and a substantial poverty America (the Census Bureau estimated 25.5 million persons below the poverty line in 1970, over one-third of whom were nonwhites).

The 1970's could be "boom or bust" or in between. Silberman states that much of America's future economy depends upon America's desire to work as well as upon the degree of governmental intervention in the economy. The changing value patterns (Silberman cites almost all of the value areas that I have discussed in Chapters II, III, IV, and V) may affect not only work but the pattern of consumption and therefore the goods and services that are produced. Certainly economic forecasting for the 1970's will not be able to depend upon an extrapolation of well-defined trends.

Peter Drucker, author of *The Age of Discontinuity,* commented (in a lecture) that the 1970's will be dominated by the international economy rather than the domestic economy and by the development of a new world money system. This will be a continuation of the trend of the past 25 years, in which world economy has been greatly strengthened at considerable cost to the U. S. domestic economy. Our international trade deficit is still huge; in the month of October 1971, for example, the deficit—more spent abroad than sold abroad—was 821 million dollars. In 1971 Americans imported 90 percent of their home radios, 51 percent of their black and white TVs, 42 percent of their shoes, 96 percent of their motorcycles, 68 percent of their sweaters, etc. (*The National Observer,* December 4, 1971). Clearly the U. S. economy of the future is tied into world economic competition.

I am not pessimistic economically, just bewildered. America has worked its way out of some tight spots before. My basic concerns are not so much the dollars involved as the attitudes which bring about dollar crises. For example, I worry about the relationship of Government spending to the meeting of urgent social need, the erosion of the private sector and the independent sector (foundations, private giving) of our economy, and growing worker-employer antagonism. For the first time in our history we have public employees striking in substantial numbers, yet the strike is against an "employer" who represents the public—themselves.

My thoughts are fuzzy on economic trends but I can write more specifically, and, yes, more hopefully on the next topic.

CHANGING PATTERNS OF FAMILY LIVING

The American family has always been in a state of crisis. Each generation has had its own interpretations of the cause and the cure. Phyllis McGinley quotes one such doomsayer who wrote at the beginning of the century: ". . . the home is perishing from our midst and civilization must perish with it. . . . If domestic virtue is decaying, the real cause is found in the rapid disappearance of the family horse and buggy. That conveyance preserved a sweet and delicate atmosphere of family ties. The citizen, shaken loose by much streetcar straphanging, takes to socialism and drinking. The matron without the steadying discipline of *having to get home in time to feed the horse* (italics are McGinley's!) gads about and grows extravagant." Some of our current explanations are, in their own contemporary sense, as ridiculously simplistic. The family is deteriorating because the mother is working, or there is a decline of religion, or the father is no longer the final authority, or it is the automobile, or the TV, and so on. Anyway, where is the irrefutable evidence that the family *is* in crisis, the urban family living in a seventies society? If it had not changed, it would not now be meeting its contemporary responsibilities as well as it does.

Within recent years in this country we have witnessed a virtual explosion of articles and books about marriage and the family. Expert and nonexpert part company on many issues, in particular that of the survival of marriage and of the family as they are known today. Some people perceive the tremendous changes within these two institutions as ones which originated outside the family and then impinged upon it. Other people seek to lay blame for society's ills on the family's doorstep.

Regardless of the point from which change was generated, there is general agreement that there is marked change in the place of woman in our society and in her self-image, which were discussed in Chapter III. Other generalizations relate to (1) reduction in functions of the family, (2) role status within the family, and (3) marriage and divorce.

Reduction in Functions of the Family

At the beginning of this century the family had a varied constellation of functions—educational, recreational, religious, moral, economic. "Today," says Max Coots in *The National Observer,* "home and family have lost their historic centrality. While the home is still the first teacher of children, it has become an uneasy creche, nurturing infancy and early childhood until the young can be fed, little by little, into the machinery of the larger institutional society." The children are funneled into Cubs and Brownies, schoolrooms, gymnasiums, and peer groups, and have their educational and moral goals shaped by schools and legal agencies, TV, and radio, Coots points out, "until in late adolescence the home becomes an affectionate hotel out of which teenage sons and daughters operate."

The extended family, with grandparents often living in the house, with uncles, aunts, and cousins usually living nearby, formerly had a vital role to play in the socialization process of the young. Someone who *cared* was always about to look after the children and in turn to be looked after and loved by them. Today there is little of that. The family is highly mobile and urbanized, relatives are scattered and "visit" the family only infrequently.

With the impersonality of urban living, with both parents frequently working away from the home, and with children staying in school over a longer number of years, the *peer group* at school has often come to have more "family" meaning than the family itself. Never before have we had so many children in school for so many hours a day and so many days a year. As the family's influence declines, there is an increasing influence of the peer group with whom children interact more hours per day than with either father or mother. The influence of peers is certainly a factor in the growing generation gap. More and more children and youth take their value cues from their peers rather than from parents or other adults.

The mobility of the American family was mentioned in connection with the dissolution of the extended family. The impact of this factor goes far deeper, however, and affects the sense of familiarity and, therefore, the emotional security of each member of the family. When father and mother are uncertain as to new values and behavior appropriate in the new location, the children tend to seek their value assurances elsewhere. Or when father and mother "carry over" values seen by children as inappropriate to the new school or community, the parents lose status with the children. Mobility leads to value uncertainty. Many recently transferred pupils should be recognized by teachers and counselors in the new school as individuals who are casting about either to test their old values or to establish viable new ones. They need help in this process and they may welcome it from adults if it is given sensitively.

As a consequence of the many changes in our society, the "New Shape of the American Family," as described in a Lutheran publication by that name, is one that does the following:

(a) includes only the small, two-generation unit of parents and their children;

(b) relies on companionship and the need for loving and being loved as the prime bonds for its inner unity;

(c) accords husband and wife relatively equal status in making family decisions;

(d) sets itself up independently in its own house or apartment;

(e) has severed close ties with blood and in-law relatives more than one generation removed;

(f) prefers to associate with families of similar race, age make-up, and socio-economic status;

(g) places high premium on comforts, conveniences, and whatever else cash or credit can buy;

(h) prolongs the economic dependency of its children while increasing their freedom to date and to marry;

(i) believes in a religious ceremony for marriage but regards the church mainly as a valuable community institution;

(j) encourages its members to participate in various worthwhile community causes and organizations;

(k) looks to persons outside the family for guidance and counsel on marital or family problems;

(l) accepts marital failure as a normal risk which should not deny the opportunity for a new marriage;

(m) has no place for the unmarried adult, voluntarily or involuntarily so, be he male or female.

From the above it would be apparent that a somewhat democratic family pattern of companionship is emerging as opposed to the more traditional authoritarian pattern. Behavior within the family is determined by mutual affection and consensus (or the lack of it) among its members. Sociologist Henry Maier proposes that a society-of-change requires a parliamentarian style of family living. This allows for cross-generational subgroupings as well as the familiar parents-versus-children alliance. In the parliamentary family pattern there is a fluid shifting of alliances. The constant aligning and realigning of family subgroups is in the service of reconciling conflicting interests, and it is this give-and-take process which replaces the older authoritarian approach to decision making in the family. In this family pattern the emphasis is on joint outcomes not the imposition of will. Consequently there is a constant seesaw balance between service to the individual and maintenance of the family. Experience *within* the family, not merely *with* the family, becomes the foundation for personal competence, the development of ego skills, and the acquisition of values.

It is clear that this description is a model, not a standard. No one knows how frequently the companionship-parliamentary family or the "New Shape Family" is found in our society. Many families still struggle with the authoritarian pattern or its reverse—the permissive, laissez-faire attitude of parents toward children. Neither is a happy one for the child. He may feel rejected by the expression of either attitude.

Teachers and counselors may find pertinent a study William Westley and Nathan Epstein made of *The Silent Majority*—the "ordinary," achieving, emotionally healthy college freshman. A study of these students and their families by this team of psychiatrist and sociologist resulted in the following findings for *this sample of subjects:*

1. Families whose distribution of power and authority is democratic, with the father having the final word, have the largest proportion of emotionally healthy children. (Of all families in the U. S. 71 percent list the father as "the head of the family.")

2. Families with a balanced division of labor are the ones in which the parents have a continuing vigorous and satisfying sex life, a positive emotional relationship, and emotionally healthy children.

3. Care of the child by the parent of the opposite sex is critical to the development of a positive sexual identity by the child.

4. Even parents who are themselves emotionally disturbed can raise emotionally healthy children if their own relationship is warm and affectionate.

5. Relative status of husband and wife is an important determinant of success and happiness in marriage; women who marry "up" educationally or economically tend to have emotionally healthy husbands and children. The converse is true for women who marry "down."

6. In the area of recognizing and solving emotional problems (in this study), it is the father, not the mother (contrary to popular belief), who is most important in the problem solution. For development of autonomy, the mother is the key figure (again contrary to belief).

Role Status within the Family

There are several suggestions in the preceding pages that indicate marked changes are taking place in the relationship between the marriage partners. Today women assume more the rule of partner (equal responsibilities in marriage) than the roles of *companion-hostess* or *wife-mother*, which Clifford Kirkpatrick outlined more than thirty-five years ago in *The International Journal of Ethics.* Few people desire a return of the parasitic hostess-companion, whose sole contribution to marriage was that she look lovely at all times and function as superb hostess for husband and his friends. On the other hand, there are built-in dangers for all family members when the wife-mother alternative is chosen, particularly in an industrialized society. When the father is away at work for the majority of the child's waking hours and is seldom seen by mother or children, the mother becomes the sole setter of values. In addition, all of her energies and frustrations are directed toward the children.

In families where "Momism" is predominant, the mother is perceived as the dominant member of the family. Studies have shown that this pattern of dominance is particularly detrimental to the development of appropriate sex-role identification. When mothers are perceived as dominant, opposite-sexed identification is more common. As mentioned earlier, when fathers are perceived as dominant, children of *both* sexes are more likely to achieve appropriate sex-role identification. To date there are no definitive studies regarding what happens when both parents are seen as equally strong.

Another factor in the family change is the overlap in roles of the husband and wife or mother and father. The tendency toward shared roles increases when husband and wife are both responsible for certain family obligations but the husband assumes roles formerly assumed by the wife or vice versa. Part of the change, I am sure, comes about because more women are working outside the home, assuming part of the man's traditional function as breadwinner. Part of the change may arise from the increasing involvement of men in jobs that do not require physical strength. A man's physical strength gives him less satisfaction than it did in pioneer, preindustrial days. He, therefore, takes on roles involving human relationships or he engages in repetitive or delicate tasks requiring brain and concentration but little muscle. In so doing, he engages in tasks for which a woman has been traditionally responsible. It seems clear that this overlapping of traditional male and female roles, this blurring of the sharp distinction between the image of man and the image of woman affects men's and women's perceptions of their roles in the family.

Psychiatrist Lief recently stated that taking out the garbage is about all that is left of the strictly masculine domain. He believes that among middle-class families no behavior is still demarcated as masculine or feminine and that in reaction there is the prevalent fear about proving one's sexuality. (I warned you he was a psychiatrist!) The concept of Unisex is still something new, and does not affect sex roles in many family patterns. But I believe that male-female overlapping of social and family roles will increase. Some will say that this is not good for the child, but how can we tell when we base "good" upon established norms which reflect change so slowly while children change so rapidly?

Working Mothers.   Some established norms have been changing at a more rapid pace. In 1970 half of all mothers with children between 6 and 17 years of age worked outside the home for all or part of the day. While it seems obvious that working mothers are far less likely to develop dependence in their children, the fact that the majority of school-age children have working mothers has one serious implication which is seldom considered. In his classic book, *The Art of Loving,* Erich Fromm points out the distinction between mother love and father love. Mother love is unconditional, while father love is conditional—it must be merited. Fromm emphasizes the merits of both kinds of love and the fact that the child needs both. Working mothers become increasingly exposed to the "production" ethic, which says that the one who produces most is valued most. May not this ethic become generalized from work relationships to mother-child relationships? If so, the implications for the school counselor are great. Counselors frequently encounter students who feel they are valued by both parents on the basis of *doing,* not *being.* If this trend is accelerated by mothers who are increasingly influenced by the production or achievement ethic, it will be more important than ever for counselors to be able to provide their counselees with "unconditional" caring and positive regard.

Other signs of the changing times: "Serial marriage—a pattern of successive temporary marriages" is thought appropriate by Alvin Toffler for this "Age of Transience;" a three-year renewable marriage contract has been proposed as a bill in the Maryland legislature; the number of communes in which marriage and family have a very different meaning have increased during the past five years from 100 to about 3,000. These innovations attract much attention, perhaps more than they deserve.

With all of the changes taking place, the family is still probably the most vital social agency for providing emotional security for the child. Parents are very important people to their children, and they should be constantly assured of this fact. Teachers, counselors, and other professionals have a tendency to play the parent down, to make him aware of his or her mistakes, or as someone has said "to regard fathers and mothers as a special breed of idiots." There is no worse service the teacher or counselor could render to the child than to erode the importance of the parent—to either the child or parent. Conversely, what the teacher or counselor does in reinforcing the parent in the parental and family roles which no one else can carry out is an act of great importance to the child. These are considerations worth remembering when one is approaching the problems of divorce and remarriage.

Marriage and Divorce

In 1970 the total number of marriages in the United States was 2,179,000—only slightly below the 1946 all-time record of 2.3 million. The 1970 number is misleading, however, because it reflects a large increase in total population. The number of marriages per thousand population was 16.4 in 1946 while in 1970 it was only 10.7—a drop of more than 50 percent. This is in turn reflected in a markedly lower birthrate of 18.2 per thousand population in 1970 as compared to one of 26.6 in 1947. However, the marriage rate is slowly climbing now, as noted earlier, because of the large number of young women in the population. The trend of the birthrate (in 1971) appears very uncertain.

The age for first marriages is slowly rising from a median age for males in 1960 of 22.8 to 23.2 in 1969. For women the corresponding median age was 20.3 in 1960 to 20.8 in 1969. Even when considering this slight (and to some people hopeful) rise in age at first marriage, it gives one second thoughts to realize that almost half of American females marry before reaching their twenty-first birthday. The divorce rates are twice as great for men under 22 years of age and women under 20 than for those who marry older.

Between 1964 and 1966 (I have no later data), 33 percent of all first births were conceived prior to marriage. For these children the chances that their parents will divorce are twice as great as for children conceived after their parents' marriage.

The divorce rate has risen steadily during the 1960's as has the marriage rate. But while the marriages were moving from 8.8 per thousand in 1963 to 10.7 in 1970 (a 21 percent increase), divorce increased from a rate of 2.3 per thousand in 1963 to 3.5 in 1970 (better than a 52 percent increase). To be kept in mind, however, in considering both marriage and divorce, is the fact that in the United States more than 90 percent of the people marry at some time in their lives and 80 percent of those divorced remarry. *Monthly Vital Statistics Reports,* 1971, and *Vital Statistics of the United States,* 1968, Vol. III, "Marriage and Divorce.")

Remarriage of those divorced took place a little more rapidly during the 1960's than during the preceding decade. During the period 1960–1966, half of the divorced men were remarried by the end of the second postdivorce year. Half of the divorced women were remarried by the end of the third year after divorce. In about 10 million current marriages in the United States (1970 figures), one or both partners have been married before. Second marriages are very likely to be successful; there is widespread agreement on that point. Paul Glick, chief of the

Population Division of the Census Bureau, makes one of the more conservative estimates in saying, "Those who remarry are much more likely to remain married until death intervenes than they are to become divorced." Every year there are about 10,000 remarriages to the first spouse! ("Probabilities of Marriage and Re-Marriage," *Current Population Reports,* July 1970.)

All of these figures on marriage and divorce (representing men and women, their love and happiness, their loneliness and unhappiness) lead up to the question, "What happens to the children?" We have talked a bit about children in the home and with parents, but what happens to the children of divorced couples? (In 1967 there were 701,000 children under the age of 18 who were affected by the 523,000 divorces granted in that year alone, according to the 1967 issue of *Vital Statistics of the United States,* Vol. III, "Marriage and Divorce.") Some children acquire a stepfather or a stepmother. When both spouses bring children into the new home, we have a "blended family." In 1961 Paul Jacobson arrived at a figure of 7 million stepchildren under the age of 18 (Ann Simon, *Stepchild in the Family,* Odyssey, 1964). With more divorces and more remarriages, that figure may now be as high as 10 million.

Divorce, "broken home," stepchild, all have negative connotations for many Americans. It is easy to forget that a divorce and remarriage may bring about a better home for all concerned, and that homes are "broken" also by death and chronic illness. Indeed, many homes were "broken" before the divorce, not as a result of it. One study of remarried women reported that 92 percent of them said that their children were either better off in the second marriage or the same.

THE URBANIZATION OF THE UNITED STATES

At one time a city was a well-defined place with boundaries that contained its people and activities. This concept is no longer adequate for describing what is happening in America. *City* has become an *area* or a *region* that may spill over county, state, or even national boundary lines. Cities have fused with suburbs of all sorts and may be surrounded by satellite cities. Authorities and special districts for this function or that (water, fire protection, etc.) have different boundaries within a metropolitan area and the identity of "the city" is lost in the complex.

In 1870 there were only 20 cities of more than 25,000 population, and 75 percent of the population lived in rural areas. A century later there were 805 such cities with a complete reversal of the rural-urban

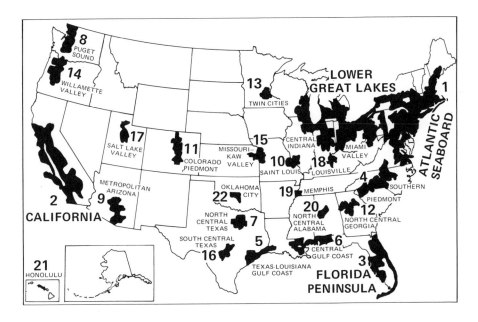

Figure 2. Population of Future Urban Regions of the United States.

Urban Region	Population in Millions 1970 (estimated)	Population in Millions 2000 (projected)
1. Metropolitan Belt	86.2	126.5
Atlantic Seaboard	45.8	67.4
Lower Great Lakes	40.4	59.1
2. California	19.9	42.5
3. Peninsular Florida	5.7	13.0
4. Southern Piedmont	3.3	5.2
5. Texas-Louisiana Gulf Coast	2.5	4.9
6. Central Gulf Coast	2.7	4.7
7. North Central Texas	2.2	4.2
8. Puget Sound	2.1	3.8
9. Metropolitan Arizona	1.3	3.5
10. Saint Louis	2.4	3.5
11. Colorado Piedmont	1.6	3.2
12. North Central Georgia	1.8	3.1
13. Twin Cities	1.8	2.5
14. Willamette Valley	1.4	2.4
15. Missouri-Kaw Valley	1.5	2.3
16. South Central Texas	1.2	2.2
17. Salt Lake Valley	0.8	1.6
18. Louisville	0.9	1.5
19. Memphis	0.8	1.4
20. North Central Alabama	0.8	1.3
21. Honolulu (Oahu)	0.7	1.2
22. Oklahoma City	0.6	1.2

Source: Jerome P. Pickard, "Is Megalopolis Inevitable?" *The Futurist,* October 1970. Published by the World Future Society, P.O. Box 30369, Bethesda Branch, Washington, D. C. 20014.

ratio. Now 75 percent of the people live in *urban* areas with about 800,000 additional people moving *each year* from rural areas into urban areas. (Higbee, *A Question of Priorities;* see References, Chapter VI.)

Not only do people cluster in cities, but the cities themselves cluster together. In 1970 there were 22 urban regions (these may contain several cities or metropolitan areas) with populations which are projected to exceed one million each by the year 2000. These 22 urban regions contained over 69 percent of the total U. S. population in 1970, projected to increase to 77 percent by the year 2000 (see figure 2).

As important as the increasing density of population in urban areas is the changing character of life in both city and suburb.

Black Majorities

In 1970 three of the 50 largest cities in the U. S. had predominantly black populations—Washington, D.C., Newark, and Atlanta. If present rates of population increase continue, the next 15 years will see 10 other large cities join these three: Baltimore, Chicago, Cleveland, Detroit, Jacksonville, New Orleans, Oakland (California), Philadelphia, Richmond (Virginia), and St. Louis. Even now in *the public school systems* of these cities the proportion of nonwhites (the majority of these being black, of course) exceeds 50 percent. A 1971 survey (by the U. S. Office for Civil Rights) added three more cities to the list having predominantly black school populations—Gary, Compton, and Kansas City (*Arizona Republic,* January 16, 1972). So-called central city increases are greatest with the black population almost doubling between 1950 and 1970 (6.5 million to 12.5 million). The white population in central cities stayed constant at 45 million during this period. There is, in addition, a strong city-to-suburb flow of blacks. Between 1960 and 1969 the nonwhite population of the suburbs increased by 37 percent while the white population was increasing by 29 percent. These percentages of increase are deceptive if taken literally, for they have very different bases. With few exceptions the suburbs remain predominantly nonblack. ("Trends in Social and Economic Conditions in Metropolitan and Non-Metropolitan Areas," *Current Population Reports,* September 3, 1970.)

These figures are only symbols, of course. It is people who are involved. A large proportion of blacks in central cities are at the poverty level. In fact, 32.6 percent of all nonfarm blacks lived in poverty in 1970. This figure jumps to 40.3 percent for related blacks under 18 ("Characteristics of the Low-Income Population," *Current Population Reports,* November 1971). The central city ghettos where most urban blacks live are inexcusable blots upon our national conscience. It is there that the least is spent upon schools and the tendency to chronic poverty remains unchecked. If this sounds extreme, it is merely a reflection of what was concluded in a 1970 report of the prestigious Committee for Economic Development, *Who Are the Urban Poor?:* "About 47 percent of all poor in metropolitan areas are in households that cannot be expected to become self-sustaining at any time in the future."

So it is not unexpected that the blacks will flow out of the central city into the suburbs in increasing numbers, seeking better survival conditions and increasing opportunities for self-respect. The late Malcolm X put it eloquently: "The black masses do not want to be walled up in slums, in ghettos, like animals. They want to live in an open, free society where they can walk with their heads up like men and women."

On the cover of the *Urban League Annual Report* for 1971 is this quotation: "Black Power is not a shout of violence or a shout of separation. Black Power simply means . . . look at me . . . I'm here. I have dignity, I have pride. I have roots. I insist, I demand that I participate in those decisions that affect my life and the lives of my children. It means that I'm somebody and that's what Black Power means." From a completely different background comes this comment by Huey Newton, Black Panther founder and present leader: "We have rejected the rhetoric of the gun; it got about 40 of us killed and hundreds sent to prison. Our goal now is to organize the black communities politically" (*The National Observer,* February 12, 1972). Newton has been retreating from violence since his release from prison in 1970, although Eldridge Cleaver, now in exile and seen by Newton as that "hidden traitor," would still depend upon it. Newton and his Black Panthers organize picket lines around stores until the owner agrees to a continuing contribution to the United Black Fund, which finances ghetto social programs, including those of the Panthers.

Malcolm X, the Urban League, and the Black Panthers may seem strange bedfellows, but their common focus is upon dignity and justice for blacks, particularly those in crowded urban areas. Only adequate education and adequate jobs will provide blacks with dignity and a sense of belonging. Subcultures serve ego needs for certain groups—religious groups, for example, or ethnic groups. Black separatism serves an important ego need for blacks, and few are going to give up the support of that subculture unless there is an adequate substitution of other satisfactions. It is useless to talk about integration of blacks or any other ethnic group with the majority culture unless there is provision for the dignity of equal education and equal job opportunity. It seems the height of absurdity for Americans to place the focus anywhere else.

The Suburbs

The 1970 census reported almost 75 million Americans living in suburbs—more than lived in either central cities or rural areas. Suburbs increased 25 percent in population between 1960 and 1970, while 22 of the 50 largest cities *decreased* in population over the same period (*Time,* March 15, 1971).

The term "suburb" is vaguely defined and has probably outlived its usefulness. Many communities called suburbs are neither "sub" nor "urb." They may be coagulations of people, independent of the city and resistant to both diversity and density. Others are small cities which again, in many ways, are independent of the larger city but connected with it (satellite cities).

Based on a survey of 1600 suburban Americans in 100 communities, a story in *Time* (March 15, 1971) describes four types of suburbs, only the first of which fits the stereotype:

1. *Affluent bedroom suburb:* Professional, white, Republican (*Time's* identifying marks, not mine!); less than half the residents work in the city and many are retired. Lewis Mumford described this historic type of suburb as "a sort of green ghetto dedicated to the elite."

2. *Affluent settled suburb:* More self-sufficient; less of a dormitory for the central city; a higher boredom quotient.

3. *Low-income growing suburb:* Blue-collar country; a sizable proportion of skilled workers earn their living close to home.

4. *Low-income stagnant suburb:* Highest proportion of nonskilled and service workers; lowest proportion of commuters to central city; highest proportion of residents who are not happy about where they live.

It is obvious that except for the relatively low population density, living and educational conditions in this last type of suburb may be little better than in the central city.

Crime in Urban Areas

The sad national picture is that of a 148 percent increase in crime during the 1960's in conjunction with only a 12 percent increase in population. Differences show up at once between cities of over 250,000 population and suburbs. In 1969 there were five times as many murders in these cities as in suburbs, three times as many cases of aggravated assault, twice as many burglaries, and five times as many car thefts.

In terms of the age factor, the city figures are the same as national figures with 10 percent of all those arrested being under 15 years of age while 26 percent were under 18. However, the figures for the suburbs show a marked downward trend in age, with 13 percent under 15 years of age and 35 percent under 18. The difference in increase of crimes by boys and by girls under 18 is also worthy of note. There was a 212 percent increase in "serious crimes" by *females* against only a 78 percent increase for *males*. Neither the higher figures for youth in the suburbs nor the higher figure for girls is easy to understand (drugs may be a factor). For teachers and counselors in suburbs these trends may be of vital significance. (*Uniform Crime Reports,* 1969, and *Preliminary Uniform Crime Reports,* 1970, Department of Justice.)

The Pollution Headache

Air pollution is a particularly crucial problem in cities because there is both a congestion of people and a congestion of the sources of pollution. For example, it is estimated that 60 percent of the cities' air pollution is caused by automobile exhausts (*Time,* February 2, 1970)—and cities abound in cars! An astonishing 25 percent of the inhabitants of metropolitan areas in 1970 had *two or more automobiles*, up from 14 percent in 1960 ("Special Report on Household Ownership of Cars, etc.: 1970, 1969, and 1960," *Consumer Buying Indicator).* The greatest increase was in the central city areas where congestion is worst and where, because of the low income level, there are probably more old cars. Of the 78 million automobiles in the U. S. in 1969, 38 percent were six years of age or older (*Statistical Abstracts,* 1970).

Noise pollution is another disruptive problem of the cities. Alvin Meyer, Acting Director of the Office of Noise Abatement and Control, reports that heavy city traffic frequently measures 90 decibels—five decibels above the level which can damage hearing capacity after continual exposure. Noise levels in city living areas, particularly in the kitchen, are said by Meyer to be approaching factory levels. Nor are the suburbs immune. Rotary power mowers run at 93 decibels and snow blowers at 92! (*Arizona Republic,* May 20, 1971.) Donald A. Belt, an audiologist at the Stanford Medical Center, comments that the onset of permanent hearing loss from noise is insidious and deceptive because there is no pain—but the loss can be real and permanent. *The Fight for Quiet* by Theodore Berland (Prentice-Hall, 1970) provides a good analysis of the current situation in our country and describes some state laws and city ordinances recently passed to reduce noise level.

The Impact of Urban Living upon the Person

In *The Pursuit of Loneliness* Philip Slater (see References, Chapter VII) suggests that American culture tends to suppress three basic human desires: the need for community, the need for engagement, and the need for dependence (sharing). This is because of our inordinate commitment to individual freedom—to drive our own car whenever and wherever we want, to consume (actually discard) as many goods as we want, to be free to be on our own at all times. As a consequence, we do not share well with others or relate to them; we do not make choices in common or purchases in common when it would be to our advantage to do so. We drive and live so independently that we get in each other's way. In other words, we are not free. *Must* we (not can we) move in the direction of more communality and less individuality? A better question perhaps—must we know how to choose situations where communality is the answer, rather than individuality? The goal, of course, is to meet personal needs within the confines of congestion.

In the crowded areas of our cities and our suburbs, these human problems are magnified. There is great impersonality and loneliness; individual freedom means competing with every other person for all that one does or gets; privacy is sought but seldom found. Our pioneer forefathers shared with others out of combined need for survival and for friendship. City dwellers find themselves in a similar wilderness of need.

Another answer is to be found in planning, in not allowing circumstances to control us but in anticipating our control of circumstances. Cities are attempting to reduce population density by developing planned satellite or independent cities, by decentralizing industry, by preserving green belts for common usage. At the same time they move in the direction of *increasing* density by a more careful use of land, by use of apartments rather than ranch-style homes. They build upward (the new Sears Roebuck Building in Chicago will tower 1,450 feet into the sky—over a quarter of a mile) and downward (Japan has a large underground center for every metropolitan area, which has the advantage of being cooler, cheaper, and safer in time of disaster).

Such planning is seen at its ultimate in the work of Paolo Soleri, who has developed the science of arcology (architectural ecology). His three-dimensional cities would tower a mile high, use little land, but be planned so that the vocational, living, and social needs of the inhabitants would all be met. The various elements of the city would operate together to produce a *social* organism just as the organs, blood vessels, and respiratory system operate together to serve a single human organism.

Soleri is almost unique among city planners in considering the manner in which city architecture can serve the psychological needs of the human organism. We know a great deal about the effects of crowding on animals, but we know much less about its effects on human beings. Calhoun's study of rats that were allowed to multiply under good conditions of food and water but within limited space (four pairs of white rats in a nine-foot-square enclosure) is nightmarish in its implications. They multiplied all right, but beyond a certain number their social order fell apart, they killed each other for no apparent reason, they lost their initiative, sexual activity fell to zero, and the last of the colony died alone in the midst of ample food and water. (Edward T. Hall, *The Hidden Dimension,* Doubleday, 1966.)

We are learning that men also have varying *spatial* needs, partly determined by their cultural heritage. Zoo keepers and designers take into account their residents' varying needs for elbowroom, but architects and city planners do not make a similar allowance for different ethnic groups in the human population. An article by Jonathan Freedman (*Psychology Today,* September 1971, 58–61, 86) provides a thoughtful review of density studies, including his own, but none of these appears to take into account ethnic differences. In general, it seems that we have adopted the melting pot image much too literally.

The liabilities and the assets of modern cities are clearly set forth in a symposium, "Are Our Cities Dying?" (*Reader's Digest,* August 1971). Three authorities offer separate answers entitled "yes," "no," and "yes, but." As in many modern social issues, different individuals draw different conclusions from the same data. To put it mildly, society is concerned about the future of people in cities. Someone has quipped, "Cities have grown so fast that their outskirts no longer cover their extremities."

THE OCCUPATIONAL WORLD

The theme of Peter Drucker's *The Age of Discontinuity* applies with particular emphasis to the occupational aspect of life in America. During the 1970's developments in technology and changes in our social institutions and organizations will mean a constant reordering of the occupational structure. New institutions will develop and old ones atrophy.

New occupations will appear and established ones fade out at a dis-
maying pace.

A world economy is emerging in which people are moving across
national boundaries to realize their economic and social aspirations. This
too will call for new economic institutions and new concepts of occupational engagement. The occupation for which one prepared at either
high school or a more advanced level will not stand still; one will retrain
for the changed occupation or move to another. This calls for re-education
and retraining over and over again during one's lifetime. This may
not mean school in a formal sense—that depends upon how well schools
keep up with social and occupational change—but it means new learnings
by whatever means. Can students face the fact that fighting obsolescence
in the occupation for which they prepared will be as important as was
the original preparation? I think *they* can accept this better than can we
of the older generation!

The English do not change their social behaviors rapidly. It must
therefore have dismayed them to hear Sir Eric Ashby, Master of Clare
College at Cambridge University, say: "The present generation of
students will still be employed in the year 2000. But long before then
their degrees and diplomas, at any rate in science, technology, and social
sciences, will have become obsolete. The only students who can be sure
of escaping obsolescence are the few who will themselves become
innovators." What is a university degree worth? However well it has
taught one how to change with the times—that is its ultimate worth.

The numbers are large and the picture complex. By 1980 the U. S.
labor force will contain more than 100 million workers, according to
present predictions. This means an increase of 25 percent between 1968
and 1980. Two-thirds of this will involve young men and women
between the ages of 16 and 34. Related to the problem for youth of
entering the labor market is the prediction that 40 percent of all women
will be working by 1980 and that there will be a 33 percent increase in
the number of blacks in the labor force. This means keen competition
for the entry-level jobs. On the other hand, opportunities for advance-
ment may be good because of the smaller number of older workers,
whose participation in certain parts of the labor force will be thinly
distributed.

It is a familiar story to counselors that the percentage of increase in
government workers will be the highest for all occupational categories,
a 42 percent increase between 1968 and 1980. The increase will be
largest in state and local government employment (heaviest in health,
sanitation, welfare, educational, and protective services).

The next highest percentage increase and by far the greatest in total numbers will be in the service-producing industries (trade, finance, insurance, real estate, medical services, amusement, and related fields). In this area there will be a 35 percent increase between 1968 and 1980 to a total of almost 60 million workers. In 1920, 50 percent of all non-farm workers were in service industries; by 1968 this percentage was 65 and by 1980 it is predicted to be 70 percent.

Of considerably less magnitude will be the changes in goods-producing industries (agriculture, mining, construction, and manufacturing). While employment in contract construction is predicted to increase 40 percent, manufacturing will increase only 11 percent, while mining and agriculture will decrease. Automation and other technological processes are causing a continuing reduction of employment in these areas.

If one cuts the cake a different way, another familiar refrain is heard. *White collar workers* will increase the most rapidly and will represent 50 percent of all workers by 1980. Within this category, professional and technical employment will increase the most (50 percent between 1968 and 1980), a trend that has been evident for the past two decades. Clerical, sales, and managerial occupations will increase at lower but still substantial rates (20–30 percent). The greatest demand will be for workers in educational and health services, research and development, computer planning and computer operating, urban planning, recreation, social work, medical technology, as well as for office machine operators (an increase of 40 percent is predicted), stenographers and secretaries (33 percent), salesmen, realtors, and insurance workers.

While the trend for *blue collar workers* generally is downward, the prediction for craftsmen and foremen is for a 25 percent increase (1968–1980. In this category, business machine servicemen will increase 100 percent. Other growing occupations will include electrician, cement mason, bricklayer, glazier, operating engineer, plumber, roofer, sheet metal workers, iron workers, and appliance servicemen. (All of these projections are from U. S. Bureau of Labor Statistics, and, in particular, *The Occupational Outlook Handbook,* 1970–71. Much that I have written in the preceding paragraphs is for those not familiar with the *Handbook.* I am afraid, however, that this includes many counselors whose efforts are largely devoted to academic advising. I would recommend also a readable 32-page Labor Department booklet, *U. S. Manpower in the 1970's,* procurable from the Superintendent of Documents for 35 cents.)

Within the total field of manpower changes, *blacks* have experienced an encouraging increase in the number employed during the past decade, and further increase is projected for the next decade. The employment of blacks increased by 23 percent between 1961 and 1969; during this time there was only an 8 percent increase for whites. It is encouraging that three-fifths of the increase in black employment took place in professional, white collar, or skilled occupations. During this same period there was a decrease in the percentage of blacks in poorly paid, unskilled occupations. In general, however, these percentage figures are misleading because the base is low. Unemployment figures for blacks, although cut in half between 1961 and 1969 (12.4 percent to 6.4 percent), are still higher for blacks than for whites. Unemployment and poverty figures for black youth are still the highest of all categories. (*Occupational Outlook Quarterly*, Summer 1970.)

The President's Manpower Report — 1970 reminds us that blacks "are still seriously underrepresented in these (professional, clerical, and skilled occupations) and other relatively high status, highly paid occupations . . ." The *Report* attributes this lag not only to "educational deficiencies and lack of skill" but also to "inadequate knowledge of better job opportunities, and racial discrimination." Our society is now engaged in many efforts to provide occupational parity through scholarship help, job training, entrepreneur subsidies, etc. These are constructive moves, but we cannot overcome a century of educational deficiency and racial discrimination quickly or without sustained effort.

Working women are another minority group against whom there is marked discrimination, a condition discussed in Chapter III. It is encouraging to note, however, that early in 1972 the U. S. Senate began consideration of an amendment to the omnibus Higher Education bill that would deny federal funds to certain types of educational institutions that engaged in sex discrimination in either admissions or staffing.

Young people, as noted earlier, will be looking for jobs in substantial numbers during the 1970's, which means that entry positions will be tight. In 1980 high school enrollment is expected to range from 14.8 million to 15.1 million while college enrollment is predicted to range from 10.2 million to 11.4 million ("Projections of School and College Enrollment: 1971–2000," *Current Population Reports*, January 1972).

Those with better educations will have an edge on entry positions in the job market. Over the long haul, the better-educated man can be expected also to earn more. For many youths, however, more money is not an adequate reason for more education. "Education for what?" does not get the answer now that it got 30 years ago. For a sizable minority of both high school and college students education should make life more livable and not merely enable one to "make a better living." They will accept more income, of course, but are even more eager for meaning, purpose, and enjoyment in life. A study by Peter Sandman, author of *The Unabashed Career Guide*, cites a survey of college students in which 55 percent cited "family" as a first source of life satisfaction, 23 percent cited "leisure," and 14 percent cited "occupation." Perhaps Buckminster Fuller's seemingly wild prediction that in 50 years the word "worker" will have disappeared from our vocabulary will not seem so incredible a decade or two from now.

Employment *now*, however, is very much a concern of millions of high school and college youths for whose lives employment and income are vital factors. If I were guessing on where youth will be most welcome during the next decade, I would not have a first, second, and third sequence of demand. For some who can absorb the learning demanded and can find educational support over a long stretch, the "first" would be the professions—in human relations, in the arts, in the sciences. The *field* chosen is, of course, influenced by background and interest, but the *level* at which entry is attempted is heavily influenced by learning potential. There were 10.3 million professional and technical workers in the U. S. labor force in 1970—one-seventh of the total work force. Yet professional and technical workers are predicted to be the fastest growing group in the 1968–80 period. (*Occupational Outlook Handbook,* 1970–71.) Brains and, even more, creative capacity and innovative ability will be highly rewarded both as to income and personal satisfaction. "Unto every one that hath shall be given."

The Biblical quotation above, however, had a sour ring to it during the summer of 1971, with 50,000 to 100,000 professionals unemployed in the aeronautic and aerospace fields and a variously estimated 50,000 "unemployed PhD's." "The knowledge industry appears to be in a decline," wrote Peter Schrag in the *Saturday Review* (August 7, 1971). If this is true, I am convinced that it is a short-term decline. The occupations that are sure to have the largest increase during this decade will be those in "the knowledge industry" and those providing services to others. There is reason to hope that many young people can engage at professional and semiprofessional levels in occupations contributing to better human relations and to needed social change.

An excellent chart of projected 1968–1980 demands in the professions is given in *Time,* May 24, 1971, as part of a somewhat encouraging article on this "Grave New World" of jobs for college graduates. New attitudes as well as prospective new careers make this stimulating reading.

For some the first choice would be for semiprofessional and technical occupations. Ordinarily qualification means an education at the junior college level of six months to two years duration. Most career programs for semiprofessional or professional aides require two years of study (after high school) and result in the receipt of an Associate of Arts degree. There were 140,000 such degrees awarded in 1968 as compared with 95,000 in 1966. More than half of the 1968 degrees (78,000) were in occupational programs; 20,000 other students were awarded certificates for programs of less than two years duration. The fields are varied and many are fast-growing. Examples are: technicians (numbering 170,000 in the labor force in 1968), forestry aides (13,000), radiological technologists (75,000), library technicians (70,000), police officers (285,000). The Fall 1970 issue of *The Occupational Outlook Quarterly* describes the growth prospects for each of these areas.

For many others, the first choice is preparation for the large cluster of occupations for which high school graduation is either required or is desirable. Most often specific vocational preparation (vocational education) is built into the high school program, but some occupations require more intensive vocational preparation such as that which is found in the postgraduate high school technical programs or in area technical schools.

Make no mistake, the employment outlook in these vocations, requiring little, if any, preparation beyond high school, is encouraging, and the activities often self-rewarding. The assumption that these are "blind alley" jobs fails to assess adequately the facts that many individuals *like* what they do and that their employment hours are regular enough to enable them to find other satisfactions outside their employed hours. *The Occupational Outlook Handbook* cites the following occupations that fall into this broad category of requiring high school plus occupational preparation: *Craftsmen* (carpenters, tool- and diemakers, electricians, typesetters, etc.) numbered about 10 million in 1968. They will increase about 25 percent during the 1968–80 period. *Clerical workers,* 2.8 million, predicted to increase 33 percent; sales persons, 4.6 million, predicted to increase 30 percent; *semiskilled workers* (operatives), 14 million, expected to increase only 10 percent; *service workers* (a very diverse group ranging from the professional aides and police workers already mentioned to barbers and restaurant workers), numbering 9 million and predicted to increase 40 percent during the 1968–80 period. In these several fields, some do not *require* high school graduation or specific vocational preparation, but those who have such preparation will be distinctly favored in employment.

IMPLICATIONS FOR THE COUNSELOR

One of the important environments in which the student lives is that of his family. As mentioned later, getting acquainted directly with this environment (visiting in the home) is not easy in terms of tact and time.

Much is learned about the home and family by listening to the student himself as he consciously or unconsciously reveals his relations with his parents. Direct questions about father or mother may be resented, whereas inquiring about how he "feels" about his parents' help or lack of help may open up a topic in which feelings are easily released. It is probably needless to say that if the student shies away from speaking of his parents, the counselor should not press. The timing may be wrong.

In sensing the student's feeling about home and parents, the counselor faces a critical problem of personal bias. His own childhood and family experience tend to prejudice him either for or against a similar kind of home. A home *different* from his own home is seen as inferior in quality or at least suspect if his own home experience was a good one. If the counselor came from a poor family, he is likely to overvalue the advantages of a "rich" home. The reverse is even more likely to be true.

If the counselor has not experienced divorce, then a child in a family where divorce has taken place is likely to be perceived unrealistically. Much has been written about the labeling effect, a process which motivates the individual to live up to the label which others have attached to him. We see this operating in the current drug crisis. A youth reveals he became a drug user because his parents accused him of being one. He may say, "If I have the name, I'll play the game." The book, *Pygmalion in the Classroom* by Rosenthal, reveals the same process in operation. Teachers were told that students (formerly labeled "slow learners") would be undergoing a learning spurt. And, presumably because of the teachers' expectations, they did!

One common label is that a child is from a "broken home." To many this signifies calamity because divorce is seen as a calamity. Consequently they convey to the child from a disrupted or blended home the negative message that something is "wrong" or that his parents have "failed" him. For the child or youth who receives such messages, the home may become a handicap to him. In actuality he may be a member of a family which had the courage to mend an intolerable situation and is now trying to build upon lessons which were learned quite painfully.

Counselors might give some thought to these comments about families and family influences:

1. Divorce is a fact of American life; let it be accepted as such. A counselor can be a negative-type Pygmalion in the counseling relationship if he gives the counselee the "message" that he is handicapped in his home. He may be, but it does not follow that his problem was caused solely by the divorce or the new parent.

2. Divorced persons marry sooner than ever before, and the majority of them are parents. Thus we are witnessing an increase in the number of

"blended" families. The counselor who is free from value judgments about such families is then free to give thought to the very real problems children in such families have. For example, teen-age youths acquire stepparents and stepsiblings at the very time they are attempting to cope with new sexual feelings. A rather straighforward book intended for children and youth (Richard A. Gardner, *The Boys and Girls Book about Divorce,* Science House, 1970) may be useful to those who counsel such children. In fact, a counselor should certainly read this book through before knowing whether or not to recommend it to a troubled client.

3. The majority of mothers now work. As they come more and more under the influence of the production ethic, they, like the fathers, may become less able to give their children the unconditional love described by Fromm (see References, Chapter XII). It thus becomes crucial that counselors strive even harder to provide them with "unconditional positive regard."

4. In urban areas where a shift in white-black ratio is taking place, counselors will be encountering students who, for the first time, are coping with the problems of minority status.

5. We are a mobile society. Within any given year at least 20 percent of the population change residence at least once (see Chapter VII). Our current ecological problems may well portend an even greater mobility as people seek healthier climates. A group approach might be the most effective one in counseling with young people experiencing the loneliness of a new location.

6. There are tremendous variations in family structure within different social, ethnic, and racial groups. Two illustrations: while 9 out of 10 white youths live with 2 parents present in the home, only 6 out of 10 black youths do so; 28 percent of black families were headed by women as compared with 9 percent for white families in 1970 ("Population Characteristics," *Current Population Reports,* July 1970).

7. Counselors who did not take courses in sociology of the family while in graduate school might be helped if they could now arrange to take such a course or courses.

The "big picture" of the urbanization process and its outcomes given in the second section of this chapter tells a counselor nothing about the particular city or urban area in which his students live. But the picture should raise some questions for which he must seek his own answers. If a counselor is to help others, he must have some understanding of the environmental pressures that surround them. He must "go and see." It would seem to me that the "caring counselor" would be impelled to become familiar with at least the neighborhood in which his school is located. What do his or her students see as they come to school? This is more important, of course, if a considerable number of them live in that neighborhood. A normal first step might be just walking about outside of school hours, observing conditions and people. How else can one get a "feel" for the world in which his students live? Where do children and youth hang out or play? In some situations one might need an ostensible excuse for being there, but there are always stores to look for and things that one might be seeking to buy.

If the students come from different parts of a city, a counselor could visit a bit in each part on succeeding weekends. With imagination alive, such travel could not only be informative but something of an adventure. I realize that the counselor's or teacher's attitude would have much to do with how these visits would be interpreted by students—and the likelihood would be great that he would meet a child or youth that he knew. But if there were a genuine concern simply to know where his students lived, with no ulterior motive such as "spying out" a given student, I believe that most students would be pleased with the counselor's interest in their world.

Visiting in a student's home, unannounced and uninvited, would be a different story indeed. This could easily be interpreted as snooping or as genuine discourtesy, no matter how reasonable the counselor's motives appeared to him. For a given situation it might be critical that he see a parent or a home, but no matter how critical, one can seldom justify the rudeness of entering another's home without some kind of prior understanding and agreement. The agreement may be with either student or parent, preferably both, but without this courtesy the counselor will be seen as making "an official" visit and resented accordingly. So he may never get into some homes even though his "need" to do so is great.

These pages may be read by counselors who will be located in towns or rural areas, in any one of the kinds of suburbs described, or in the inner city. And in the inner city the reader may or may not be of the same ethnic or cultural origin as the majority of the students in his school. And *each* of these different urban or nonurban communities carries its own mores of what is acceptable behavior on the part of a "visitor." So my comments are carefully general in nature. The *need to understand* the environments of one's students is equally great for each counselor, but each must seek his way of best achieving this.

Because some attention is given later to career counseling, little will be said here—except for one point, and this again is a warning on bias. Counselors are likely to be academic in orientation and to favor unconsciously students who plan to and who can begin preparation for the professional or semiprofessional fields. There could be no worse "favoritism" than this. This is the age of the technical man or woman—the one who can install and maintain the machines, computers, and appliances of our industrial society. It is also the age of the professional aide, the craftsman, and the paperworkers. Do not "play down" these occupations or the students who should plan for them. Omitting the semi-skilled workers, they still outnumber the professional worker by almost four to one *(Occupational Outlook Quarterly, 1970–71).*

Perhaps it bears repeating (see Chapter III) that rapid changes in occupations mean that students should be helped to see that vocational education is a lifetime endeavor. A change in kind of occupation or level of occupation will be considered again and again, and the need for periodic re-education will continue throughout the student's working life. President John Schwada (Arizona State University) recently described the present situation very vividly:

"The useful life of knowledge in some fields may be no greater than five or ten years. Among the most saddening human tragedies in our society today are those who were well trained for the world of ten or twenty years ago but are either inadequately equipped or largely obsolete in the technological world of today."

References for Exploration

Angelou, Maya. *I Know Why the Caged Bird Sings.* Bantam, 1970.

Berg, Ivar. *Jobs and Education: The Great Training Robbery.* Praeger Publishers, 1970.

Brown, Claude. *Manchild in the Promised Land.* Signet Book, 1965. (A vividly told autobiography of a young black's childhood and youth in the slums of Harlem. A remarkable story of a man who "made it" and in the process makes the reader feel that he was right there with him.)

Galbraith, John. *Economics, Peace and Laughter.* Houghton Mifflin, 1971.

Gardner, Richard A. *The Boys and Girls Book about Divorce.* Science House, 1970.

Gordon, Leonard. *A City in Racial Crisis.* W. C. Brown Co., 1971.

Hedgepeth, William. *The Alternative: Communal Life in New America.* Macmillan, 1970.

Kirsten, George. *The Rich, Are They Different?* Houghton Mifflin, 1967.

Malamud, Bernard. *The Tenants.* Farrar, Strauss, and Giroux, 1971. (Two writers, one white and one black, and their intellectual and love life in the ghetto. Dynamically written in the contemporary mood.)

Mead, Margaret. "Future Family." *trans*action, September 1971.

Montague, Ashley. *The Concept of Race.* Collier Books, 1964.

Otto, Herbert. *Family in Search of a Future: Alternate Models for Moderns.* Appleton, 1970.

Rothman, Jack. *Promoting Social Justice in the Multigroup Society.* Association Press, 1971. (Fascinating case studies—23 of them—of social inequities between groups in our society. Most of these are ethnic groups—blacks, Jews, Chicanos, Puerto Ricans, Indians; some are cultural—Catholic, women, white suburbanites. No broad answers are given, but individual situations are described to illustrate what can be done.)

"The Suburbs: Frontiers of the 70's" *City,* January–February 1971.

Theobald, Robert. *The Economics of Abundance.* Pitman Publishers, 1970.

Hey Mama (film). 18 minutes. Creative Film Society, 14558 Valerio St., Van Nuys, Calif. 91405. ("A candid unpretentious documentary of the black subculture in Venice, California.")

I Am Joaquim (film). 20 minutes. Canyon Cinema Cooperative, Room 220, Industrial Center Building, Sausalito, Calif. 94965. (A montage history of the Chicano from Indian Mexico to the beginning of a "Brown Power" ethic in the United States.)

Natural Habitat (film). 18 minutes. Canyon Cinema Cooperative, Room 220, Industrial Center Building, Sausalito, Calif. 94965. ("A poem about dehumanizing work.")

That's Me (film). 11 minutes. Contemporary Films, 330 W. 42nd St., New York, 10036 (*Evanston, Ill.,* 828 Custer Ave., 60202; *San Francisco,* 1714 Stockton St., 94133). (A gentle but moving story of a young Puerto Rican living in New York with nothing to do.)

A Time for Burning (film). 58 minutes. Contemporary Films, 330 W. 42nd St., New York, 10036 (*Evanston, Ill.,* 828 Custer Ave., 60202; *San Francisco,* 1714 Stockton St., 94133). (The struggle—in Omaha—that whites have in "seeing" blacks.)

CHAPTER X

Some Major Trends
in Education and Psychology

It would be presumptuous indeed to assume that I could cover all the trends in these two fields, education and psychology, in a short chapter, even if I knew them all. So without even defining "trends" I will simply present three or four developments I consider major in each area. There is an enormous literature and I have not covered it all. So "major" means to me those movements which appear frequently or prominently in the literature, some of them supported by my personal experience. This selection will also be shaped by the things I consider especially significant for counselors.

SOME ISSUES IN EDUCATION

If popular concern and trenchant criticism are indicators of significance, it looks as if formal education (schooling) will undergo radical changes during the next decade. The immediate post-Sputnik period was a time of change toward more science and technology in the schools, more structure, and more arbitrary performance standards. A reaction to these emphases is now being felt, and the changes to be anticipated are in quite a different direction. As noted in earlier chapters, the United States is currently in a postindustrial phase of development. The beckoning frontier belongs less to technological knowledge than to better understanding of human relationships, less to knowledge *per se* than to *use* of knowledge, less to ideas and things than to that most puzzling phenomenon, the human being.

Perspective

In any attempt to gain a perspective on the past twenty-five years, one must pay attention to the shattering impact upon schools and colleges of both a flood of new knowledge and a flood of more people. The sharp rise in the birth rate that marked the 1946–1966 period meant overwhelming increases in enrollment, first in the elementary schools, then in the secondary schools. By 1965 the colleges and universities felt the first peak of the population growth (high birth rate of 1947). Schools struggled merely to *absorb* the swelling tide of students. This attempt to adjust to numbers has doubtless reduced the amount of attention that could be given to desirable changes in content and method. This may be a rationalization; yet I have observed that criticisms of education most often emanate from those who have not had to

worry about more and more classrooms, more and more college buildings, more staff, more money, more students. Pupils in increasing
millions have had to be accommodated.

Another factor that has influenced schools during this recent period
is the American passion for education. We are a people who look to the
schools for everything—vocational preparation, development of citizenship, self-understanding, ability to get along with people, morals, and so
on. During this period the unsettling effect of both the rapid change in
knowledge and the challenging of established values has made parents
even more dependent than before upon the schools. Much of what home
and church formerly felt responsible for now falls upon the school. The
burden has proved excessive and the expectations unrealistic.

The decided increase in the amount and variety of informal education
which children have been given represents still another factor. Many have
learned much more than any previous generation from mass communication and from travel. They come to school informed and sophisticated. They are far from *tabula rasa* beings upon whom the school can
imprint an education. Furthermore, what they have thus learned often
seems more recent and meaningful than what the school offers them.
They are often unmotivated for formal education by the amount and
nature of their informal education. Aye, that's the rub—where does the
school fit into their "education"?

All of these "perspective" factors undoubtedly will influence the
future; it is not likely that enrollment numbers will grow much less, for
although currently the birth rate is low the record shows a steady
increase in the proportion attending schools and colleges; the flood of
new information that quickly makes texts and teacher preparation
obsolete will doubtless increase, along with more stress to decide what
kinds of information and experiences are important. Along with these,
the American tendency to expect more and more of schools and to
expect each generation to increase the numbers of years spent in school
may grow less, but paradoxically, only if education out of school continues to be more seemingly relevant than education in school. It would
seem that the schools of America are in serious trouble—they have
competition.

Recourse to a perspective in the area of higher education invokes some
striking memories. Forgotten by now is the influx of veterans on campus
that jammed all facilities just following World War II. This memory dims
because of the more recent vivid experience of enrollments which
climbed to over 7 million in the 1960's and to 8.5 million by 1971. The
overwhelming immediacy and magnitude of the Vietnam War dims our
recollection of the disruption of college life by the Korean War. College

students in the 1950's were called complacent and passive, a characterization that was seldom used in the 1960's! Not yet forgotten are the thousands of new campus buildings and billions of education dollars that were made possible in large part by grants from the Federal government.

The end of the last decade and the beginning of the 1970's was a stormy period on college and university campuses, marked by many student demonstrations, burned buildings, and lost lives. Violence on the part of students and pseudostudents was met with counterviolence upon the part of "the authorities." College administrators often appeared bewildered and inept. Clashes occurred over a complex of issues: the Vietnam war in general, the draft, racial conflict and apparent discrimination, local college regulations long resented but heretofore endured. Often the students themselves were unable to differentiate among these various factors and to specify how the college was at fault. On university campuses in particular there developed a smoldering resentment against faculty preoccupation with government-sponsored research and the faculties' indifference to students. Much of the research was directly or indirectly related to the military and to the conduct of the hated Vietnam war—which added fuel to the flames of some ROTC (Reserve Officers Training Corps) buildings.

The precipitating cause of a demonstration was often trivial or un-related to predisposing factors. It became clear as the demonstrations developed that one basic predisposing factor was resentment against the "authoritarian attitude" of the college or university and the administration's apparent indifference to those matters which seemed important to students. A contravening factor also became clear. The demonstrators were often stimulated by nonstudents who represented organizations opposed to the authority of society in general. The university was merely a convenient and rather defenseless symbol of this authority.

The colleges and universities responded to the protests—and are still responding—with some seemingly desirable changes. Residence hall regulations were eased or abolished. Students were not only included in general policy making but were often given jurisdiction over the regulation of social life on the campus. Coeducational residence halls, pass-fail grading, reduction of uniform graduation requirements, screening of government research contracts, voluntary rather than compulsory ROTC —all of these developments were direct outgrowths of student demonstrations. Some of them would have been made anyway but student action speeded up the process of change. Sometimes the concessions were made reluctantly and with faculty and staff far from united about the changes, but made they were. And there are more to come.

One additional point should be made clear, student protests occurred in high schools as well as in colleges. The majority of inner city high schools experienced turmoil in the form of protests or strikes. These were most often against school regulations or discriminations; few were expressions of resentment on social issues. The fact that they occurred at all is significant—youth who in mid-adolescence are still living at home have little freedom to develop organized protests. The explanation of this unanticipated reaction of high school students must lie in the protest "spirit of the times" or in the increasing unreality of the school's program; likely it is a combination of the two.

Some Critical Decisions for Schools

It is becoming increasingly apparent that "education" and "schools" are not synonymous terms. That learning is more inclusive than schooling, that it is as inclusive as life itself, has always been easy to see. Now much "education," planned and labeled as such, is to be found outside of schools: education via TV, films, camps, extension and correspondence courses given by nonschool agencies, and educational programs within industry. David Bazelon (Professor of Policy Sciences at Buffalo) writes: "Here is a fact to keep you awake nights: today in the United States a young person leaves high school having spent 15,000 hours in classrooms and 18,000 hours staring at television" (*Change,* May-June 1971, p. 46). This is indeed a startling ratio. It is mandatory that school people understand the magnitude of the education that takes place out of school settings. This phenomenon is not restricted to the United States alone. In France, for example, where tens of thousands of *lycee* (secondary school) students staged hunger strikes, occupied buildings, and fought police, the Minister of Education Guichard commented: "Fifty years ago, four-fifths of teen-agers' knowledge was acquired by lycee teachers. Today, four-fifths of what they know comes from other sources—television, movies, newspapers, teen-age magazines."

Ivan Illich's new book, *De-Schooling Society* (see chapter references), involves a radical concept which the title only suggests. More explicitly stated as "The De-Schooling of Education" the question becomes: will schools remain?

I am sure that the mere thought that schools are waning in their influence and are facing vigorous educational competition will appear shocking, even "subversive" to many readers. Most school personnel are too close to the assumptions and ideals of schools to discern their weaknesses and are also aware of the efforts to improve schools. Yet some leading critics, to use as examples Illich (a former Catholic priest

who heads up a free university at Cuernavaco, Mexico), Elliot Richardson (the current—1972—Secretary of the U. S. Department of Health,
Education and Welfare), and Robert Hutchins (former President of the
University of Chicago and currently head of the liberal Center for the
Study of Democratic Institutions at Santa Barbara), think the change is
not rapid enough. To them education in the United States has become
too completely institutionalized. The "educated" are restricted to those
who are taught in small groups by certified teachers, who for a certain
number of hours per day and a specified number of years, take courses
prepared by educators. All of this is directed toward the goal of completing specified graduation requirements. Illich is very pointed in
believing that all schools have a "hidden curriculum." From this curriculum "students learn that education is valuable when required in the
school through a graded process of instruction; that the degree of
success the individual will enjoy in society depends upon the amount of
learning he consumes; and that learning *about* the world is more valuable
than learning *from* the world."

"Universal" education under these conditions is not universal at all
since smaller and smaller numbers complete each successive level in the
system. Because the requirements are the same for all it is likely that
only smaller numbers can complete the successively higher standards.
Beyond this, attainment of these institutionalized school requirements
becomes the only currency with which youth can buy access to jobs and
the earning of a livelihood. Richardson (HEW) decries this concept of
education as "investment" saying that education as "preparation for
life" has become merely "preparation for making a living." Education
has become training. Conceiving of education as investment, writes
Richardson, classifies it with all other investments where the enjoyment
of consumption is deferred. We should have on hand a "consumption"
theory associated with an immediate sense of enjoyment.

Learning is our basic concern, not education or training. If we are to
become a "learning society," says Hutchins, we must deinstitutionalize
education and let other agents have free access to the learning potential
of the individual.

So write some of our critics and it is probably more than coincidence
that they echo what many youth are saying. The reply may be made,
"There have always been critics of the school and yet the school persists."
This has been true, but there is a new element in the current scene.
What is questioned at this time is not what schools do but whether or
not schools should *exist* if they continue to assume that education is
synonymous with schooling. (As my wife typed these pages she said that
what I had written both irritated and upset her. She and I are of the

same generation, only two months apart in age. Why do my ideas bother her? My citing of the criticisms of a personally experienced and loved institution is painful to her. Perhaps I have been through the painful stages and she as yet has not. The goal of criticism is to leave the person criticized with the feeling that he has been helped. In my criticism of schools and school people, I may not have achieved that goal.)

What is called for, it seems to me, is the recognition by schools that sources of learning other than themselves exist, and that these provide valid learning experiences. How can the school *complement,* not ignore, these other learning sources? How can schools provide more varied ways of learning, provide experience in living, not ideas about life? This might mean not only offering more school content that is contemporary but also requiring less learning time in the school itself. More hours, more years, of formal education tend to reduce the amount of time available for learning from all other experiences, useful experiences and "educational" experiences. In addition more formal education, more hours in school, may result in further disillusionment of students and a greater estrangement of the schools from society.

I hope that schools (and here I mean teachers and counselors) will do something to relieve the continuing frustration of adolescents. In our highly organized society schools contribute far too much to the discontinuities between biological life stages and cultural life stages. We postpone gratification of needs at the various stages of normal life-stage needs to an incredible degree. Everything is designed to prepare for the future which to youth seems as if it will never arrive. Entry into marriage, into vocational life, into a sense of being accepted as "grown up," into a satisfying sense of identity, all are frustrated by being "kept in school," restraining and delaying satisfaction. It is true that these discontinuities between readiness and realization are a part of our total society, but youth sees the school as the major restraining influence. In this manner the school harms the youth, builds in him a bitterness. As a consequence too many youths view compulsory education as similar to the compulsory draft.

In a recent issue of *The Counseling Psychologist* (Nov. 4, 1971) Moser and Sprinthall quote a professor of clinical medicine as concluding from his study of several hundred drug-addicted youth that compulsory education was heavily responsible for their addiction. They hated school so much they saw it as their jail. First they attempted to destroy it and then to escape it through drugs. These are unpleasant thoughts and some readers will think they are too extreme. Even though we do not change the compulsory education system, counselors and teachers *can* give students more immediate satisfactions, can have students engage in activities that meet immediate developmental needs, can acknowledge and share their nonschool satisfactions, and can reduce the discontinuities. Were I a teacher today I would have a heavy conscience if I saw myself glossing over the gap between the nature of youth and the nature of schools. Somewhere I have seen the rather bitter comment, "If God had really understood what schools would be like, he would have made children different."

All of this is not to say that educators are unaware of the need for change (witness the hard-hitting book by educators Neil Postman and Charles Weingartner, *Teaching as a Subversive Activity,* see chapter references). Much is being conceived in the way of change; a little less is being done. The question is, can enough be done before critical reaction crystallizes still further?

One of the most far-reaching legal decisions of the past few decades was the recent ruling by the California Supreme Court that to depend upon local property taxes for the support of schools violates the equal protection clause of the Fourteenth Amendment to the U. S. Constitution. The ruling reads that such school support "invidiously discriminates against the poor because it makes the quality of a child's education a function of the wealth of his parents and neighbors." One case cited in the argument was that of a wealthy suburb of Los Angeles that needs to tax itself at the rate of only 2.38 percent to provide $1,231.71 worth of education for each child, while another, poorer suburb taxed itself at the rate of 5.48 percent to provide $577.49 worth of schooling for each of its children. By early 1972 three other states had followed California's lead. If this ruling is upheld by the U. S. Supreme Court and pooled state or Federal taxes become the basis of school support, we will have taken a giant step forward toward equal opportunity of education. What will the schools do with this golden opportunity? Will more money for the less affluent schools merely mean "more of the same"?

Another outcome of these court decisions may be the inability of state governments solely to finance local education and the tendency then to turn to the Federal government for the money. What the states won't do, the Federal government will have to do. One wonders what may happen in the next decade or two to the whole question of the sovereignty of the 50 states. They were established as "independent" states within the Republic under social conditions that no longer prevail today. The postpioneer, postindustrial, highly mobile and mass-communicating conditions of today may speak for far less state sovereignty. Will schools then become more Federalized?

I will comment later upon what I think might be the developments within the field of psychology during the next decade. I believe that during this period formal education will see more drastic change than psychology. "Surely," you say, "a science changes more rapidly than does a social institution!" Perhaps so, but the social pressure for change upon both schools and colleges will be greater than upon psychology because *the average school curriculum* (the total of school experience) is further from social reality than is the practice of psychology. Schools will make the changes or society will act. Schools will not be wrecked—they will simply become less and less significant for all ages and will be replaced by other influences. They will expire slowly, "not with a bang but a whimper."

Changes Taking Place in Schools

Networks. Perhaps I am giving undue attention to the criticisms. Changes are being made—significant changes in both structure and process. Not only are numerous individual schools experimenting with innovative changes, but also several models have been developed for a network of schools to work cooperatively. The Model Schools Project of the National Association of Secondary Schools is one of the more ambitious programs, involving 35 schools in all parts of the country. The model makes provisions for five basic changes to take place in each school: (1) for the school principal to devote about three-fourths of his working time to the improvement of instruction; (2) for teachers to have the help of various clerks and instructional assistants, to have about two-thirds of the school day to prepare and improve evaluations, and to serve as counselor to 30 to 35 pupils; (3) for the pupil's day to be spent primarily in "informal, planned learning environments," in and out of school, which are not under the constant supervision of the teacher; (4) for the innovative curriculum to draw more "from the real world that the pupil knows rather than the adult world of the teacher"; (5) for buildings, equipment, and supplies to be directly related to the objectives of instruction. This model makes drastic changes indeed!

Other "networks" reported in *The Journal of Secondary Education* (April 1971) are: The League of Cooperating Schools, An Educational System for the 70's, and Project PLAN (Program for Learning in Accordance with Needs).

This last project, with which I have had some contact as an *ad hoc* consultant, had its initial tryout in 1967 with 2,000 students of three grades in 12 school districts. By 1970 40,000 students in grades 1 through 12 were involved. The model is based on a system of individualized units of learning completed by each student at his own pace. A unit is given to a student on the basis of tests of his present knowledge in a given area and his educational objectives. He is guided individually by a teacher; tested individually; and goes on to the next unit after having had success with the earlier one. The significant elements of the model are: (1) determination of educational objectives in the four areas of language arts, social studies, mathematics, and science; (2) selection of learning materials and methods; (3) evaluation of student progress; (4) guidance and individual planning of each pupil for both immediate and long-term goals; (5) a program of teacher development.

It is clear that the role of the teacher in all of these models is quite different than that of the teacher in the traditional classroom model. Richardson writes of the present teacher role in indignant terms: "How extraordinary, how absurd, that we have fostered this—what?—this rigorous toilet training of the mind, expecting our teachers to be disciplinarians, force-feeders, almost anything but teachers in a grim and relentless process of getting our children through their school years!" We "produce" graduates, using assembly line concepts. Richardson's four goals of education assume quite different concepts of teaching: to maintain the curiosity of a child throughout his formal education and to awaken it when it slumbers; to build self-confidence in each student; to cultivate a love of learning; to develop competence according to each person's ability. These goals fit well into the network models.

Schools. In the literature can be found exciting descriptions of individual schools that are creating a new atmosphere of learning for their pupils. For example, the John Adams High School in Portland, Oregon, was described in *Phi Delta Kappan* (May 1971) as "a school where students and teachers from different backgrounds could work together toward common goals in an atmosphere of freedom and trust." This objective has an idealistic ring to it, but after the first two years of operation there is ample evidence that the goal is realistic too. The concept of freedom to work is rated high by both teachers and students as the most distinctive characteristic of the school. Not everything has worked, of course, and there is "freedom" also in admitting this. But those most desired qualities of student responsibility and a positive student-teacher relationship seem to dominate the scene.

Or take a look at Wilde Lake Middle School, Columbia, Maryland (*Time,* June 21, 1971), where freedom is present to a high degree and where originality is the order of the day. The curriculum is organized; there is not complete permissiveness; tests are given regularly; but the freedom to think and perform in one's own style is again dominant. Competence? During each of the past two years Wilde Lake's students have outscored students in all of the country's other middle schools on standardized tests.

A different example is the Up With People High School. This is a mobile high school that serves the educational needs of the youth singing groups called Up With People. It is an accredited high school of the Tulsa, Oklahoma school system which combines "formal" education with all of the learning experience of constant travel and public appearances. Last year the school traveled approximately 1,500 miles a month. Its juniors and seniors stay in 50 different homes a year. In 1970 60 students graduated from this high school, two of them as National Merit finalists.

Behavior Today (June 21, 1971) reports that students from six Tacoma, Washington elementary and high schools would return to a varied school year of experimental opportunities including work experience and foreign travel for senior high school students. To graduate from high school the student must prove that he has held down a job. The Palo Alto, California High School District has some 500 students enrolled in an Exploratory Experience course involving more than 100 industries and offices. The Kinkaid School in Houston, Texas, has a similar "Career Research Laboratory" offered in both the regular school term and their Interim Term. (I have some comments later on this question of school and job experience.)

Packages. The use of "curriculum packages" or "instructional packages" contributes to the individualization of learning. These provide a carefully developed form of self-paced learning. The "package," whether commercially purchased or homemade, is a unit of learning, complete (ideally) with behaviorally stated objectives, varied learning activities (or content), indication of outside resources and aids available, tests of progress, and suggestions for futher activities in depth. It is designed for a student who is "ready" for this particular unit and who will develop a sense of achievement by exposure to it. It is personalized instruction to a high degree. Teachers become instructional managers and learning diagnosticians. This is the core of the previously described Project PLAN.

An extension of the package concept is EVR—Electronic Video Recording. Someone has termed the educational potential of EVR as providing "A Teacher in a Cartridge" (*Change,* Jan.–Feb. 1971, p. 40). The EVR cartridge stores pictures with sound for playback through a standard television set. This is a development over which Marshall McLuhan and Alvin Toffler would grow lyrical. The contents of the entire *Encyclopaedia Britannica,* for example, can be stored in a single cartridge and priced under $15.00. For sets such as this or for books, a device has been perfected that enables the viewer quickly to find a given page. Although few "educational" cartridges have been developed as yet, expansion in this direction could be very rapid. The University of West Virginia is experimenting with a mathematics teaching program which employs these same audiovideo tape concepts. In their study the students participate in the making of the tape and may make their own tapes for review purposes. This element of student participation has a marked learning advantage over the prepared commercial cartridges, which tempt the viewer to be a passive learner. There is little doubt, however, that schools and homes will soon have libraries of such tapes for class and individual use, for "education" and "recreation." Perhaps these two experiences will not be quite so far apart in this new learning world!

In general the teaching-learning trends that appear to be on the move in education incorporate such general principles as: an individualized learning experience in which the pupil initiates what he wants to learn and at what pace; a new teacher role as facilitator rather than director of the learning process; teacher-student relationships in which there is less teacher threat and more teacher help; teacher encouragement of peer to peer learning; more utilization of technological aids to learning; more freedom of personal movement in the school and less directed movement.

Michael Marion pulls these trends together in what he terms a basic, long-term trend in education (*The Futurist*, December 1970, published by the World Future Society, P. O. Box 30369, Bethesda Branch, Washington, D.C. 20014). His anticipation is of movement from "closed teaching systems" to "open learning systems." This distinction is illustrated by Marion with some 40 to 50 goals, learning concepts, curriculum objectives, etc. Excerpts from his chart will make his main point clear.

FROM CLOSED TEACHING SYSTEMS	TO OPEN LEARNING SYSTEMS
Learning requires discipline, work, drill, memorization, pain control	Learning is enjoyable, follows from pursuit of interests
Teacher as source of knowledge, student as passive absorber	Learning from many sources, including peers; student as active participant
Curriculum is narrow, fixed, retrospective. Classics, Principles, Truth, facts, deduction, Maxims	Curriculum is broad, changing, present and future-oriented. Methods, principles, induction, creativity, intuition, randomness

FROM CLOSED TEACHING SYSTEMS *(continued)*	TO OPEN LEARNING SYSTEMS *(continued)*
Curriculum is programmatic, sequential; Lesson plans strictly followed	Curriculum is interchangeable pro-grammettes, Modular learning; Lesson plan as guide to options
Teacher as Authority, student as follower; control as instrumental technique	Professional as Learning Facilitator or Senior Learner; student as junior colleague
Compulsory attendance; no choice of institution	Optional participation; alternatives offered
Dropping out is fault of student; shaming for ignorance	Many possible sources of failure; environmental, institutional and individual
The Goal is getting an education, being educated, terminal education	The Goal is learning how to learn, lifelong learning, education as a beginning

H. B. Gelatt stated the case succinctly in two quotations: " 'If you give a man a fish—you feed him for one day. If you teach him how to catch a fish—you feed him for a lifetime.' Or to put it another way: '. . . we are giving our young people cut flowers when we should be teaching them how to grow their own plants.' " ("Confronting the Status Quo," *Focus on Guidance*, October 1971, p. 2.)

REFLECTIONS ON HIGHER EDUCATION

The word "reflections" was chosen deliberately. There is so much change and so much uncertainty in our vast complex of more than 2,500 colleges and universities that I question my ability to identify trends. Public reaction which is more prominent here than at lower levels of education, complicates one's assessment.

The public is critical, that much is certain. A 1971 Special Report by the Editorial Projects for Education carried the title *Are Americans Losing Faith in Their Colleges?* The editors of the report comment that five years ago such a question would have been absurd; today it is highly relevant. A personal experience carried the same theme when I took part at the University of Hawaii (summer of 1971) in a symposium which bore the almost insulting title, "Can the University Be Guided Out of the Middle Ages?" An entire issue of *The Humanist* (September 1970) is devoted to the topic, *Does the University Have a Future?* In that issue Jacques Barzun bears down fully as hard upon the university as does

Ivan Illich on the secondary school. "If we had a coroner on the scene he would readily pronounce the American University dead, and if he were astute he would call it a suicide rather than murder by persons unknown." Noam Chomsky believes that universities are fully responsible for their ordeal of student protests and demonstrations because their arbitrariness encourages confrontations. Sidney Hook, on the other hand, blames universities for policies of appeasement when dealing with student extremists. Still he writes that, as a consequence "colleges and universities today face the gravest crisis in their history."

Other questions are raised in connection with the wealth of informal education that is available throughout life. Will the liberal-arts function of higher education ever be as distinctive as before? Some are sure that the university must divert its emphasis from vocational specialization. One career for a lifetime is not viable; one cannot define himself by his profession or educate himself for life by preparing for that profession. It has been said, "People are working smaller and smaller portions of their longer and longer lives."

A few large issues are clear:

1. The college or university must decide whether it is to be a *student* of political and social change and therefore remain neutral and objective, or whether it is to be an *agent* of change and take stands on social and political issues. There are impassioned arguments in the literature for each position. If I argue that the university has its greatest influence as a detached, noninvolved "student" of social issues, I deny students the great advantage that results from their becoming involved in these same social issues, of having learning experiences *in* the world of reality rather than from *outside* it. Can a university compromise in these matters? Can it "eat its cake and have it too?" President James Robinson of Macalester College says that his college can: "Across this divided country, one voice urges colleges and universities to limit their exertions to the acquisition and transmission of knowledge—to divorce their efforts from such contemporary issues as war, racism, and pollution. Another voice urges colleges to act upon the basis of feeling rather than knowledge, to become involved. . . . These alternative formulations . . . are an apparition, not a choice. Macalester College has long been dedicated to the symbiotic goals of scholarship and service, science and society, knowledge and policy." Perhaps Macalester College can continue these combinations but such a policy is likely to stir up some discussion among students, faculty, and the board of trustees.

2. Should students participate in the governance of their college or university? If so, to what extent—a token participation or a substantial responsibility? If given such responsibility, will students have time and

continuing motivation to take it as seriously as do the continuing staff or faculty? (The proponents of participation would reply immediately by saying, "Of course only some students will work at it just as only some faculty are willing to devote time and thought to policy-making!") If students are not allowed to contribute to governance how does the college avoid the highly objectionable *in loco parentis* stance?

3. Will private colleges and universities survive financially without becoming elitist institutions which only students of certain economic levels can attend? Will public universities get enough financial support to enable them to avoid an increasingly selective admission policy meant to keep the numbers down? The financial magnitude of the total operation of higher education in the United States is staggering: a physical plant investment of $38 billion, annual operating cost of $14 billion, involving about 10 million people directly—students, faculty, and staff. When there are financial headaches in this kind of an operation the money shortage is seen in hundreds of millions and the people involved in hundreds of thousands. College consultant Paul H. Davis drew this comment from an anonymous educator:

> Higher education will most probably undergo a marked reconstruction during the next ten or fifteen years. In this reconstruction two marked points of change will be reduction of the influence of the independent liberal arts colleges and reduction in line with current trends of the importance of privately supported higher education. . . .
>
> The function of the liberal arts college as a provider of general education for all, even if the faculties were willing so to define their function, is being cut into at several points: A. The high schools have absorbed much of the work previously given in the freshman year of college. B. Professional schools have been tending to shorten the period of training required, notably medicine, and the shortening has meant a reduction in the liberal arts component. C. Professional schools are tending to give work in supporting academic disciplines which previously was given by the colleges of arts and science. D. Community colleges as you (Paul Davis) suggest are working hard to provide a program that includes essential liberal studies and in many instances succeeding very well. E. The cost of higher education as you well know is at a level which pushes to get the student into productive work at an earlier age. This is another powerful factor to shorten exclusive programs of liberal education and encourage a mixture of liberal and professional goals.

One major change is widespread. This involves the rapid increase in the number of two-year post-high school institutions, often called "junior colleges." There were over 1,000 public and private junior colleges in the United States in 1970. Frank Jennings (The Two-Year Stretch" in *Change,* March 1970) predicts that there will be 500 more junior colleges established by 1975. He states that the two-

year colleges now enroll more than half of all the students in higher
education." He must mean freshmen, for the 1970 junior college enrollment was only 2,440,000 out of a total college enrollment of 8.5
million, but even so, this is a move of massive proportions. Jennings
comments that junior colleges "are the surest growth stock on the
educational exchange." The age of the students ranges widely although
as yet the majority are recent high school graduates. Just as there is a
great variety of types of institutions, from elaborate campuses to down-
town store-fronts, there is a wide variety in the motivations of students.
Some, perhaps a third, come with serious intentions of graduating and
transferring to a four-year institution. Most, though, come for vocational
preparation at a post-high school that offers less academically than a
B.A. program. Many of these are "the emerging students," those who in
the past would not have chosen higher education and those who could
not afford to go to four-year colleges.

This strong vocational thrust worries some commentators of the scene.
Will there be adequate counseling help available? An experienced junior
college administrator, Johnnie Ruth Clark, proposes that "career counseling and guidance may by the most important function the school may
provide for some emerging students." As a detached but penetrating
observer, David Riesman comments that both society and the students
would be better off if after high school it became general practice to
enter some form of employment or voluntary service and to expect
further education only as an adult. He believes that too many "emerging
students" are "neither mature enough nor eager enough to profit from
college." Others would reply that the junior college must be flexible in
its program to care for "academically unmotivated" students—that many
young people would be continuously unemployed without this type of
specific vocational preparation.

In a chapter just written for another book (Henry Borow, ed., *Career
Guidance for a New Age*, see References Chapter XI), I express a
concern that is similar to David Riesman's reservation about this continuing build-up of education.

> Many rejoice at this wealth of education but I have a caveat. Education through-
> out life, yes, but 14 years at a continuous stretch for all, no. I have no doubt
> that each succeeding generation will get more schooling or at least more edu-
> cation from various sources. This will not be a luxury but a necessity in a world
> of rapidly expanding knowledge and increasing social complexity. However, I
> plead for staggered education, short periods of it at intervals throughout 60 or
> 70 years of life. We have not really become accustomed to the continued
> schooling of adults, but we will. Adults have been educating themselves for a
> long time, but I speak here of planned, formal periods of education, often in a
> school or college, perhaps soon by television and other decentralized means. . . .

For both adequate motivation and a sense of realism in life I propose alternating periods of educational and occupational experience. I would wish that millions of those entering junior college immediately after high school would taste the occupational world instead. One to five years experience in an occupation would diversify and broaden personality development much more than would continued education. When the student returned to school his motivation would be sounder, he would want to acquire knowledge in certain areas. . . .

Failing to stem the drive "to stay in school as long as you can" I would hope for a healthy improvement in cooperative vocational education and in other work-study educational opportunities. Any school or junior college could build such community-centered programs if it took the initiative to get in touch with the local occupational world. If there were too few paid jobs for youth, then non-paid apprenticeships, or internships in occupational experience could be developed. I have a feeling that many employers in the community would be flattered to find that experience in their occupation or business was considered an essential part of a young person's education.

This may be a dream, I know, education for education's sake still holds a favored spot in the value structure of many in our society. But I can dream that some day a better bridge will be built between education and occupation, to support the personal development and career adjustment of individuals.

Too much will be expected of the junior college just as too much was expected of the junior high school and senior high school. We will load it with too many community functions. But here is where I make a distinction between the "junior college" seen as just that (the first two years of collegiate education) and the "community college" which may serve that function but is geared to serve many other community needs at the adolescent, young adult, and adult levels. A community college does not establish itself by being "proudly academic" but by gaining support and gratitude from different segments of the total community. Much that is socially significant can be legitimately expected of community colleges. And some of them, perhaps most, will produce well.

Arthur Cohen and Florence Brawer are the co-authors of two recent books on the community college—*Confronting Identity* and *A Constant Variable* (intriguing titles!). They provide a briefer statement of this identity crisis (*Change*, Winter 1971–72, pp. 55–59) which shows that this fairly recent arrival on the educational scene is, although fumbling, a lusty youngster indeed. A decade ago Clark Kerr described the "multiversity" as the King of the educational jungle. It just could be that the community college represents the brawny young male of the tribe, eager to challenge the battered and aging chief!

Other developments to be anticipated:

1. Already some four-year private colleges have "gone under" financially and more will—perhaps scores or even hundreds. The Carnegie Commission staff estimated that in 1971 two-thirds of the nation's

colleges and universities were either in financial trouble or headed for it.

This same commission report predicted a "stop-go" sequence in enrollment. College and university enrollment doubled between 1960 and 1970; it will increase only 50 percent during the 1970–80 decade; it will have a zero increase during 1980–90 but it will make a one-third increase between 1990 and 2000. This will mean that by the end of the century about 50 percent of those of college age (75 percent of high school graduates) will enroll in college. The "breathing spell" of 1970–1990 could mean that colleges will increase the *quality* (relevance, depth, and personal significance) of college education.

2. The colleges that survive will provide more freedom of choice, more alternatives to choose from, more contact in the curriculum with off-campus realities, fewer fixed requirements that apply to all, opportunity for learning without the external pressure of letter grades. Such colleges will also continue the loosening of social and residence regulations or they will see their students living in apartments on the perimeter of the campus and away from "parental" influence. Many other innovative measures will be tried. The Interim Term is well established, the three-year bachelor's degree is not (England has had this for centuries). All moves will be to lessen two kinds of pressures, financial and regulatory.

3. Universities will change in many ways as yet unknown. Graduate school enrollment is currently decreasing. Will that continue or will the graduate pattern change? Will "open universities" develop, requiring no set campus but using parts of existing campuses, television, and correspondence? (The Union Graduate School is now an "open" institution using short intensive seminars, consultants from many campuses, and much independent study and responsibility.) A national open university is projected by Lawrence Dennis, Provost of the Massachusetts state educational system which will open its own "University of the Commonwealth" in 1972.

Views of the future were given at a recent conference of the American Association for Higher Education by such significant leaders in the field as Samuel B. Gould and Clark Kerr. "Within 15 years you won't recognize the American University as we know it today," said Gould. "Twenty-five years from now one out of every two adults will be involved in the educational process as a teacher or learner, or, more probably, as both" (reported in *Chronicle of Higher Education,* March 22, 1971.) Clark Kerr predicted continued tensions in higher education for at least the next three decades and continuation of a poor job market for college graduates. By mid-1971 over 50,000 PhD's were unemployed or employed out of their field and level of preparation.

As earlier stated, almost 100,000 professional workers were "unemployed" in the aeronautic and aerospace fields alone.

Perhaps it is unkind to end our discussion of education on such a negative note and yet it is negative only if interpreted in terms of what we have now and hope to continue to have. Much of our present and of our nostalgic past will not be continued in even the near future. Much that is new, however, and might be even "better," could leave us hopeful and optimistic. President John Schwada of Arizona State University proposes the possibility of a compromise between a "liberal" education and preparation for a vocation. He suggests, "What is required is a general education which broadens the world and the vision of the individual, and which concurrently provides career and professional training." This is entirely possible, says Schwada, if students are given reasonable choices and some counseling help during their early years in college. In many respects exponents of higher education are seriously examining alternatives to the traditional—by defining liberal arts in terms of relevance, by acknowledging the public accountability of both faculty and administration, by permitting more freedom of choice for students, by admitting students to policy problems that apply to the entire academic community. I am hopeful; only I am wondering whether changes will occur rapidly enough to restore public confidence and support before institutions are seriously damaged.

SOME TRENDS IN PSYCHOLOGY

Unity of Mind and Body

One of the most significant developments of this decade is the appearance of new conclusions relating to the ancient mind-body issue. A dichotomy of the two is traditional and appealing but it is too simplistic and increasingly unrealistic. Gardner Murphy seems to have taken one of the broadest looks at what may be developing in the field of psychology ("Psychology in the Year 2000," *American Psychologist,* May 1969). In making what he believes to be "a systematic and reasonable extrapolation from identifiable trends . . ." he finds that five out of ten trends relate to psychology's growing concern with the unity of the human organism.

1. *Psychophysiology.* Murphy foresees within the next few decades "a thoroughgoing isomorphism (convergence) of physiological process and psychological process right across the board." This includes psycho-

pharmacology which has at its command the initiation of hundreds of new psychological experiences by chemical additions to the body.

2. *Internal scanning.* The identification of messages from the world of reflex, involuntary muscle action, the development of a capacity to observe objectively what has been considered as involuntary and beyond conscious understanding.

3. *Direct confrontation of the unconscious.* An increased understanding of the inner world of affect and impulse both through direct experience and experimentation.

4. *Voluntary control over the inner world.* A mastering through conditioning of the "autonomic" nervous system.

5. *Psychology and biology.* An awareness of biological growth potential which can be modified by new psychological environments as well as new psychological beings made possible by genetic selection.

Murphy writes that "the twenty-first century can offer less terror and more joy, but only if psychologists have learned both *how to look inside* and *how to look outside;* how to recognize the reciprocities of inner and outer. . . ."

Two trends that have the support of current evidence are "internal scannings" and "voluntary control." Peter Lang, in an article entitled "Autonomic Control or Learning to Play the Internal Organs" (*Psychology Today,* October 1970) initiates his account of the history of internal scanning and of voluntary control by explaining one method Houdini used to escape from his chains. He had mastered his gag reflex and was able to hold a key suspended in his throat. When no one was looking he just coughed up his means of escape!

The Russians pioneered the research on voluntary control. Luria has reported a man who could slow his own heartrate and raise the temperature of one hand while simultaneously lowering the temperature of the other simply by imagining one hand was near heat while the other was exposed to extreme cold. Then in 1958 another Russian psychologist, M. I. Lisina, reported success in training subjects to dilate and constrict blood vessels in order to avoid painful stimuli. She was unsuccessful in this attempt until subjects were allowed to monitor their own vascular responses. With this feedback system they were successful.

Lang in 1962 "built an apparatus that allowed a subject to 'drive' his own heart." Again utilizing feedback, this apparatus was similar to the driving skill booths in penny arcades. The subject could watch a spot of light on a screen. Movement to the right indicated slower beats, to the left indicated faster beats. With practice the subject became quite skillful in "driving" his heart down the middle of a narrow road—955 to 1,045 milliseconds wide. Shock avoidance and other indirect incentives were necessary. Success was its own reward. Indians practicing Yoga can slow the heart rate materially, apparently by controlling chest muscles used in breathing. This did not seem to be essential to subjects trained by Lang and his associates—they could control the heart rate directly.

In 1968 Joseph Kamiya reported that his subjects could control their brain waves—notably the alpha wave. When individuals were presented with a 400-cycle tone upon spontaneous emissions of the alpha, they learned to *produce* this particular brain wave. The implications are immense. If one can condition things as autonomic as brain waves and heartbeat then it follows that other parts of the autonomic nervous system can be controlled. The day may come when the physical symptoms of anxiety and emotional disturbance can be reduced voluntarily without the aid of tranquilizing drugs or intervention in the form of psychotherapy.

This beginning of control portends the reunion of mind and body. The neat dichotomy of voluntary and involuntary responses is out of the window. New victims of high blood pressure, irregular heartbeat, asthma, etc. may be "taught" to control these functions voluntarily. Already there has been some success with epileptics who have been conditioned to alter the brain patterns that usually precede seizure.

Another implication of alpha wave control is found in what are called mind-control classes, now offered in 40 states and developed over many years by Jose Silva. Voluntary entrance into the alpha state enables one to project himself outside of his body in what is called "affective sensory projection." The claim is that you can enter the body of another person or into a situation removed from you and both read and influence the person or situation. This sounds fantastic and unbelievable but it is one of the popular accounts within this area of sensory control.

An interesting inference is drawn from the Kamiya data by the humanist Abraham Maslow. Under a heading "The Mind-Body Correlation" (*American Psychologist,* August 1969) Maslow draws attention to Kamiya's finding that the alpha brain waves produced by operant conditioning result in a psychological state of serenity and meditativeness. He likens this to the serenity sought by those who follow the way of Eastern mysticism, Yoga, or Taoism for example. Some confirmation of this is found in the fact that those who achieve a state of serenity through meditation emit the same pattern of brain waves as those induced in Kamiya's subjects. Thus it seems possible to train oneself to bring about a bodily condition (the emission of alpha waves) which is accompanied by a psychological state of what might be called happiness (serenity).

In the same issue of *Psychology Today* with Peter Lang's article there is something old and something new on the mind-body issue. The "something old" picks up the long-standing question of a relationship between body build and personality. Going back to Lombroso and his physical stigmata of the criminal, up through Kretchmer to Sheldon, the evidence has been long argued but always suspect. Cortés and Gatti use Sheldon's definitions of three body types—endomorph (round, fat), ectomorph (tall, thin), and in the middle the mesomorph (athletic and muscular)—but then make a more objective temperament-rating scheme than that used by Sheldon. The authors report some well-validated body-personality relationships involving delinquency, sex drive, and male-female differences. One's confidence in their research is encouraged by their modesty in evaluating the importance of their findings. They say: "Body build is a relevant factor in many variables of personality. . . . However, physique is merely one factor and many others are very relevant. . . . If we deal mainly with some biological and constitutional aspects, it is . . . not because we consider them all-important or the most basic."

The "something new" includes two reports by Sam Keen on what he terms "counter therapies," using the body rather than the mind in therapy. The result is improvement in the joy of living of the *total* person in which body and mind are one. His vivid account of a personal experience with structural integration leaves the reader tingling with a bit of the exhilaration Keen experienced.

The separation of man's mind and body has been assumed and "practiced" for centuries. We seem to be entering a period when this separation is being attacked as artificial. Sydney Harris states the situation in lively language: "This artificial split, inspired by the arrogance of medieval ascetics, has been institutionalized by the learned professions. Medicine repairs the visible parts; priests, teachers, and the uplift tradesmen tend the invisible side." He goes on to say there is now new hope of an acceptance of mind-body unity. "This important new thrust promises a sounder view of man and leads away from the medical notion of man as a maze of plumbing that comes with or without a cognitive attachment" (*Psychology Today* Symposium, October 1970).

The implications of this development for counselors are found in the Harris statement. If a counselor deals only with cognition or even with emotion he is as much out of touch with reality as is the physician who has a "plumbing" concept of the human being. No one expects counselors to condition alpha waves or heartbeat or to teach students to become Houdinis. The important thing is to know that the body is involved or could become involved in any "mental" decision or even value determination. Most counselors accept, I believe, the indivisibility of cognition and effect in learning and in counseling. The next step is to appreciate the unity of the total organism. To be aware of this unity in the counseling relationship is one implication. Another is the appropriateness of engaging in research on the factors of this unity as part of one's professional preparation for counseling.

Humanism As a Philosophical-Psychological Stance

The development of humanistic therapies is, of course, often associated with what is thought of as their opposite number, the behavioristic therapies. That relationship will be presented later but at this point I wish only to give a brief glimpse of humanism and its significance for the counselor.

In Chapter V attention was given to existentialism as a philosophical viewpoint and to phenomenology as a way of interpreting behavior. Humanism incorporates both of these concepts. It is perhaps an amalgamation of both, but humanism may also embrace Freudian concepts and behavioristic methods. It is integrative and it is eclectic (for some humanists at least) utilizing theoretical concepts and procedures as they are needed in the consideration of a given human being.

The goal of humanistic psychology is the understanding of a person as a unique, irreplaceable organism. The goal of humanistic counseling, individual or group, is to help a person develop himself as a unique and worthwhile individual. Humanism is a sweeping psychological social movement in the United States, which uses as a major tool of expression the widely used and warmly debated encounter group. Sometimes it seems that the individual is overstressed, that others and society itself are ignored. To overstress the individual would be unrealistic, for a person's "life space" always includes not only himself but significant others (and their life space may include him). Even if humanistic, or what may be called existential, counseling sometimes seems too self-preoccupied, this is to be preferred to the concept of the self as Object, to be observed and studied but seldom recognized. Humanism views the self as Subject, warm, vital, and real, perhaps the ultimate reality.

Abraham Maslow and Charlotte Buhler, leaders in the humanistic field of thinking, have both presented humanism as person-centered in contrast to concept- or method-centered. Although Maslow divides all theories of behavior into (1) psychologies that originate in Freudian psychoanalysis, (2) psychologies that are behavioristic, mechanistic, and methodological, and (3) psychologies that are personalistic, experiential, and humanistic, he seems to accept *within* his humanistic psychology the concept of unconscious motivation, the value of emotional catharsis and other Freudian elements. He also accepts readily the contributions of operant conditioning and the reinforcement principle. Buhler contrasts the "science" of psychology which stresses ideas but not necessarily persons with a psychology which is wholly *about* persons. She quotes Nevitt Sanford's wry observation that "the advocates of a . . . psychology-without-a-person . . . have been able to gain and maintain power through putting across the idea that they are *the* representatives in psychology of *true science.*" Not so for humanists. A psychology without persons is not psychology, whatever else it may be.

As the term implies, the distinguishing characteristic of humanism is that it is always and without exception focused on the totality of the human being. Maslow goes further. He proposes that biology, like psychology, move away from the value-free or value-neutral model of science that has proved so useful in physics, chemistry, and astronomy. This model, he believes, "is unsuitable for the study of life." Living creatures are reacting organisms not objects that remain inert as they are manipulated. They not only react but in the higher forms, they act and initiate behavior from within themselves. Rosenberg has commented that the human being is "an open system capable of change and endless growth." I liked also his statement that "the individual is a private experience that cannot easily be categorized." A wise Chinese gentleman who once tried to distinguish for me the difference between "experience" and "knowledge" said that experience is "an awareness of all of your five senses and more, it is an awareness of you."

Humanism focuses upon man as central in life (akin to existentialism in philosophy), and the study of individual man as central in the science of psychology. (An excellent brief description of humanistic psychology that takes into account several dimensions that I have not touched upon is an article by Charlotte Buhler in the April 1971 issue of the *American Psychologist.* Opposition (to be expected in psychology or any behavioral science!) to humanism and wholeness is also found in the *American Psychologist* ("Psychology in the Year 2000: Going Structural?" March 1970) where Foa and Turner propose that the future may see more attention to the *structural components* of the whole.)

The Struggle Between Behaviorism and Phenomenology

I have written thus far enough incidental material about these two schools of thought to suggest how differently they view man. The behaviorist sees man only in terms of observable behavior—the real is what he does. What is *outside,* observable, counts. Man is passive, acted upon by external stimuli. He is totally what his environment has made him. "Behavior modification" means just that—a person's behavior is modified by the behaviorist, with or without the individual's knowledge of what is happening. Operant conditioning, the method most frequently used by the behaviorist, "operates" upon the person by altering the environment of his act by giving him reinforcement (a rewarding environment) or withholding it (a punitive environment). As a result of this the person is more likely or less likely to engage in similar behavior again. His behavior is thus "shaped."

The phenomenologist, on the other hand, contends that reality is how a person *sees* the world, phenomena are real in terms of each person's perception of them. Reality is based upon what is inside the person, with each person's perception of anything being largely unique to him. Man himself is, at least in part, the source of his behavior. He can control, in part, his behavior from within rather than being controlled entirely from without. Behavior is changed by the person as the result of changed insight and self-understanding. The counseling or therapeutic relationship is designed to contribute to this enhanced understanding.

Neither behaviorism nor phenomenology-existentialism is new. The one had its origins during the early part of this century but it was Skinner in the 40's and 50's who originated and developed the concepts of operant conditioning. There is a large literature on behaviorism and a substantial one on behavior therapy and behavioral counseling and names that may be frequently found by counselors are Greenspoon, Krasner, Bijou, and Krumboltz. Research in psychology has experienced a marked swing toward behaviorism during the past decade.

The other school, existentialism, phenomenology, and existential counseling, had its birth during the last half of the last century in Europe with such leading figures as Husserl, Kierkegaard, Schelling, and Nietzsche. Its leading contemporary proponents in America are Rollo May, Van Kaam, Bugental, Maslow, Rogers, and others. The field of counseling has been greatly influenced by this school of thought although the counseling utilization of the concepts is often simply labeled client-centered or when groups are concerned, group counseling.

The most consistent exponents of the two schools are Skinner and Rogers and it is these names which may be most familiar to counselors. While the differences between the two approaches are marked, it has been disturbing to witness the dogmatism regarding these movements that is shown by many psychologists and counselors. So fierce is their defense of their own approach that they may literally know nothing of the other school. They do not examine evidence, read the literature, or even listen to an exponent of the other side without becoming rigidly defensive—and sometimes offensive! Intolerance of this sort ill becomes a counselor faced with the nuances of individual behavior, or a psychologist who deems himself a scientist drawing conclusions upon the basis of evidence.

Skinner and Rogers are tempted sorely to be dogmatic and at times they are, but often because their followers expect it! Each has held appointments in large universities—Skinner at Minnesota, Indiana, and Harvard (I occupied Skinner's former office when I first went to Minnesota in 1936, but all I knew about him at that time was his controlled environment for the infant called the Skinner Box); Rogers at Ohio State, Chicago, and Wisconsin—preceding that by early beginnings at a child guidance clinic and present experience at his adult "clinic" in California. Both men are courteous and fair to each other although their followers attempt to pit them against each other like Roman gladiators in the Colosseum!

Mrs. Wrenn and I once listened to Rogers and Skinner engage in a three-day dialogue at the University of Minnesota at Duluth before an audience of almost a thousand (which they had not expected!). Each was trying to understand the other, not "put him down." The exchange was earnest but always courteous. As we followed the dialogue it became increasingly clear that Rogers and Skinner were in reasonable agreement on all major points except for Rogers's assumption of an "inner Self." This Skinner contended was entirely unnecessary. He conceded that the fiction of a "Self" might be convenient at our present state of knowledge, but that it was still a fiction. Rogers, on the other hand, said that he would be unable to understand how he had seen people behave in a counseling-therapy relationship without the construct of a self that was at least partially autonomous. Input of stimuli, yes, but there was an intervening variable within. The self not only digests input but gives it meanings which result in changed perceptions of self and others, a changed outlook upon life. As we listened to their conscientious and unimpassioned dialogue, we wondered how much each had been affected by his individual life environment. Skinner had created his system of thought while working with animals, and Rogers had built his while working with people. In a sense this supports Skinner's theory of environmental influence!

There has been much to suggest that behaviorism and phenomenology can learn from each other. Each is seen to have something so important to contribute that research effort is now being expended to discover the conditions under which one approach is to be preferred to the other. A person confused about himself and his world may learn to trust himself and others through client-centered (phenomenological-existential) help. Another person may want desperately to change a behavior pattern or make an informed decision, and here the behavioral counselor may direct the process of change. Nor do the two approaches lack points in common. *Reflection,* a major principle of the client-centered counseling approach, has within it many elements of *reinforcement,* which the behaviorist uses so successfully with both animals and men.

A singularly helpful comparison of the two schools is given by William Hitt in "Two Models of Man" (*American Psychologist,* July 1969). He outlines 10 points on which the two schools *seem* to part company:

1. Man can be described meaningfully in terms of his behavior; or man can be described meaningfully in terms of his consciousness.

2. Man is predictable; or man is unpredictable.

3. Man is an information transmitter; or man is an information generator.

4. Man lives in an objective world; or man lives in a subjective world.

5. Man is a rational being; or man is an irrational being.

6. One man is like another; or each man is unique.

7. Man can be described meaningfully in absolute terms; or man can be described meaningfully in relative terms.

8. Human characteristics can be investigated independently of one another; or man must be studied as a whole.

9. Man is a reality; or man is a potentiality.

10. Man is knowable in scientific terms; or man is more than we can ever know about him.

To examine these pairs of concepts, as Hitt does, is to reason that each of the pair is a valid assumption or procedure for some situation or is present in many situations to some degree. No concept, on either side, is adequate for every situation. Both models are useful but, as Hitt comments, "it would be premature for psychology to accept either model as the final model." For me, a crucial concept for counselors is the enormous potential locked into every individual. Pick up an old dictionary and you may find uranium defined as "an almost worthless ore." A person is still as unknown in his or her potential as was uranium. To call anyone except the permanently damaged, "worthless" or "hopeless" is an act of stupidity, callousness, or defensive anger upon the part of the speaker.

B. F. Skinner's 1971 book, *Beyond Freedom and Dignity* (see References), will intensify the debate between the two schools of thought. I can hope that this will not delay what I believe to be the developing use of procedures from both schools to meet different situations. Skinner's book adds little to our knowledge of behavior therapy or behavioral counseling. It is not about procedures. It is a philosophical-social treatise written by a scientist. It is Skinner writing as a positivistic philosopher. Its goal is to outline the development of a society, not the development of man.

Beyond Freedom and Dignity is a landmark book, not only because of its bold attack upon the two basic human attributes of its title but for its clarity of language and marshaling of logic to prove the points made. Skinner abjures most of what I have said about freedom and the dignity of the individual, but it is a timely work. Skinner offers a solution to a politically tense, pollution-smothered world. Whether it is *the* solution will be hotly debated for some years.

Columnist James Kilpatrick characterizes the book as "at once monstrous and terrifying—monstrous in its error, terrifying in its truth." The truth lies in Skinner's coldly analytical description of man's movement toward destruction of the race, the error lies in Skinner's solution—a controlled society. Who will select the controllers and designers—and control them, asks Kilpatrick. Richard Rubenstein in a more complete review of the book (*Psychology Today,* September 1971, pp. 28, 31, 95–96) again is both fascinated and alarmed by the truth and error that he sees in the book. He digs deeply into Skinner's singlemindedness and overassurance and ends his review with the sentence, "In spite of Skinner's assurance to the contrary, his utopian projection is less likely to be a blueprint for the Golden Age than for the theory and practice of hell." Both reviewers are deeply concerned because they concede Skinner to be one of the most influential psychologists in the world today.

It is at this point that we again see the either/or phenomenon. For Skinner there is no degree of freedom, no value in individual dignity. I opt for *some degree* of both. I cannot throw away the inner self as nonexistent even though I readily accept the terrific power of environmental conditioning. I cannot accept the dictum that if society is to survive through more stringent control of people, passions, and pollution (and this is a stark reality) then all pretensions to individual human dignity must be abandoned. Am I a compromiser? or am I a realist? Time will tell. Leonard Krasner, himself a leader in behavior therapy research, wrote in the 1971 *Annual Review of Psychology:* "The decade of the 1960's covered the childhood and adolescence of behavior therapy (its birth was in the 1950's). The 1970's should see its development into adulthood and even maturity. Ahead will almost certainly lie old age and senility in the 1980's, but by that time it will have given birth to a newer and at this point (at least to this observer) an unpredictable paradigm."

I can accept this evolutionary concept of Krasner's, except that his "it" (behaviorism) is for me a compound of behaviorism and phenomenology. So much has been done for people by the therapies associated with phenomenology-existentialism that they seem to be sure to play a major part in the future unknown. So much also has been done with programmed learning and the beginnings of behavioral counseling in schools and with reinforcement control procedures in the treatment of social and emotional deviates. My evolutionary picture must take both into account.

I do not see behaviorists as exploiters (I recall Skinner's commenting on the hazard involved in Rousseau's "benevolent" control by teachers), and I champion their alternatives to punishment. They too can "care" by providing a reinforcing, healthy environment. Nor do I see existential counselors as sentimental, rationally deluded psychologists. They care in different ways, they help people to learn from each other in groups, and their assumptions of some degree of autonomy works—for many people. A thoroughgoing and helpful analysis of "Existential Counseling" is found in *The Counseling Psychologist,* 1971, Vol. 2, No. 3, with C. Gratton Kemp providing the major analysis while ten others give shorter additional insights—Tyler, Arbuckle, Brammer, et al.

Fred Massarik in his presidential address to the Association for Humanistic Psychology ("La Force est Morte: Vive les Forces," *Newsletter* for the Association, December 1971) attempts to depolarize humanism and "the rest of psychology." He thinks humanism can no longer afford "psychological isolationism" . . . as being those who are "the lucky few who have the road to Nirvana in our hip pocket." Humanism—and existential psychology?—must engage in a process of cross-experiencing, of seeing its point of view as *part* of the whole.

Julian Rotter has established the finding that human beings are on a continuum of responsiveness to internal control versus responsiveness to external control. People who are high on the internal-control scale are different in a number of ways from those low on the internal-control scale—those decidedly responsive to external control (*Psychology Today,* June 1971). It is reasonable then to conclude that individuals vary with regard to the methodology to which they respond. It is the person as a total entity to whom I must respond, and the method used will follow.

All three of these trends in contemporary psychology that I have been sketching (mind-body unity, humanism, and *the complementary nature* of behavioral and existential counseling) have a common thread running through them, *seeing people whole rather than in parts.* We have learned how to disassemble and study the parts, how to label and categorize each part. But as psychology puts the parts together it becomes apparent that the whole is greater than the sum of its parts. In terms of living creatures collectively, the added element is that of relationship. Seemingly discrete elements are interdependent. All creatures are interdependent as well—ecologically man's survival may be dependent upon the smallest creatures in the sea. We have learned very well how to discriminate differences; now we are beginning to understand the importance of discovering similarities. We are seeing the significance of the kinds of psychological cement that binds the parts into the whole. It is no accident that the current times see us striving heartily to end social separation based upon skin pigment, separation based upon gender, separation based upon language and superficial cultural differences.

Buckminster Fuller ("Planetary Planning," *The American Scholar,* Winter issue, 1970–71) defines *synergy* as "the behavior of whole systems unpredicted by the behavior of any of its separate parts." One cannot predict how the total organism man will behave by measuring ever-so-carefully any of one of his parts or subsystems. Yet that is where so much of America's psychological effort has been expended to date. Fuller provides a corollary of synergy—"the known behaviors of the whole plus the known behavior of some of its parts may make possible the discovery of other parts. . . ." Perhaps we can discover the parts or processes that bind the marvelous complexity of the human being together.

The enduring parts of psychoanalysis, of psychological measurement, of behaviorism, of phenomenology are being sifted out by time, other parts will be found, and we will move closer to the total meaning of man. Psychology and philosophy have been engaging in a pleasant flirtation, marriage has been proposed in the form of Existentialism. If a stable union takes place then their progeny may provide some of the successors to our present actors in the never-ending drama called "Understanding Man."

Trends in the Employment of Psychologists

Any discussion of the employment of psychologists must begin with the perspective of the 25 years since World War II. This period saw a proliferation in the kinds of psychologists that would have been interpreted as science fiction in 1940. To some degree "many kinds of psychologists" is explained by the increased variety of settings in which psychologists are employed. The adjectives preceding psychologists' names are as frequently representative of setting as of function. The following major types of psychologists are listed in order of frequency (with the accompanying number representing percentage of total—1966 figures): clinical (36), experimental (12), counseling (11), educational (9), industrial (8), school (6), social (5), developmental (3), personality (3), engineering (3), psychometric (2), other (2). Other descriptive labels are represented by the titles of various divisions of the American Psychological Association—military psychology, community psychology, consulting psychology, etc.

One should not assume that the "counseling psychologists" of this study represent those working in schools. Three-fourths or more of this sample are psychologists with their doctorate, and not many of these are in schools. Many are in colleges and universities, as well as in hospitals, social agencies, industry, and government. Most "school psychologists" at the doctorate level are likely to be on university faculties (colleges of education or departments of psychology) rather than in the schools.

The employing institutions are also varied: colleges, universities, and medical schools (employing 44 percent of the total in 1966), government (15), public and private schools (12), nonprofit organizations, hospitals, and clinics (11), self-employed (6), business and industry (6), and other (5). The "principal activity" of these psychologists falls under these labels: clinical, counseling, and consulting (23 percent), teaching (23), administration and management (19), research and development (15), testing and test development (10), other (9). (*1966 Register of Scientific and Technical Personnel.*)

There was an increase in unemployment among PhD's of the social sciences in 1970 and 1971 but this did not seem to affect psychologists. One summary published in October 1970, indicated that the number of vacant positions for Ph.D.'s in psychology was considerably in excess of the supply. In health settings alone, 750 to 1000 vacancies were said to exist. The *1970 Manpower Report of the President* projected employer needs to be greater for "psychologists" than for any other professional field outside of "systems analysts" and "computer programmers."

I do not know of any pronounced trends with regard to the type of psychologist except, of course, for the general increase in all types of *applied* psychologists. New fields, such as community psychology, absorb small but increasing numbers. There seems to be little sex discrimination in the employment of psychologists, except for the tendency in all fields for higher and administrative positions to be disproportionately held by men. "A psychologist" increasingly means a man or woman possessing a doctorate in the field, although many professional as well as technological positions are held by psychologists at the M.A.

or post M.A. level. The members of the American Psychological Association (some 34,000 in March 1972) who have doctorates increased from 69 percent in 1962 to 80 percent in 1969.

Other Developments

There are, of course, many other situations in psychology that justify discussion. If space permitted I would particularly like to look at some changes in the field of ethics. An ad hoc committee of the American Psychological Association is currently (1971) working on a revision of the APA principles of ethical conduct. The intention of the committee is to give particular attention to principles for group situations, for private practice, for student protest situations, and for community psychology. I have served both national and state committees on the ethical conduct of psychologists and have become convinced that the great majority of those who violate ethical principles do so from ignorance or hasty action rather than from intent. The American Personnel and Guidance Association has also had ethics committees which resulted in a published "code of ethics."

Counselors should be familiar with these codes as a protection to themselves and their clients. Mere ignorance of ethical principles is no excuse for anyone who deals with human lives. The latest statement of the ethical principles of the American Psychological Association (the first version was published in 1953) is found in the *American Psychologist*, 1968, 23: 357–361, while those of the American Personnel and Guidance Association is found in the *Personnel and Guidance Journal*, 1961, 39: 206–209. Both codes can be purchased as separates from the appropriate Association as can Case Books for each code. The APGA code in full and a helpful chapter on "Legal and Ethical Counselor Behavior" are provided by J. J. Pietrofesa and John Vriend in *The School Counselor As a Professional*, Peacock, 1971. Any counselor reading both codes will find much to aid him in his professional development. The December 1971 issue of the *Personnel and Guidance Journal* is a special issue devoted to "Ethical Practices."

If I had more space I would *like* also to look at the challenging new field of community psychology (see article by Lehman in the June 1971 issue of the *American Psychologist*). Other things I wish I could get into are: the thrust in psychology toward an increased sense of social responsibility (APA has a new Board of Social and Ethical Responsibility for Psychologists); concern for all of the stages of life development, attention given to the psychology of minority and underprivileged groups—

youth protesters, old people, women and blacks, the field of engineering psychology; common concerns in biology, physiology, and psychology; the soulsearching of clinical psychology; a search for new systems to disseminate psychological information; and the amazing popularization of psychology and its implications. An example of the last is the journal *Psychology Today* started only four years ago. Today (1972) it has a rapidly growing circulation of over one-half million; it was sold recently to a corporation for $21 million. Highly respected professional psychologists publish in this slick, vividly illustrated journal. The publication itself is a new phenomenon in psychology.

Psychology is a lively field of study. No counselor can afford to neglect it. Knowing about the behavior of people is an important adjunct to the experiencing of people. "Knowing" is sometimes more common among those who have no aspirations to counseling than among those who do. A salesgirl in a candy store had customers lined up waiting for her while other girls stood idle. The proprietor said, "What's the secret?" "It's easy," said the popular girl. "The others scoop up more than a pound of candy and then start taking it away. I scoop up less and then add to it."

References for Exploration

(A larger selection of references is given for this chapter than for other chapters under the assumption that fewer would be new to a given reader.)

Bruner, Jerome S. *Toward a Theory of Instruction.* Harvard, 1966.

Bugental, James F. T. (ed.). *Challenges of Humanistic Psychology.* McGraw-Hill, 1967

Cole, Michael, et al. *The Cultural Context of Learning and Thinking.* Basic Books, 1971. (A carefully conducted cross-cultural study—Africa and U. S. A.—that throws much light not only on the topic but on the varying methods used by anthropologists, linguists, and psychologists.)

Cook, David R. *Guidance for Education in Revolution.* Allyn and Bacon, 1971.

Dennis, Lawrence E., and Joseph F. Kaufman (eds.). *The College and the Student.* American Council on Education, 1969. (A thoughtful presentation by 45 of the best qualified writers in the field. A semiclassic only mildly dated.)

Greene, Maxine (ed.). *Existential Encounters for Teachers.* Random House, 1967. (A remarkable collection of 64 excerpts from the writings of 15 of the "greats" in existential thinking. Excerpts from such classics as Rilke's *Letters to a Young Poet,* Buber's *I and Thou,* Camus's *The Plague,* Dostoevsky's *The Brothers*

Karamasov, Nietzsche's *On the Genealogy of Morals,* Kierkegaard's *Works of Love,* Tillich's *The Courage to Be,* Marcel's *The Philosophy of Existence*—each with an editor's comments on the implication of the excerpt for teaching. An excellent small library of classics, all within 166 pages.)

Hart, Leslie A. *The Classroom Disaster.* Teachers College Press, 1969. (A layman's analysis of what is wrong but with a constructive proposal for what will be right and a list of schools that are making these changes.)

Illich, Ivan. *De-Schooling Society.* Harper and Row, 1970.

Lamont, Corliss. *The Philosophy of Humanism.* Unger Publishing Co., 250 Park Ave. South, New York, N.Y., 10003, 1968.

Leonard, George. *Education and Ecstasy.* Dell, 1968.

Lifton, Walter M. (ed.). *Educating for Tomorrow.* John Wiley and Sons, Inc., 1970.

Macrorie, Ken. *Uptaught.* Hayden Book Co., 1970. (The chapter you have been reading is not about teaching—or humor. But this book is about both. The book is compelling. I got up three times one night to read more. There is life and reality and humor here, whether you teach or help teachers.)

May, Rollo. *Psychology and the Human Dilemma.* Van Nostrand, 1967.

Piaget, Jean, and Bärbel Inhelder. *The Psychology of the Child.* Basic Books, 1970. (A beautiful synthesis of Piaget's lifetime of work—his cognitive theory of learning applied to children from infancy to adolescence.)

Postman, Neil, and Charles Weingartner. *The Soft Revolution.* Dell, 1971.

Postman, Neil, and Charles Weingartner. *Teaching As a Subversive Activity.* Delacorte Press, 1969. (The contents are not as harsh as the title. "Subversive" teaching is teaching for change which is subversive to those who maintain *status quo.* The authors are well informed and constructive. They see the faults but have many suggestions for change, for subversive teaching. One of the most penetrating satires in print is found on pp. 39-41.)

"The Reform of Urban Education." Special Issue of *Phi Delta Kappan,* February 1971.

Rogers, Carl R. *Freedom to Learn.* Charles Merrill Publishing Co., Columbus, Ohio, 1969.

Silberman, Charles. *Crisis in the Classroom.* Random House, 1970.

Skinner, B. F. *Beyond Freedom and Dignity.* Knopf, 1971.

"Sorting Out the Seventies." Special Issue of *Change Magazine,* September 1971. (A very readable journal in the area of higher education. This particular issue contains some searching articles on the future of colleges and universities.)

"33,000 Graduate Students' Views Dissect Education and Society" in *Chronicle of Higher Education,* November 22, 1971, pp. 104-105. (Since many readers will be graduate students themselves this digest of a Carnegie Commission on Higher Education report will be of considerable interest. The figures provided on both the characteristics of graduate students in all fields and their reactions to their education are normative for a total population of almost one million graduate students in 153 graduate schools.)

Airplane Glue, I Love You (film). 20 minutes. Creative Film Society, 14558 Valerio St., Van Nuys, Calif., 91405. (A school dropout, at age 30, returns to school. What follows is charm, innocent humor, nonsense, and satire.)

No Reason to Stay (film). 28 minutes. Contemporary Films, McGraw-Hill, 267 W. 25th St., New York, N.Y., 10001, 1965. (Why *should* he stay in school?)

Zero for Conduct (film). 44 minutes. CCM Films, Inc., 866 Third Ave., New York, N.Y., 10022. (A French avant garde classic of a revolt in a French boy's school.)

CHAPTER XI

Counseling and Caring 1: Priorities and Perspectives, Developments and Decisions

THE IMPORTANCE OF CARING

The counselor is a knowing person, but he is also a caring person. Many people can know all that a counselor knows, but unless a person cares, he is not a counselor. A counselor cares about how the other feels and uses all of his skills to communicate that caring. He cares about the decisions the other makes. He cares so much that he works hard to help the other learn how to make decisions. He cares about the other's having a chance to express himself fully and without fear of censure. He cares enough to see that the implications of feelings and doubts are explored and the options made clear. He knows about options in the educational, vocational, marital, and personal-relationship areas of living, but he is concerned more for the person than the options. *Counseling is caring.*

The first ten chapters of this book have been focused on the counselor's *knowing*, and only the last two are on his *caring.* The proportion seems out of line, but there is so much to know just to keep even with what the counselor's contemporary, now-oriented client knows. And the client *expects* you to know, to know a little of how he feels, of the outside-of-school world that he lives in. He expects or hopes that you will have some knowledge of the educational, occupational, adult-responsibility world he is going to live in and that you will help him take the next step toward it. Yet with all that you know, the small spark of caring is what fires the engine; it may be a small spark, but without it the car will not move. It is easier to write about knowing than about caring, for caring is your attitude toward yourself and others—it is a way of life. You can store up knowledge quickly, but learning how to care is more difficult and sometimes quite painful when you realize you have failed at it. For many it takes most of a lifetime to learn how to care.

Much has been happening to counselors and to ideas about counseling during the ten years since *The Counselor in a Changing World* was published. The sheer increase in numbers mentioned earlier has been striking. But more significant are such developments as viewing the counselor as a consultant or as the group facilitator or as struggling with soul-searching ethical questions that face him and the counseling relationship in a contemporary world—his attitude toward patriotism and responsibility, abortion, drugs, etc.

Of all the exciting developments that have been taking place, there is none more basic for me than the realization that a counselor can gain the whole world and lose his or her own soul. He can know a lot, dress modishly, belong to powerful professional organizations, go to summer school regularly "to learn the latest," get advanced degrees to his ego's content, but if he doesn't really care, he's a flop as far as students are concerned. He has failed the test of trust—of his trust in the student and the student's trust in him—regardless of how many university tests he has passed.

A little later in this chapter I shall look a bit at some of these professional developments in counseling, but to me the most striking personal discovery of the past decade has been that people respond to my degree of caring more than to my degree of knowing. The Psalmist said it well a long time ago, "With all thy wisdom, get understanding." People quickly sense a counselor's or teacher's degree of caring—his trust in them, his respect for them, his attempt to be himself rather than to play a role. I now see that I have played roles all of my life, most of the time not knowing that this was what I was doing. Occasionally, and often without awareness of the significance of what I was doing, I have openly shared myself with a class or a person. They have responded to me upon such occasions with warmth and closeness, but I saw it only as an unexpectedly "good day" or a happy circumstance. Only recently have I begun to appreciate that much of the reaction of others to me was the result of my reaction to them (or to him), that when I was open and personal, sharing and enjoying it, concerned about them and showing it, then they responded!

There has been some research on affective response, but it is too often overshadowed by much more research which is cognitively oriented. Why it took me so long, I do not know, but finally I have learned that one can do the wrong things, say the wrong words, but if he shows that he cares, he is accepted. To care who the other person *is* and what is happening to him, means that one's attention is upon him and not upon what *you* are doing, how *you* are progressing. This focus of attention, of concern is what he senses.

There seem to be two basic ways in which I (and perhaps the reader as a counselor) can develop a client relationship that is meaningful both to the client and to the counselor. One is to be the agent through whom the client has a positively reinforcing experience, either with me or with a situation apart from me. I have given him meaningful information or helped him to a decision that worked. He feels reinforced within himself and I am seen as part of this positive process, either directly or indirectly. The other way is to show that I am concerned, even though I don't know the answer to his question or problem. To be sure, if I both *know* and *care,* all the better, but the key word of the two seems to be *care.* This is not always true. I am generalizing too much. When the need is for information that will help a client come to a decision, or the need is to learn *how* to come to a decision, or the need is for an understanding of a wider range of options then what I *know* is very important. But still there is something positive between us even when I lack the knowledge, if I *care* enough to work with him or her so that we may discover jointly what is needed.

I have said that knowing is part of caring. A counselor must know a bit more than the contemporary world in general. He needs to be abreast of what is happening in the world of counseling. First, permit me the luxury of a brief perspective, then I want to talk a little about some professional developments and impending decisions that are at the top of my list of priorities. After that we return to some final thoughts on caring.

COUNSELING IN PERSPECTIVE

Before picking up a few recent developments in counseling and out-lining some projections for the future, we should take a broad look at the current counseling scene. The 1970 figure of 60,000 counselors in various settings was projected from a 1967 study by economist Eli Ginzberg in his *Career Guidance* (see References). I arrived at somewhat similar figures in 1970 from direct estimates at that time. School counselors were estimated at 35,000 full time (30,000 secondary and 5,000 elementary) and 20,000 part time (18,000 secondary and 2,000 elementary). College counselors were estimated at 3,000, employment counselors at 3,000, rehabilitation counselors at 7,000, and counselors (mostly counseling psychologists at the doctoral level) in business, industry, government, Veterans Administration hospitals and centers at 2,500. Thus I arrived at a total of 50,500 full-time and 20,000 part-time counselors in all settings. (These estimates were more than guesses, but because no one agency reports year-by-year figures there is at least a 10 percent possible error factor in any category. All figures were rounded off in order to eliminate any assumption of exactness.)

These 1970 figures represent impressive increases in the number of school counselors and rehabilitation counselors, resulting from the Federal subsidy of professional training programs in those fields. Earlier I mentioned the increase in secondary school counselors from 7,000 full time in 1958 to 30,000 in 1970—an increase of over 400 percent. Few, if any, professions have increased as rapidly as that over a 12-year period. With the assumption of a *continuation* of greatly reduced Federal subsidies in these fields, future increases will be more modest.

These figures sound encouraging. But in 1970 there was a counselor on regular assignment in 90 percent of the public secondary schools but in only 22 percent of the public elementary schools (*School Staffing Survey,* National Center for Educational Statistics, U. S. Office of Education, reported in APGA *Guidepost,* December 1971). These and other figures of the *Survey* suggest that millions of children never have a chance to see a counselor.

There is, of course, a wide variation in what these thousands of counselors do, a much wider variation than for counselors in any other part of the world. I have lectured on various occasions in other countries about the American counselor, and the variety of activities he performs is as much a matter of curiosity as is the large number of counselors involved. In other countries the counseling focus is quite often restricted to educational planning and adjustment, sometimes only to vocational planning. In England, for example, vocational planning and personal emotional adjustments are largely cared for by agencies outside of the school. (It is only fair to say, however, that the professional education of "school counselors" in England dates back only to 1965–66 when Gilbert Moore at the University of Reading and I at the University of Keele helped to launch the first programs. The movement in the present programs is toward a more varied set of roles.)

Some English observers see American school counselors as stressing a continuity and globality of concern for the client—the total person of the student and his needs, active client participation in the process and a preventive rather than crisis-oriented concern. Such observers comment that much of this would not be seen in "average" English counseling today. I fear that the same would be true of the "average" of American counseling. These emphases are characteristic of the "best" of practice and are emphasized in the literature. On the other hand actual logs of the way in which school counselors' time is spent would indicate that registration advising, test recording, and various kinds of paperwork occupy far more of the average counselor's time than the literature suggests. One-to-one counseling and much paperwork all too often fill up the counselor's day. A 1970 study of Colorado counselors by Professor Donald Frick (Colorado State University) disclosed that 35 percent of the secondary school counselor's time was spent in individual counseling while 42 percent was spent in registration advising and paperwork.

The Occupational Outlook Handbook describes duties of school counselors in broad terms: "educational, vocational, and social development of students." A 1966 study by Patricia (Lawler) Reed of a 20 percent sampling of the membership of the American School Counselors Association reports that 80 percent checked "working with students individually" as one of "the *three* activities considered to be the most important aspects of the counselor's job." This is in contrast to the only 40 percent who checked "working with students in groups" as one of the three most important aspects and 40 percent who checked "consulting with parents" or "consulting with staff." Only 12 percent checked "working with administrators" as one of the three, and only 6 percent checked "performing liaison functions between school and community." The mean age of this national sample of counselors was 43 and the mean age at entry to counseling was 35. The implications of this rather late entry into the field will come in for later attention.

One large city high school lists ten major duties for its counselors, six of which involve working with students individually. A counselor in this school, reporting to the Board of Education, made clear that little time was left for other duties: for "group guidance," "liaison with other agencies," "consulting with staff and parents." This, by the way, is one of the more progressive and well-organized high school departments in the country (Phoenix Union High School District, Phoenix, Arizona).

The picture then is that of a large and growing number of school counselors who have a wide variety of possible activities suggested for them, but whose time is actually restricted to a great deal of individual counseling and academic advising. At one time I would have said, "Fine. Individual counseling *is* the counselor's major job." Now I am much less sure of the validity of this type of reasoning.

SOME CONTEMPORARY DEVELOPMENTS IN COUNSELING

It would be sheer effrontery to attempt to detail or even summarize all of the innovations being attempted by 60,000 people working in thousands of different situations. The most that I can do is to point up four or five current developments that I think have promise for the future. Some of these are practiced by only "the growing edge" of a minority of counselors, but it is my opinion, and I stress that it is only an opinion, that these movements in counseling will increase consistently and perhaps rapidly over the next few years. It is hazardous to select only a few out of the many, but these are at least among the most significant forward thrusts.

Group Counseling

Perhaps most striking is the counselors' adaptation of a sweeping social movement, that of learning about oneself from others in a group setting: sensitivity training (T-groups), encounter groups, group psychotherapy. There are many forms with group leaders (more often facilitators of group interaction) from psychology, education, psychiatry, social work. One of the rapidly growing specializations involving the group process is family therapy in which the whole family is the client. School counselors are still in the process of developing a form of "group counseling" appropriate to student groups as distinct from adults, business executives, or hospital patients. Some are moving in from the "group guidance" base where shared information is the focus. Others develop encounter groups for which they are often ill prepared. Still others use group counseling situations to help students see themselves more clearly as developing personalities, to achieve a better sense of self-identity.

Gloria Zeal of the David Douglass High School in Portland, Oregon, gives a description of a working group. She meets with at least one group a day; a group meets one period a week for ten weeks. Often the groups request an extension; she reports that one group met for more than a year. Some of the students become so skilled that they become group leaders of other groups. She writes: "One happy benefit is that these group meetings alleviate the terrifying loneliness experienced by so many adolescents, particularly those entering the school from other places. Students express this in their gratitude for each other *just for being there,* in their feelings of safety, openness, trust for the eight people in that room. This in spite of the fact that these people were formerly complete strangers, chosen at random from a class roster. Their ability to *help each other* is exciting."

It is unfortunate that, for all their enthusiasm, most counselors have little or no preparation or experience in capitalizing upon the potentials of group interaction. They are only prepared for one-to-one counseling relationships, but they are trying. Many are excited and hopeful; others are threatened by the unfamiliar; but all are aware of the phenomenon. (Some excellent books on group counseling in schools have appeared recently. Those by Fullmer-Bernard and by Mahler come to mind at once—see References—as well as Gratton Kemp's *Perspectives on the Group Process,* Houghton Mifflin, 2nd edition, 1970).

Counselor As Consultant

There is a modest amount of practice, with much discussion in the literature, of the counselor as consultant to and counselor of the teacher. This has occurred over a longer period of time in the elementary school than in the secondary school. In fact, in the elementary school it is taken for granted that the counselor and/or the school psychologist will spend as much (or more) time with teacher as with children. This development has significant implications for schools in general as part of a marked change in the role of the counselor.

Manuscript commentator J. Jeffries McWhirter (Arizona State University) writes in this connection: "Please don't forget the parents as sometimes needing consultation or counseling. I am concerned about the number of negative comments that *good* counselors make about both parents and teachers. I see this setting up an adversary system, and I-They dichotomy that is harmful to the youngster. This came to me most clearly last year when I accepted a case involving child beating. I have a fantastic anger at parents who are child batterers but after I helped the father look at his behavior and his own development I found that I could really care about him as a person and could separate out his behavior from him."

McWhirter is right, parents are often more important to the counselor than teachers. They are certainly more important to the child. When the parent is the most significant person in the development of the child or youth, then the counselor must consider one of two alternatives. The first is that he take the time to help the parent understand the child, and in the process, he hopes, the parent will understand himself or herself a little better. Helping a parent in this way may be the most important thing by far that a counselor can do for a particular student. Some systematic work is being done with parents in helping them to communicate better with their children. One widespread program is called Parent Effectiveness Training (see References).

The other alternative is that the counselor help to see that the school experience compensates in part for what is lacking in the home—affection, self-respect, recognition of achievement, being liked and accepted. Parents are certainly important, but I see the teacher as more important to *the school learning environment* of the student. More of this in a later section.

Peer Counseling

Faint beginnings are discernible of what is called "peer counseling." As adult counselors and teachers have developed increasing uncertainty regarding their understanding of the contemporary world of youth, it seems natural to turn to those who might understand—other youth. Peer counseling is predominant in drug treatment centers or in information services which deal primarily with youth. Peer influence has visibly increased during the past decade, and the enlistment of selected young people who could be given some training and supervision to help other young people has been initiated at a few schools and colleges in the country. The results appear to outweigh the risks. We will see more of this in the years ahead. A junior college program of peer counseling and the training of the student counselors involved is described by Robert R. Pyle and Fred A. Snyder in the *Journal of College Student Personnel* (1971, 12:4, 259–262). Another account of a peer counseling study is one by T. J. Vriend, "High-Performing Inner City Adolescents Assist Low-Performing Peers in Counseling Groups," *Personnel and Guidance Journal,* May 1969, pp. 897–904.

An extensive ongoing program of peer counselor training and supervision is found in the Palo Alto, California, High School District, directed by Barbara Varenhorst. A great deal depends upon including students who are both motivated and mature, and in the extensiveness of the training given them. Ten training sessions were given in the spring of 1971 for the 98 peer counselors who began to serve the next fall. These were truly professional training sessions with such topics as life career games, small groups, communication, experience in one-to-one relating, experiences in relating to a group, counseling issues, planning and goal setting, counseling strategies, etc. In reading reports from Palo Alto, I got the impression that the peer counselors gain as much from the experience as do the students they see. Casual is the word, either one-to-one or in groups, but it is an informed and skillful informality in which the student being helped feels no condescension from the peer counselor. In other words, the psychological climate of the program seems healthy and wholesome.

Computer-Assisted Counseling

Faint beginnings and a substantial literature again are the picture. The idea of computers as substitutes for counselors or even as aides frightens some counselors. Much of this fear or reluctance is the result of ignorance of the basic principles involved or ignorance of the fact that computers can be used to *supplement* the "humanness" of counselors, that they cannot become full substitutes for counselors. If a counselor is now performing only the functions of a computer (information retrieval, cognitive analysis), then he *should be* concerned, for the computer can surpass him at this game! The development of computer assistants will require the counselor to identify his more distinctive human qualities (sensitivity to nonverbal cues, responsiveness to group interactions, etc.) and capitalize upon these.

Basic work in this field has advanced far enough to provide several prototypes that are currently in operation. In some, the client feeds in information about his abilities and preferences and gets back a structured and limited set of suggestions such as "college to attend" or "vocations to consider." There is no feedback from client to computer and no chance for refinement of the questions asked. Many of these systems with names such as Search, Select, Match are commercial systems in which one enrolls for a fee. In other systems, all of which are research-oriented and in use at schools or colleges, the client sits at a console or keyboard and types in coded questions to the computer, receiving back typed answers. These answers are based upon information programmed into the computer about both the individual at the keyboard and the options open to a person with his characteristics. The more advanced of these systems (with long titles such as The Education and Career Exploratory System, The Computerized Vocational Information System, The Information System for Vocational Decisions, etc.) provide for what is called "monitoring." This has been defined as "the overseeing capability of the computer program which keeps a record of the alternatives chosen by the user. It has pertinent data about the user himself, relates these data to the chosen alternative, comments on the consistency of these two in accordance with a decision table determined by the systems designer, states the probability of success in appropriate alternatives, and reviews a path of decision-making."

The above quotation is from one of the latest documents on the topic, the 1971 report of a committee of the National Vocational Guidance Association, "The Commission on Computer-Assisted Guidance Systems," JoAnne Harris, Chairman. (I was a hanger-on member of this commission, struggling to keep my head above the sea of technological knowledge of the other members!) The publications of the leading workers in this field—Joseph Impellitteri, John Loughary, David Minor, Robert O'Hara, Donald Super, David Tiedeman, John Vriend, Garry Walz, and others—are reviewed in this report (for Super, see References).

Behavioral Counseling and Decision Making

Another of the developments in counseling has been the thrust forward in behavior modification and decision making. I link these two in a rather unorthodox fashion by assuming a common factor of overt behavior. For a long time the world of counseling has been troubled by the problem of demonstrating the behavior resulting from counseling.

Repeatedly the question is raised, "What does the student *do* after he makes verbal commitments or comes to verbal conclusions?" I believe that some counselors have sidestepped this issue much too neatly. The answer most often given has been some paraphrase of Proverbs, "As he thinketh in his heart, so is he." So the counselor has said, "As a client changes his perception of self and his attitudes, he will change his behavior accordingly." Perhaps he will, but all too often the proof has been lacking.

Recently attention has been upon *behavior* changes—overt, observable behavior changes. The issue is not yet joined regarding the sequence of changes, whether attitudes change first and behavior follows, or whether changed behavior will result in changed attitudes. It is likely to be the first sequence in one situation and the second sequence in another, but there is no weight of evidence to show that one sequence or the other is invariably true. This points up the crux of the behaviorism-phenomenology issue described in Chapter X. Outcomes of behavior seem the more important to some counseling theorists and research workers. They focus on behavior changes and care little about changes of attitude. They can afford to, perhaps, because behavior changes are the ultimate outcome. The case is not so clear from the other approach. It *is* important that behavior changes follow changes of perception and attitude.

So counseling to bring about desired changes in specific units of behavior has been on the increase. The reinforcement principle and its skillful application is the core of the method.

Likewise decision making that leads to action has been vigorously advocated recently. The process of making a decision is stressed, as it often is in behavioral counseling. The process is learned by *doing* things in sequence, moving from broad categories of choice to more specific categories. The decision to be made is always personalized and is thus unique to the individual. Although the steps to be taken in coming to a decision may be similar in one situation and another, they are always toward goals determined by *that* individual's personal values. From a decision, the movement is to alternative plans, to the advantages and risks of each alternative, to the final action chosen. All of these are in terms of what has meaning for that particular client, what he has found rewarding in past experiences, what appear to be trends or changes in his personal value system. Two recently developed decision-making models appear to have much promise. One of these is entitled *Vocational Exploration Group* (developed by Calvin Daane of Arizona State-—Studies for Urban Man, P. O. Box 1039, Tempe, Arizona), a model based upon counselor-led small-group interactions, including each person's account of successful experiences and self-attitudes in a series of increasingly specific choices. The second is called *Deciding* (developed by the Palo Alto team of H. B. Gelatt, Barbara Varenhorst, and Richard Carey—College Entrance Examination Board, New York City), a model again of teacher-led or counselor-led small-group participation in discussions at junior or senior high school level, using a series of self-involved exercises in each of several areas—the process of choice, crucial decision points, risk taking, identifying alternatives, etc.

From those specific developments that are under way, I want to move to some broader issues that need resolution. These affect counselors in a total sort of way and give some different answers to the question, "Just who is a counselor, anyway?"

SOME CRUCIAL DECISIONS AHEAD

On his return home from a dinner, a man was asked by his wife, "How was the talk you gave at your dinner club?" "Which one," asked the man, "the one I was going to give, the one I gave at the club, or the one that I delivered so brilliantly to myself on the way home?"

I am not sure which speech you have heard me giving thus far in this chapter. There are two themes—a major theme full of faith and enthusiasm for the field in which I have spent my life, and a minor theme of concern and discouragement for this same field. This minor theme has been displayed fleetingly, and the discerning reader may have seen it in earlier sentences or phrases.

My concern is that school counselors are opting for development in the wrong direction for the decade 1970–1980. They ask merely for "more of the same," more counselors, lower counselor-student ratio, higher certification standards. "What is wrong with these goals?" you ask. Well, almost everything.

Many More Counselors?

Those in the counseling field have always been unrealistic about the projected increase in numbers. Ginzberg (see References) cites the 1967 Interagency Task Force as calculating the additional "need" for school counselors for the period 1966–1971 on the basis of a counselor-student ratio of 1:600 in the elementary schools, 1:300 in the high schools and junior colleges. This results in a figure of 116,000 school counselors, an increase of 81,000 over a five-year period! I myself have played with statements of need, based upon a lowered counselor-student ratio, knowing even then that I was playing a "numbers game." As chairman of the Panel on Counseling and Selection of the National

Manpower Advisory Committee, 1962–1967, I fought for "more and better" counselors in employment offices and schools throughout the country. The panel sponsored a national conference on counseling in 1965 that projected the need for large increases in the number of counselors, similar to those later proposed by the Interagency Task Force.

In the 1960's, such increases were based upon appeals to the Federal government for subsidy of both professional training and employment of counselors. It was a good decade for those appeals, but the well of Federal concern began to dry up before the end of the decade. Nor was this merely a change of administration which another change might reverse. The decrease in enthusiasm and support came about, in part, because of competition with other social needs. These needs will grow no less in the decade ahead. In part, too much was expected of counselors operating within schools and colleges in which too little reform had taken place and which were too far out of touch with contemporary youth needs. Ginzberg put it well in saying that the government tried to buy its way out cheaply by supporting reform in guidance rather than broader reform in education.

I do not think the public, at either local or Federal level, will provide the funds needed to educate and employ school counselors in the numbers that we have been proposing. I know that this prediction will disturb some readers, but let us all stop deluding ourselves. There are solutions other than greatly increased numbers. There will be some increase in the total number of counselors, of course, and I will welcome that. I believe, however, that the substantial support that counselors want from the public will come only after they have moved in at least some of the directions suggested in the rest of this chapter and in Chapter XII.

One major move in the direction of obtaining continued public support would be for school counselors, guidance departments, and departments of student personnel in colleges to give careful attention to providing an *accountability record.* This term has a nasty ring to it when it suggests only accounting for numbers of students served. But the criteria of accountability can be much more meaningful than is implied by the numbers game. An accountability record can involve, in a very simple fashion, such matters as a daily log of the way in which time is spent—time spent with teachers and staff, time spent *out of office* with students or staff, proportion of students seen who are self-referrals, etc. More comprehensively, an accountability record could be formulated in terms of *feedback* from various areas of the public to get at needs to be met and feedback from various clients on the counseling process; feedback from the public on the extent to which stated outcomes have been met and feedback to the various areas of the public on the results of evaluation. In the previously (Chapter X) cited article by H. B. Gelatt, it is proposed that accountability be reported in terms of contributions made to change the *status quo,* the changing of schools to fit the students. It is suggested that accountability be in terms of *evidence* to the extent to which previously established objectives are met.

In any event, if counselors and school people do not establish a program of accountability, the public will hold them accountable and to objectives only vaguely stated and often inappropriate. From my point of view, counselors should be held accountable not only for helping individuals, whether student, staff or parents, but for evidence of the extent to which they have contributed to the whole school function and to change in that function. (Accountability profiles that could be useful to others have been developed by the Palo Alto, California, High School District—H. B. Gelatt—and the Colorado Springs Public Schools—Julian P. Tatum.)

One-to-One Counseling Revisited

The 1960's were good to counselors, as I earlier suggested. The number of school counselors increased to more than 50,000, full time and part time. And by far the greatest increase was in full-time counselors with at least basic professional education. Our task now is to see that the available time of existing counselors and a reasonable flow of new blood are utilized in the most effective fashion. The maturing of the developments described in the preceding section would go a long way toward this enhanced effectiveness. Even more, perhaps, might happen if the total stance of counseling would change in the directions suggested in this and succeeding sections.

Although I have been a lifelong advocate of one-to-one counseling as the core of the counseling effort, I am convinced by now that we in counseling can no longer afford this luxury. Nor am I so convinced as I once was that we *should* go this route even if we could. Counseling is increasingly seen as ineffective and even wasteful if it spends its efforts in a constant succession of repair jobs. I have used the analogy before of building a guard fence or straightening out the curve at the top of the cliff rather than operating a hospital at the bottom to do first aid or surgery on drivers who cannot make the curve. Counselors have been doing learning repairs on individuals rather than improving the learning environment. They could be giving vigorous leadership to some of the educational reforms suggested in Chapter X, for they, of all educational personnel, are acquainted with student need. It is student need that must be considered early in educational change even though meeting societal need is also one of the goals sought.

The counselor will have the time to contribute to educational planning if he stops relying so heavily upon one-to-one counseling. He can help students to help each other through peer counseling and small-group interaction. He can assign routine work to counselor aides, housewives or interested young people of the community, on either a volunteer or paid basis. He can, eventually, save counselor time by utilizing computer programs to aid students in narrowing down the alternatives available to them in a decision situation. The counselor has other technological resources at hand for helping students make educational and vocational choices, such as films and audio tapes. These and a flexible supply of written materials can be used to help small groups explore social and personal problems as well, such as drug usage, interpersonal relations, effective personal communication, etc.

Most of all he can *find* time to do that which he thinks is most important. He will have to believe, however, that improving the learning environment in addition to counseling individuals is a major concern of the counselor.

I believe that the counselor must accept the responsibility for helping teachers and other staff members as well as directly helping students. Expediency is one reason for my believing this. It is likely that the 1970's will see greater accountability demands made upon all school personnel. Unless schools rapidly become more relevant (it *is* an appropriate word even if overused!), parents and taxpayers, influenced by the reactions of youth and possibly of employers, will be asking penetrating questions. The counselor will come in for his and her share of them. Counselors who appear indifferent to school improvement or incompetent to contribute to such improvement will be vulnerable. A more essential reason for counselors to help teachers is that they contribute to the growth of both students and teachers when they do so.

The Counselor and the Teacher

Some years ago Verne Faust made me aware of the power behind the concept of the counselor as a consultant to teachers and staff as well as a counselor to students. This concept was well defined in his 1968 book *The Counselor-Consultant in the Elementary School.* Faust wrote that the counselor could and should also be a counselor to the teacher, but that playing the role of both counselor and consultant to the same teacher was difficult. In acting as a consultant, the counselor works with the teacher on learning situations that are *external* to the person of the teacher, such as classroom situations or particular students. He serves as a specialist in human behavior, but with most attention given to student behavior or classroom situations. When he serves as a counselor to the teacher, the focus is on the personality and needs of the teacher, not something outside the teacher. As a counselor, his goal is to help the teacher *become a more effective person* and in this way contribute to the improvement of the learning environment of the student.

Faust, in a recent paper and in personal communication, now holds strongly to the view that the counseling relationship between counselor and teacher is more important than the consulting relationship. He therefore has counseling as his primary and overshadowing role, but more of his time is spent in counseling teachers than in counseling students. A major distinction between the consulting and counseling roles is the development of a much greater degree of trust in the counselor as counselor than in the counselor as consultant. This results in greater freedom for the teacher to examine himself and to risk himself in the relationship.

Be it in counseling or in consulting, it is critical for the counselor to give attention to helping the teacher more than he has in the past. Why critical? It is critical that the counselor make the most effective use of his time, and assistance can be given to a wider range of students by helping the teacher directly. Some counselors may be more comfortable and more effective in a consulting relationship with teachers; others are more effective in a counseling relationship. The key is that there be a close and helpful relationship between teacher and counselor. Wayne Maes in commenting upon this section wrote, "Counselors may stand to gain much personal and job satisfaction from playing a helping role that is readily recognized by teachers, one that does not leave the counselor marginal either professionally or socially." I agree.

Teachers in some schools can be helped by counselors to become effective in planned "classroom guidance." Counselors can provide materials and supervision for teachers that will enable them to lead small groups of students in discussion about concerns and problems that are vital to students: plans, present worries, personal relationships, and the like.

Plans are being considered (1971) for a statewide program of this sort in Hawaii. Farrington High School in Honolulu has thirteen teachers especially designated to give this type of small-group leadership on a systematic basis. The decision-making curriculum mentioned earlier calls for just such a teacher-led service to students.

Counselors *and* teachers: this team concept is vital to schools which want to keep faith with their students. Harold Munson has suggested that the increased teacher involvement in the guidance function "could be interpreted as coming full circle historically." Well, it could be so interpreted, but conditions are radically different from those of 50 years ago. Then there were only teachers. The 50,000 school counselors of today have many new contemporary responsibilities to discharge. Teachers and others can be enlisted to help discharge some basic functions if counselors are to meet new needs which only a counselor can meet.

The Counselor and the Outside World

A common criticism of the school is that it is too self-contained, removed from the world of community reality. Here the counselor can meet one vital "new need." The counselor, perhaps of all people on the school staff, hears about this world of reality from students. He hears as he helps the student to plan for his educational and vocational future, as he hears of home situations and frustrations, as he struggles to help the student who feels lonely or alienated in his world. Does the counselor ever *sample* this world, visit it with student eyes? Earlier I suggested that the counselor who was not interested in the ability of the school to meet contemporary situations or was not competent to give leadership in this connection was indeed vulnerable. He can easily be shunted aside or assigned clerical duties. David Cook, in his edited *Revolution* volume (see Chapter X References, p. 489), writes: "The counselor who presumes that he can fullfill his role in the school by remaining in his office and seeing students one at a time is already becoming an anachronism." This may sound truly "revolutionary," but I am convinced that Bob Dylan's theme is almost desperately apt, "the times, they are a-changin'." If the counselor cannot get close to these changes, then he is not "a-changin' " and he is not likely to survive long.

This means, literally, "Get out of the office into the school and into the world outside the school." To work with teachers, to meet parents, to understand the employment and social considerations of his community is important. What about community drug programs, church programs to help the young, community attempts to provide recreational and work experiences? Do you, reader-counselor, know what your State Employment Service is doing? You say, "I haven't the time— I cannot see my 400 advisees a year if I do this." I reply, "If you aren't 'a-changin' with the times,' seeing your 400 advisees is only one thing that you will *not* be doing." I am deadly serious about this. Seeing more than your 400 advisees is highly essential if you *and* the school are to survive. Contract services and contract schools are a new but very present reality.

At the 1970 White House Conference on Children some brutally frank facts were reported: "Millions of our children are turning to drugs.

Venereal disease rates are soaring. The teen suicide rate is shocking. FBI reports show the juvenile crime rate hitting highs. Welfare rolls are swelling. Policemen and others representing authority are under attack. And great numbers of young people are alienated from their parents." (Louise O. Eckerson, "The White House Conference: Tips or Taps for Counselors?" *Personnel and Guidance Journal*, November 1971, pp. 167–174.) If counselors are to appreciate these social conditions in their own communities, they can do so *only* by seeing more than the school.

Edson Caldwell (*Personnel and Guidance Journal*, December 1970) describes how one enterprising young counselor established the terms for a job in a junior college. The record of the preceding year at that college was one of increasing unrest among students, and everyone was apprehensive. The young man who was invited to become the director of the counseling services first spent an intensive day or two interviewing students, deans, other counselors. He then told the president that he would accept the position under one condition: ". . . that counselors leave their offices half of the day and get out where the action is—out where the students are. . . . Students open up best on their own territory where you can see them as they are. . . . I want to see them (the counselors) active in both individual and group counseling sessions that arise out of the very context of the conflict wherever it occurs, be it on the campus or in the classroom." He got the terms he wanted for the job. Caldwell asks some penetrating questions about contemporary counseling and zeroes in on making counseling real for the student, "a part of campus life and his own world—not an activity apart or reserved only for a cloistered office." This is not really revolutionary although it may sound so to "established" counselors. It is simply carrying the concept of counseling to its logical conclusion, that of meeting the student where he is, not where the counselor is.

There is no way to suggest in specific terms what this new emphasis means. What is done will vary with the character of each counselor, school, and community. What I do suggest is an application of what the first three-fourths of this book has been about. If you, the reader, do not see changing values, changing social conditions, changing expectations of education as meaning changes for the role of the counselor— then read again or give this book to someone you do not care for anyway! Up to this point, studies of persons to whom students go when critical issues arise in their lives have not been very complimentary to the school counselor. Could this mean that the counselor is seen as merely another school functionary, not someone who senses what outside reality is all about?

Career Counseling

Munson might have hit a more appropriate note with his "coming full circle historically," had he been referring to vocational counseling. This was a very early emphasis in the guidance field but at a time when choice was simpler and, unfortunately, when information about the vocations was the only material available. Now more kinds of pertinent information are available, and the situation is infinitely more complex. New vocations are being added almost daily to a vast array of many thousands on the scene; educational expectations are more extensive and often specialized; the choice to be made is one of a sequence to be made throughout one's lifetime; one looks no longer to choosing an occupation but to choosing a life vocation or career. This situation has been already touched upon in Chapters IV and IX.

Eli Ginzberg discusses ten contemporary conditions that affect career counseling in *Career Guidance,* pp. 315–320 (see References):

1. The unrealistic assumption of "the younger generation" that there will be jobs available whenever they want to work.

2. A heightened tension between the inherited verity that rewards come only from hard work and the TV version of the easy life.

3. The tendency of youths, who have been exposed for so long to the impersonal organizations of our current society, to respond to an attempt at sympathetic understanding rather than to a critical, objective analysis.

4. The indifference of many youthful clients to shaping their lives for achievement of conventional goals.

5. Consideration by more and more adult men and women, from both necessity and choice, of marked vocational shifts in their lives.

6. The desire for a sense of vocation by the first postdepression and fully involved generation of Social Security men and women who will reach retirement in the 1970's.

7. The years facing the millions who will reach retirement in the 1970's with from one-quarter to one-third of their life span still remaining. Death for them is a long way off—in the meantime?

8. The continued trend toward increased female participation in the labor force. What do counselors really know about career counseling for women?

9. The increased entry of minorities, particularly blacks, into the labor force. Can non-black counselors assimilate the "black revolution" and at the same time engage in appropriate career counseling? What do such counselors know about career counseling for other minority groups such as Spanish-Americans, Puerto Ricans, and American Indians?

10. The slow, rather than rapid, decline of poverty in our society. Can we counsel on "jobs for survival" as well as on "careers for the advantaged"?

These identifications of need clearly suggest Ginzberg's concern not only with youth but with adults and retirees, with women, and with minority groups in the labor force. School and college counselors must consider these groups because schools will increasingly have students at all age levels and from all strata of society. These new demands for counseling also suggest many job opportunities for counselors outside of the academic world that will be developing within the next few years. The new needs will certainly have meaning for qualified professionals in social agencies, employment services, youth organizations, and private practice.

A "career" is a planned sequence of jobs or even occupations that extends over a large segment or the total of life. A "vocation" is a commitment to a sense of significance or achievement, to some combination of paid employment and unpaid activity that makes life meaningful. "Vocational counseling" or "career counseling" is counseling for more than an occupation; it is counseling not only for making a living but also for making a life. When conceived of in these terms, career or vocational counseling becomes the most significant single responsibility in the counselor's relationship to students. *It is counseling for finding meaning in life and for what one gives to and gets from life* (see p. 60).

Usage of the phrase, "counseling for a life style," has begun. There is a Life Style Center in Gunn High School, Palo Alto, California (see *Planning for a Life Style,* published at that school). The Career Resource Center at the Marshall-University High School, Minneapolis, Minnesota, has also developed a broader life-style approach. Career development there means *life* planning. That center was developed through the coordinated efforts of the Minneapolis Public Schools and the Minneapolis Section of the National Council of Jewish Women. Coordinator of the two is Lorraine S. Hanson of the University of Minnesota.

Currently too much of a counselor's efforts are piecemeal—helping toward "a job," toward "college," toward "finishing" high school, toward the selection of a course or a curriculum. There is an enormous waste here because it is *counseling without a goal,* or no more than a short-term objective. It is a counseling of tactics but not within a strategic context. It is often unsatisfying to both counselor and client. I do not suggest that every student is expected to have a Grand Plan or that a plan once set is satisfying without frequent modification. I propose that the tactics of a job choice or a program choice be seen within the context, however faintly visible, of a strategy for life. Educational demands are often too explicit for choices to be made without a plan, a purpose. Occupations are too varied and too fluid for choices to be made without some sense of *sequence,* some understanding of *families* of occupations, some knowledge of the process of choice, some appreciation of the need to *look ahead* and be prepared for change. The specific and fragmented counseling for "college choice" or "a job" that is so frequently seen is highly unprofessional and almost unethical. There is an ethics for professional counseling that involves much more than confidentiality or accuracy. There is an ethics for counselor competence.

References for Exploration

Borow, Henry (ed.). *Career Guidance for a New Age.* Houghton Mifflin Co., 1972 (estimated publication date).

Fromm, Erich. *Man for Himself: An Inquiry into the Psychology of Ethics.* Holt, Rinehart, and Winston, rev. ed., 1964.

Fullmer, Daniel W., and Harold W. Bernard. *The School Counselor-Consultant.* Houghton Mifflin Co., 1971.

Gartner, Alan, Mary Kohler and Frank Riessman. *Children Teach Children.* Harper and Row, 1971. (Provides convincing arguments and evidence that children can teach other children; one important change that *can* be made in our schools.)

Ginzberg, Eli. *Career Guidance.* McGraw-Hill, 1971. (Contains some far-reaching conclusions and recommendations based upon a nonrandom but still convincing national survey.)

Gordon, Thomas. *Parent Effectiveness Training.* Peter H. Wyden, Inc., 1970.

Herr, Edwin L., and Stanley W. Cramer. *Vocational Guidance and Career Development in the Schools: Towards a Systems Approach.* Houghton Mifflin Co., 1972.

Krumbolz, John, and Carl Thoreson. *Behavioral Counseling.* Holt, Rinehart, and Winston, 1969.

Mahler, Clarence A. *Group Counseling in the Schools.* Houghton Mifflin Co., 1969.

Osipow, S. H. *Theories of Career Development.* Harper and Row, 1968.

Peters, Herman J., and Michael J. Bathory (eds.). *School Counseling: Perspectives and Procedures.* Peacock, 1968. (Last section on "Developments.")

Roth, Thomas, David B. Hershenson and Thomas Hilliard (eds.). *The Psychology of Vocational Development: Readings in Theory and Research.* Allyn and Bacon, 1970. (Includes some of the most visible writers in the field—more than 80 in all.)

Shertzer, Bruce, and Shelley C. Stone (eds.). *Introduction to Guidance.* Houghton Mifflin Co., 1970. (The last two sections, "Issues" and "Trends.")

Super, Donald E. *Computer-Assisted Counseling.* Teachers College Press, 1970.

The Golden Fish (film). 20 minutes. Brandon Films, 221 W. 57th St., New York, N.Y. 10019 (*Chicago:* Film Center, 20 E. Huron St., 60611. *San Francisco:* Western Cinema Guild, 244 Kearny St., 94108). (A fantasy about tenderness and the look of it.)

CHAPTER XII

Counseling and Caring 2:
Reformulation of Role,
Priorities in Preparing,
and a Consideration of Caring

THE COUNSELOR'S EXPECTATIONS OF HIS ROLE

In *The Counselor in a Changing World,* I presented the counselor's "program responsibilities" in the following frames of reference:

a. *Counseling with students* on matters of self-understanding, decision making, and planning, using both the interview and group situations.

b. *Consulting with staff and parents* on questions of student understanding and student management.

c. *Studying changes in the character of the student population* and making a continuing interpretation of this information to the school administration and to curriculum-development committees.

d. *Performing a liaison function* between other school and community counseling resources and facilitating their use by teachers and students.

Ten years later the counselor's situation seems more complex and more fluid. These terms now sound a little too pat.

Joseph Bentley in *The Counselor's Role: Commentary and Readings* (see References) has made clear the distinction between *role expectations* (by others) and *role perception* (by the counselor of himself). All too often others' expectations of the counselor and the counselor's expectations of himself do not correspond. Then appear *role conflict* and the need for the counselor to consider *role compromise.* The compromise may be to attempt to meet others' expectations to a degree consistent with maintenance of self-respect but to do this only as a temporary measure while planning to move to a better environment as soon as possible. The compromise, on the other hand, may be to meet others' expectations but over a period of time attempt to modify them to a pattern closer to that of the counselor's. I am not suggesting that the movement should be only in one direction; the counselor may well learn from the situation and modify his own role perception. The danger is real, however, that the counselor will have so vague a role perception that he will be "shaped" by the situation and allow expediency to determine professional performance. A number of studies have shown this disparity between the two sets of expectations. A recent one in the burgeoning junior college field, which concludes with some constructive conclusions, is reported under the title, "The Administrator and the Counselor: Perception of Counselor Role in Two-Year Colleges" (George W. Herrick, *Journal of College Student Personnel,* 1971, 12: 365–369).

All four of the program responsibilities listed in the earlier book are still valid, but I would state them somewhat differently. Today I would not put them in terms of program but in terms of the person of the counselor, in terms of expectations of himself that bring about certain behaviors. Within the context of society today and the educational scene today, these might be his major expectations (goals) for himself.

1. *To help students indirectly by contributing to the improvement of the learning environment of the school.* This would mean behaviors helpful to teachers in their work with their students in the classroom and out, in groups and individually. It would mean being an ally and helper of the teacher. Some behaviors would be in the form of consulting about students and situations, some would be in the form of helping the teacher as a person, counseling with him or her about himself. To the degree possible, other behaviors would involve helping the principal, other student personnel specialists, the curriculum committee, in fact, any agency of the school or community that affects the school learning experiences of the student.

2. *To help students directly, both individually and through groups.* The behaviors called for here are again varied but this time in terms of the student and his world rather than the teacher and the school world. The realities of the student and of his world might call for much counselor time with students in groups, where they learn from each other as well as from the behavior of the counselor, perhaps as much time as with students in an interview relationship. These student realities would also mean time with students in natural settings out of the counseling office. Counselor behaviors would include working with selected peer counselors and counselor aides. Within the near future, counselor behaviors will include working with computers as learning aids in decision making.

3. *To keep myself, the counselor as a person, in constant touch with the changing world around me.* The behaviors indicated here are those of observation and reading, of study and travel. They are both personal and professional; indeed the two cannot be separated if the goal is that of being a contemporary person. This means not only traveling in the world but traveling in the students' community; it means not only professional study but engaging in a cultural world that enhances the richness of one's personal being.

Two prickly professional perennials not touched upon in the above paragraphs are: is the counselor concerned with changing *attitudes* or with changing *behaviors,* and will he engage in *crisis* or *preventive* counseling? In a sense these are not issues at all but are questions of emphasis and time expenditure. One school of thought places attitude change first in the expectation that behavior change will follow. Another school focuses on direct behavior change but says that of course attitude

change will follow! Both kinds of change are desired; there is no either/
or dilemma.

As far as crisis counseling is concerned, the counselor will of course
handle immediate and emergency needs. The question is how to avoid
being absorbed by them. Merville Shaw, in *School Guidance Systems:
Objectives, Functions, Evaluation, and Change* (Houghton Mifflin, 1973),
makes a clear distinction between "remediation" and "prevention" in
the guidance program, but sees both as necessary parts of the whole. The
danger is that unless there are *planned* counselor behaviors in the prevention direction, it is all too easy to have expediency and crises rule.

In proposing the three major role expectations and the resulting
counselor behaviors, I have tried to avoid allotting specific proportions
of counselor time or emphasis to each role expectation. In some situations, one hopes in many, the counselor would spend a major portion
of his day in indirectly helping students (role expectation number one).
In other situations much more time would be spent directly with
students. In addition, the proportion of direct to indirect help will be
affected by each counselor's personality and personal needs. Some will
receive more reinforcement from making direct contact with students,
others from helping teachers and the school environment. Just as there
is no adequate basis for setting an ideal counselor-student ratio (although everyone tries his hand at it!), so there is no foundation for
suggesting that everyone should spend a certain portion of his time in
specified behaviors.

With regard to expectation number three, some kinds of growth will
occur in day-to-day student and teacher contacts, particularly if the
world of the student is entered even to a small degree. The behaviors
contributing chiefly to this expectation, however, will occur during
out-of-school hours, weekends, and summers. Parents and taxpayers
often ask, "What do teachers do with all of their spare time?" This is an
infuriating question, to be sure, but educational personnel, *as professionals,* do not always have adequate answers. A professional must be
forever at the job of learning. I am proposing that to learn about one's
self and the nonschool world around one is as important as it is to read
new texts and attend summer school. Perhaps it is more important. If a
counselor sees himself as dealing primarily with learning outcomes that
are pertinent to students and with the constellation of human relationships that are a part of this process, then surely he or she is most vitally
concerned with the changing patterns of our society.

It is of the greatest significance that there be a *balance* between the
three sets of role expectations and behaviors. The pattern of this balance
will vary from person to person, but *some amounts of each set of*

behaviors should be in each counselor's life. This is a flatly arbitrary statement to be sure, but perhaps the reader would profit from examining the pattern of *his* daily, weekly, yearly life against the background of these expectations.

COUNSELOR SELECTION AND EDUCATION

Selection

No dimension of counseling has been held up to more question than the two basic issues of a careful selection of counselors for professional education and of a professional education that is more than exposure to abstract ideas. In both of these issues there are weaknesses compounded by the unrealistic certification prerequisite that all counselors must first be certified and experienced teachers.

Thoughtful commentators from outside the field of professional education almost invariably question this prerequisite. Counselors are likely to reply, "They simply don't understand." I wonder if *counselors* understand, or are they merely perpetuating a custom that originated under conditions of society, of schools, and of counseling that no longer prevail? Eli Ginzberg (see References, Chapter XI), for example, wonders why counseling is the only profession which requires one to master another profession before preparing for it. Beyond this, there is the strange anomaly that in three major counseling fields, school, rehabilitation, and employment counseling the prospective counselor is frequently selected by the employer to *work* at counseling before he prepares for it! Does this speak well for counseling as a *profession*? I do not think so, not until such practices as the above are rare rather than prevalent.

Ten years ago I proposed that one alternative to the teaching-experience requirement be the substitution of a supervised internship (at least three of the larger states now provide this alternative). This proposal drew some adverse reaction from my critics, who inferred that I was abolishing teaching experience as a background for counseling. I was not, of course, denying teaching experience as one major alternative, but currently I would almost accept my critics' inferences without struggle! Certainly I am convinced that "successful" teaching experience is *not* an adequate criterion for admission to counselor education and the prospect of becoming a counselor. Yet in 1965–66 over one-half of the 300 institutions providing some degree of counselor education required for admission to the program only a bachelor's degree, a teaching certificate, and a principal's recommendation—nothing more!

Let me put it succinctly; some forty years in counselor education have convinced me that the priorities have been wrong. Counselor educators should spend more time on the process of *selection* and less on developing and teaching didactic courses in counselor education. (More relevant experiences, perhaps, but not more "courses.") Careful selection in terms of the humanness of the applicant takes time, but time spent at this end of the process would save time and frustration at the other end.

The *person* of the counselor applicant is more significant than the amount of cognitive materials to which he is exposed. And it *can* be done. As an example, it is instructive to read the description by C. B. Truax of a selection program that is in action (*Counselor Education and Supervision*, Fall 1970). This selection process involves: (1) the employer's judgment (assuming that many counselor candidates begin preparation after having had vocational experience) regarding the usual criteria for employment—dependability, responsibility, appearance, and the like; (2) five scales and three indices of the *Minnesota Multiphasic Personality Inventory* and eight scales of the *Edwards Personal Preference Schedule*; (3) a rating-scale analysis of tape recordings of the applicant's reactions in a group counseling situation. A substantial investment of time? Yes, but the advantages to the program, to the profession, and to future counseling clients are incalculable. For years I have heard frequent criticisms of teachers, that some are not trusted by students, are not helpful to students. Too many counselors are rejected by students for the same reasons. Part of this is "the system," but part lies in the fact that they should not have been counselors in the first place, should not have been admitted to a counselor education program.

My contention that one should select counselors for their human qualities has indirect support in several reports of *untrained* counselors who were carefully selected. These are reported to be doing quite as well in counseling as those who are professionally prepared. Truax provides one such illustration. Another might be a report by Robert Lindberg and myself on a situation in which *carefully selected* minority teachers, given the beginnings of a supervised counseling experience (practicum) were almost immediately effective in counseling minority clients—as testified to by both students and counselor observers (*Personnel and Guidance Journal*, January 1972, pp. 371–378).

I have begun to think that the ability to *listen* with understanding, and without apparent threat to either counselor or client, is a most important attribute of an effective counselor. This quality would not be difficult to observe in the selection process, and yet I doubt that it can *be taught* to everyone admitted. Counselor educators can far more easily teach the process of behavioral counseling, for example, to those who have the essential personal attributes than they can develop those attributes within a period of, say, a year's time.

Of course, there must be selection in terms of the ability to master content courses. Graduate schools always consider this factor. The tragedy is that it is often the only factor stressed in the admission process. There may be an analogy in the selection of students for schools of art or music. If one selected students for these schools on the basis of brains, there would be many "false positives" (the group selected would contain many who could not achieve artistically). If one selected on the basis of artistic ability, most of these would have enough brains because intelligence is a factor in artistic performance (there would be *fewer* false positives). So if I had to choose between human warmth and brains in selecting for counselor education, I would choose the warmth—adequate brains would often enough accompany it. But intellectual ability alone will not make a counselor—a research worker, or perhaps, a university professor. Is this what counselor education programs are looking for? Sadly, I must reply, "All too often."

Counselor Education

It is easy to criticize and difficult to modify the structure of counselor education. Tradition and laziness both work against change. I can speak plainly here because I have helped to establish some of the tradition that I now seek to overturn! Yet some developments that I consider constructive have already taken place: practicum is a necessity in any program; the study of developmental psychology (or personality development) and the study of group processes are offered to at least a strong minority of all counseling candidates. The stronger programs provide candidates with a personal experience in a group (or group practicum) and some contact with the social sciences as part of their graduate curriculum.

Many suggestions for modification come to mind in connection with the changes proposed earlier: understanding of the psychology of learning, the nature of the learning environment, and the psychology of the adult; knowledge of and contact with the community and the occupational world; practice in working with peer counselors and counselor aides; experience with a systems approach which utilizes both man and machine (computers, audio tapes, and other technologies).

I am convinced, however, that the most basic change in the counselor education curriculum would be to provide students *early contact with people* as well as ideas. Students frequently ask for it: "I entered this field because of people. All I get, at least for the first few months, are ideas *about* people. Ideas without people seem sterile and unreal." I believe we have overcome our earlier fears that we "endanger" the client by permitting the counselor candidate to have early contact with the client. Paul Meehl's argument against the "spun-glass theory" of personality is widely accepted, that is, that a person is not made of spun glass which shatters at the first awkward movement by a therapist. There may be much danger, in fact, in postponing client contact until after the graduate student has had several courses *about* human nature. Courses and books which present ideas apart from people lead the student in counselor education to make generalizations which may be completely untrue when applied to a given client. If a student "learns well" from books, he may believe in an idea about people more than in the person. This results in an unconscious movement to make the person fit the idea!

My proposal is (1) that the counselor candidate see people as prospective clients from the first month on and (2) that ideas about people be presented parallel with flesh-and-blood realities. This not only protects the student in counselor education from making unrealistic generalizations but makes ideas come alive as they are seen in people.

It is all a question of sequence. Everyone would agree that client contact is crucial in counselor education, but the question is, "When?" I say early in the program and continuously. The early contacts could be by observation, of course, or under supervision that would offer the client some protection against an impulsive counselor candidate. Some writers have proposed that the *only* early experiences in counselor education should be with people as prospective or actual clients. Only after the student has developed "a listening ear," should he be trusted not to distort what he reads of ideas about people. One university has developed a "block program" of rather free, self-motivated learning in which there is more contact with people than formal contact with ideas. Such a structure, or any program structure, must be tested, of course. I am sure only of the principle—early and parallel contact with human realities must be introduced if candidates are not to turn out to be cognitive skeletons as counselors.

If we select with some care, then counselor candidates can be trusted—from the first. In terms of reality, I would certainly trust observations of people at least as much as I would trust compilations of ideas about people. So the counselor educator must answer two decisive questions: (a) does he or does he not trust the counselor candidates whom he has selected? And (b) does he believe that the reality of a person is at least as significant as the reality of an idea?

Some people are warm, knowledgeable, and sharing counselors despite, not because of, counselor education programs. This is a harsh statement, perhaps, and I have probably done as much harm as any counselor educator. It is so easy to get out of touch with reality, so easy to be self-deluded into thinking that the professor's perception is reflected in that of his students. In one of Freud's last papers he proposed that a psychoanalyst needs to be analyzed every five years, for in the process of working with people, he hears many patients ascribe to him the attributes of God. In time, he begins to believe *some* of this—so he needs analysis to find out whether he is changing in undesirable ways. Similarly, every graduate adviser should do some counseling and design or a Ph.D. thesis of his own every five years!

THE NATURE OF CARING

I opened these two chapters about counseling with an emphasis on the importance of caring. I now end the chapters and the book with an attempt to discover the meaning of caring. "To care" immediately suggests caring for another. It does mean that, but it also means caring for yourself. The relationship is very close between the two kinds of caring. In fact, caring for yourself is a vital factor in how much and in what manner you *can* care for another. If you care little for yourself, you are less likely to be able to care for another. It would be reasonable then to discuss "caring for self" first. But "caring for another" provides our most vivid association of the word and we will look at this first.

My very helpful editorial consultant has been admonishing me that I shift from second person to third person and back again throughout this book! In the remaining pages of the book where I am being very personal about caring, I am also being reckless. Don't expect consistency at all! "You" means the reader, as a counselor or as a person; "we" means you and I, sometimes as counselors, sometimes just as people. So bear with me. I am *talking* to readers, not writing to them or about them. Most of all I value you, the reader, as a person more than you, the reader, as a counselor.

Caring for Others

In the middle of writing the first draft of these last chapters, I found that the time had arrived to fulfill a commitment to the University of Nevada at Las Vegas. For a week I served there as seminar leader for a group of forty graduate students—counselors from various settings, nurses, teachers, probation officers, etc. They proved to be a delightful and responsive group, so I asked them for help in analyzing the nature of caring. From their forty short papers (two were in verse form!) and a lively group discussion, I have selected the following as the more commonly accepted definitions.

Caring is:

Knowing enough about the environment and the process of learning to understand the client's learning problems. In general, knowing is a form of caring.

Communicating that you care by saying so, by listening completely, by giving time completely. (One counselor defined caring by describing six hours of time that week with an alcoholic, three hours with a depressed father of five—voluntary time which she gave because she cared for these two lives.)

Reinforcing positively the other's concept of himself as a worthwhile person.

Being available, all of you, when you say you will be available—caring enough to keep your promises.

Saying "no" firmly at times, but with a willingness to give reasons for the "no." If this is not done, then blanket permissiveness may be interpreted by the student (or by the child in relation to his parent) as *not* caring, not taking the trouble to consider the issue, to become involved.

Giving without expectation of return (an attribute of caring widely accepted by members of the seminar and one which I want to discuss later).

Supporting without directing, showing that you want the other to remain autonomous and self-directing.

Rejoicing with the other when he is happy as well as to be "with him" when he is troubled.

Effecting a change in the other's feelings or behavior, not merely expressing or showing caring.

Empathizing, projecting yourself into the other's world as much as you can while retaining your own self-awareness; being subjective yet objective; "being with" yet retaining autonomy.

A *general caring* for all, an attitude, a giving of your surplus of good will or time or money; a *specific caring* for an individual in a sense that you sacrifice some of yourself, becoming involved enough to risk yourself for that person's sake; that is, a caring at two levels.

Some quotes from the seminar papers are included because they cast intriguing even though individual highlights upon the topic:

> The brightest blaze of intelligence is of less value than the feeling that some one cares for you.

To live is to care, else one merely exists.

My definition of caring approaches my definition of religion, which from its cognate *religare (religo)* means to bind together. Caring to me, is also "to bind together."

To care means to constantly expand your own knowledge and resources so that the quality of your giving can grow with you.

To care means to pick him up after he has failed again and again and making him know that you still believe in him.

Caring means listening when you would rather be talking.

Caring means hearing what remains unsaid.

The essence of caring is contained in the story of the Japanese sculptor who confounded the curator of an American museum where his works were being shown. At the base of each statue the sculptor had placed a polite little sign. The signs all read, "Please Touch."

It is apparent that caring has various meanings for different people. It would be a fruitless gesture to attempt to summarize them. Your own perception of caring is a reflection of the person that you are. But *you* change and so your perceptions of caring can change. You can enrich your pattern of caring by seeing new facets of expression, new dimensions of being.

Since I have shared these perceptions of seminar members with you—and pondering them has enriched me—I can do no less than add to them some persuasions of my own. Adding to them is all that I will do. I will not urge any perception of mine as meaningful for all. Each reader must select his own if the perception is to become related to behavior.

Kinds of Love. I cannot distinguish between caring and love, and love without expectation of return was stressed in the seminar. This is love in the *agape* sense. Three kinds of love are frequently mentioned—*erotic* (sexual love), *filial* (brotherly, or family love), and *agape.* Filial love is an expected love, a love within a structured relationship. The counselor is often seen by others as exhibiting this kind of love within a school setting. He is *expected* to care, it is part of his duty, and in turn he at least hopes for some response of appreciation from the students.

In "The Three Worlds of the Counselor" (*Personnel and Guidance Journal,* October 1970, pp. 91–96) I have said:

On the other hand, I interpret *agape* to mean a love for those to whom one does not have any structured responsibility. It is a concern for a person as a person, with *no expectation* of a return from the other individual. It is an open love, one which is a condition of life and is inherent in the nature of people and their relationships to each other. I think students suspect that a counselor's love is *filial,* a kind of professional obligation of a counselor, while their whole being cries out for *agape,* love freely extended to them as a person. Edwin Markham's famous couplet is pertinent here: "He drew a circle that shut me out—heretic, rebel, a thing to flout. But Love and I had the wit to win—we drew a circle that took him in." This love has no professionalism in it.

Robert Heinlein (see References, Chapter VI) defines love in a manner that has come to have much meaning for me: "Love is that condition in which the happiness of another person is essential to your own."

Style and Agape.   Do we care for another because we "should" or because we cannot help caring? The "should" is only a style, the fulfillment of a "professional expectation" that a counselor care. Recently I have read expositions on "style" by Maxine Greene, a professor of English at Teachers College, Columbia University, and by Seymour Halleck, a psychiatrist at the University of Wisconsin. Both are analyzing style as many young people think of it today—being modish, contemporary, expressing oneself freely, dressing as one likes. These comprise style, but they are shallow. Halleck says, "You can go to Hell with Style," your own particular hell of trying constantly to be "hip" (a dated word no doubt!). Greene goes back to Sören Kierkegaard, who distinguished between the aesthetic person and the moral person. Many youths, says Greene, never get beyond the style, the art form of life— they have not made a moral choice of that to which they are committed and which will determine what they do. They have the clothes but not the commitment or the sense of personal responsibility.

If counselors do not care beyond the style level, they are not seen as caring at all. To care is not a professional garment to be donned in one's office—it is so very apparent there as a garment. Recently I wrote somewhere that it is an insult to a client to offer him a role rather than a person.

Can I continue to love when it is not returned? I fully believe in the principle of reinforcement, that one continues doing what he is rewarded in some way for doing. Does this concept conflict with *agape*? With no feedback, will I persist in caring? No, I would reply, but I will get feedback from some, from enough people "to keep me going." Caring (loving) is an attitude, an integral part of me, a way of living (Erich Fromm). If I care for the unlovable, those who return little or nothing at all, I will also care for those who return some or much. So I am rewarded—and can, occasionally at least, live *agape*.

I have not thought through whether it would be possible for me to continue loving *only* those who give no return. Perhaps a saint could, but I am not one. It would also be unrealistic to conceive of my world as not containing many returns (feedback of love) from others. It is immaterial that their appreciation of me often seems undeserved. My perception of myself is not always the image that I project to others and they give feedback to the image, not necessarily to me. It has taken me a long time to understand this. I can accept "undeserved" appreciation more gracefully now that I see that it is of *their* me, not of me as I perceive myself. So I can live *agape* to the limits possible within my personality, and the rest of my world will reinforce my caring. If my inferences are valid, this makes *agape* love possible—for anyone.

Moments. Caring for others means to me "moments of caring," sometimes hours of caring but never days. Therapist Gerald Haigh once commented that counselors had as their major function that of creating a relationship in which clients experienced "moments of humanness." It may be only for moments, said Haigh, that a client can feel entirely open to himself, unguarded, freed of internal restraints. These are precious moments, deeply rewarding ones, and the counselor who makes them possible for a client is fulfilling a high mission. As I reflect upon these "moments," I am reminded of Maslow's "peak experiences" and of C. S. Lewis's transcendental moments in *Surprised by Joy.*

Loyalties. Caring also means an ordering of priorities. Where is your primary loyalty? What will you risk in order to care? In a *Time* story in 1970 a young psychiatrist drafted into the army asked to be restored to civilian status because of his inability to reconcile the goals of psychiatry with his function in the army. As a psychiatrist in the army, he was a member of a "mental hygiene team" on which he served merely as a consultant, with the decisions made by his commanding officer. His purpose, as defined by his commanding officer, was to serve the army, not the individual.

This interesting commentary suggests a clear analogy with the dilemma of many counselors. The counselor, when employed by an institution, be it social agency, school, college, or hospital, is immediately faced with a question of the primacy of his loyalties. In his professional preparation, he has learned that he is to serve the interests of the individual, to keep the confidence of the individual, and to be more concerned with the individual than with the institution. If counseling is to have any specific meaning, it is that the counselor operates in the interests of the person with whom he is counseling, except under most stringent circumstances threatening the welfare of other individuals.

When a professional serves as the agent of an institution, and *in the interests of the institution primarily,* then I very much doubt that he can be called a counselor. This is not to mean that a counselor has no regard for the welfare of society or that he has no consideration for the institution that is paying his salary. In the counselor's hierarchy of values, however, the individual ranks higher than the institution. There is simply no way around this. When a psychiatrist represents an institution, he always has problems because, although he has responsibility to the institution, he has even more responsibility to the patient. When this institution is war, then the institution or the nation becomes paramount, and the welfare of the individual is secondary to the good of the whole. This is why another psychiatrist recently said, "Military psychiatry is a contradiction in terms."

The theme of this book is that the contemporary counselor must know the world he lives in, its trends, and its moods, but that beyond this he must care for what happens to the client and care for him as a person. Knowing and caring are both in the interests of the client. Caring for his client is not to neglect or deny society but to serve it indirectly rather than directly. I am reasonably convinced that when the best interests of the individual living in a contemporary culture are served, then the best interests of that society are also served. The point is that the start must be made with the individual and his needs, rather than with the society and its needs.

Caring, then, means making some decisions, taking some risks. How much do you care? School people generally are loyal to order and follow consensus. They are likely to be suspicious of liberty which disturbs order. David Cook quotes a 1969 Massachusetts court decision, which says in part, "Order can be defined properly only in terms of the liberties for which it exists, as liberty can be defined properly only in terms of the ordered society in which it thrives. As Albert Camus implied in *The Rebel,* order and liberty must find their limits in each other." Does a counselor care enough for students to encourage the expression of liberty as well as the maintenance of order? Is a counselor to "help students" express themselves, even at some risk to himself? If helping shows caring, then look at your priorities—for whom and about what do you care most?

Caring for Self

A counselor can be helpful, as I said earlier, can assist others in powerful ways, even when he knows little, if he cares. You and I have been touched by people like that, people who listened to us, and for a few moments perhaps, lived with us as though they really cared who we were. And these were important people to us. We never forgot them.

Essential to my truly caring for another is self-respect for all that I am, fully admitting to myself all that I am not or have failed in doing. Numerous counseling protocols have shown that as a client increases in respect for himself (self-acceptance without defensiveness), he increases in ability to care for another. Counselors are people as much as clients are and doubtless respond in the same manner. Long ago Rabbi Joshua Liebman commented that "to love another one must first love oneself." What was a far-out doctrine then (for a religious leader speaking in philosophical terms) has now become a psychologically validated reality. This is why meditation, or a continuing relationship with a deeply respected person, or group experience which contributes to positive feedback are essential for a counselor.

Both Strengths and Weaknesses. It is of first importance that you care about yourself. You are a person unique in all the world. Most of us are more aware of our liabilities than of our assets, because our particular home and school cultures have stressed more what was wrong about us than what was right. Our weaknesses and errors were under-lined, and our assets and successes were taken for granted. Do we, regrettably, pass this heritage along to our clients, our family, our friends?

What is sought is a balance, an awareness of both strengths and weak-nesses, successes and failures. Self-respect or self-confidence means self-assurance tinged with humility. If you are open to all of yourself, then you know the boundaries of your knowledge and the limitless extent of your ignorance. In your self-awareness you know that you do not at all times have a high level of good judgment, sensitivity to others, caring for others. Humility, which makes you aware of the limited scope of your own knowledge and effectiveness, your own uniqueness, con-tributes to your acceptance of the uniqueness and limitations of the other. That self-respect and humility are complementary to each other, that one exists *within* the other, I learned only recently from a warm and sensitive young woman in the previously mentioned Nevada seminar. I had never considered the relationship between self-respect and humility before. I should have and I am grateful for the insight. Humility means that I could learn something every day—from someone. It means that life can be exciting!

Both Head and Heart. Caring for self means that you respect the various elements of yourself, not downgrading some to the benefit of others. You are one, the parts are inseparable and interdependent (remember some of the trends discussed in the psychology section). Take head and heart, do you consider one more important than the other? Let the story of the Tin Woodman make the point, retold in Don Fabun's *Dynamics of Change,* see References, Chapter I). Two familiar citizens of Oz, the Scarecrow and the Tin Woodman, are overheard as they travel down the main road to Oz. They have been discussing the Scarecrow's lack of brains. He has just asked the Tin Woodman if *he*

has any brains. "No, my head is quite empty," replied the Tin Woodman, "but once I had a heart and brains also: having tried them both,
I should much rather have a heart."

From this conversation it is easy to discern that the Tin Woodman is
truly a citizen of the Western world, one who is totally caught up in the
either/or dichotomy. He experienced his choice as between head and
heart rather than experiencing a choice which could include both.

So it is with counselors. I have heard much discussion among graduate
student counselors-to-be about the relative importance of cognition and
affect, head and heart, knowing and caring. To care for yourself means
acknowledging all of you and acknowledging that one part of self is
dependent upon the whole. This book has focused upon the counselor
who "knows and cares." There is no either/or—knowing enough means
caring, and caring is often dependent upon knowing. In any event I
cannot pluck out either heart or head from an indivisible me! And I
respect *me*, not my heart or my head.

Enjoyment not Duty.   If I care for myself in the sense of self-respect
and humility, then I am free to *enjoy* others—not everyone to be sure,
but enjoyment would be the rule, not the exception, If I enjoy people,
then some of my needs are met in the counseling relationship, group or
individual, and I am freed to recognize the needs of the other. If I do
not have *to prove something to myself,* then I will not press the client
for decision or commitment, will not push him in the direction of the
decision that will give me a glow of satisfaction. Assurance about myself
contributes to my effectiveness in the counseling relationship.

Respect for self means also that you do not let clients impose on you.
You are concerned for them, but they cannot abuse your time or self-
respect. They may be hostile toward you, but you may see this as an
expression of their need rather than an exploitation of you. Openness in
showing hostility may be an indication of their trust in your ability to
absorb it without threat to them. If I sense strength in another, I can be
more open with him without threat to him—or without fear that he will
retaliate. No, I am not speaking of openness between you which may
involve an expression of anger. This may show *respect* for you. I speak
of the abuse of your time and of the tendency to throw emotional
burdens on you, asking you to carry the load. These *are* acts of exploitation; you do not have to endure them. As one counselor expressed it,
"I am not a sacrifice upon the altar of my client."

"Sacrificing yourself" is a kind of egotism. When you begin "feeling
sorry for yourself," then you are not caring adequately for either yourself or the other. You are lowering the dignity of both.

It Takes Time.   Finally, a counselor must take time to consider himself, enrich himself, refill drained reservoirs of physical and emotional energy. You as a person deserve some attention. This may mean a little solitude, time in which to reconsider goals and regroup activities. It may mean music, reading, worship, some companionship with nature. Refurbishing your self means something different to each person. Recently a counselor shared with me the experience of herself and her husband. Their marriage of several years had become strained and brittle. They agreed upon a complete separation for three months. "During that time, and since we have been back together we have each done a lot of searching within ourselves about caring," she told me. "We both learned to like ourselves more and to care for ourselves. This was the missing ingredient in our former relationship. As a consequence we have had nearly a year now of peace, understanding, and deep caring. I think we had to have the time alone to examine ourselves and appreciate who we are."

Commitments. A counselor has three commitments: (1) a commitment to himself as a person of worth, (2) a commitment to his clients, family, and friends as people of worth also, and (3) a commitment to the society of which both his client and he are a part and to that institution of society which he serves. Of these three, the first commitment is the most important. The most significant growth upon the part of the counselor lies in learning to trust himself. I have seen much frustration, ineffectiveness, and unhappiness in counselors over the years that could be traced back to their lack of trust in themselves. Growth in self-trust is not without agony, but it can also result in moments of exhilaration. It is a liberating experience to increase in one's sense of openness, to move toward a complete sense of being, to become more willing to admit others and share oneself. To grow in this way is to increase the worth of the most potent single element in the counseling relationship. This is the person of the counselor, his sense of reality, his self-trust, his increasing awareness of the beauty and joy of living, and his open regard for others.

Dreaming and Doing. One night recently I had a dream (literally) that I was reading an article in the *Saturday Evening Post* which closed with a long section on slowing down to "be," not constantly speeding ahead to catch up. The article said that someday a counselor would become famous for advocating being, not doing; that it was essential that you stop occasionally and let things catch up with you, allowing them to nestle down around you comfortably like little chicks around a mother hen, little fox kits around a vixen. Then both *things* and *you* could become comfortably aware of each other in an atmosphere of trust and affection.

This dream awakened me and, as I lay meditating upon it, I felt that I could stop and rest only for a time, that *being* required that I be up soon and moving ahead. If I did not, then life would move on around me, and I would be part of the flotsam and jetsam left behind by the eddy of the flood in the dry wash of the desert. I have followed down these washes after a storm, making rare "finds" of desert-whitened driftwood, lacy bits of saguaro skeleton, shining rocks, and charred wood from campfires, all dead, all left behind. One might change the metaphor and think of the beach after a storm, where driftwood, kelp, and shells all are left high and dry beyond the highest waves. For awhile they were afloat, but were finally flung high on the beach, spent and helpless.

We (all people) are different from the driftwood. We have some degree of autonomy, of self-directed motion. We can move out of the eddy, off the beach and get back into the surging stream or morning tide. We *must,* after our quiet time of becoming more intimately aware of ourselves, or our bones will whiten in the wash or on the beach. Eventually some curious wanderer will pick us up and marvel, "John, come and see. Look what *was.*"

If the analogy has any degree of pertinence, the conclusion to be drawn is that *being* without *doing* results in nonbeing. There is a sign at the entrance to the Washington Monument, where long lines frequently form in front of the elevator. The sign reads, "There is no waiting for those willing to climb the stairs."

References for Exploration

Bentley, Joseph C. *The Counselor's Role: Commentary and Readings.* Houghton Mifflin, 1968.

Bugental, J. F. T. *The Search for Authenticity.* Holt, Rinehart, and Winston, 1965.

Fromm, Eric. *The Art of Loving.* Harpers, 1956. (A classic slender volume, well known to many readers. I encourage a revisitation.)

Gardner, John W. *No Easy Victories.* Harper and Row, 1968.

Hamachek, Don E. *Encounters with the Self.* Holt, Rinehart, and Winston, 1971.

Jourard, Sidney. *Self Disclosure: An Experimental Analysis of the Transparent Self.* John Wiley & Sons, 1971.

Maslow, Abraham H. *The Farther Reaches of Human Nature.* Viking Press, 1971.

Morris, Desmond. *Intimate Behavior.* Random House, 1971. (Yes, I am hooked on Morris. This is the third book of his that I have listed. And with confidence. Zoologist-anthropologist, he compares the intimacy of mother-child relationships among animals with intimacy symbols of humans. It makes much sense to me. This is a personal reaction, I am a "touching" person.)

Otto, Herbert, and John Mann. *Ways of Growth: Approaches to Expanding Awareness.* Viking Press, 1969.

Otto, Herbert A. (ed.). *Love Today: A New Exploration.* Association Press, New York City, 1972. (Twenty-one contributions by some excellent writers on different dimensions of love. To me, it is an engrossing and intellectually stimulating book. Not sentimental. "Love's creative role in a world of alienation and destruction.")

Rogers, Carl, and Barry Stevens with Eugene Gendlin, John M. Schlien and William Van Dusen. *Person to Person: The Problem of Being Human.* Pocket Books, 1971. (This is Barry Stevens's book. Her 100 pages of comment on the seven professional chapters by the other authors are intensely personal and appealing. Entitled "From My Life," her comments reveal a warm and sensitive person whom you feel privileged to know. Beyond this, you get some feeling of how *you* might become more spontaneously human.)

Schutz, William C. *Joy: Expanding Human Awareness.* Grove Press, 1967.

——. *Here Comes Everybody: Bodymind and Encounter Culture.* Harper and Row, 1971. (*Joy* is a beginner's book; the second one takes the reader further. The two subtitles partly suggest the content of each—but only partly. These are books about encounter groups, to be sure, ideology, goals, and techniques. But they are about honesty and joy in living. They are about Schutz also, his long experience with groups, what he has learned about himself as well as others. Personal books.)

Tournier, Paul. *The Seasons of Life.* John Knox Press, 1961.

Ungersma, Aaron J. *Escape from Phonies.* Westminster Press, 1969.

The Smile (film). 18 minutes. Contemporary Films, McGraw Hill, 267 W. 25th St., New York, N.Y. 10001. (An artistically directed French film about a Buddhist monk and his 12-year-old novice as the youth awakens to life around him.)

Index of Topics

Index of Authors